64-18251

6-17-66

The Crossroad Papers

A LOOK INTO THE AMERICAN FUTURE

The Crossroad Papers

A LOOK INTO THE AMERICAN FUTURE

EDITED AND WITH AN INTRODUCTION BY

Hans J. Morgenthau

W · W · Norton & Company · Inc · New York

CONTENTS

5

The Crossroad Papers

A LOOK INTO THE AMERICAN FUTURE

Introduction:
The Great Issues

HANS J. MORGENTHAU

THE United States must come to terms with five great issues, interconnected and overlapping: the issue of nuclear power, the economic issue, the issue of race, the issue of education, and the issue of democratic government.

The issue of nuclear power puts into question the very survival of our society and of the civilization of which it forms a part. It is an illusion to believe that this issue, because it is not continuously as acute as it became in October 1962 on the occasion of the Cuban crisis, has lost its threat. As long as governments threaten, and prepare for, the use of nuclear weapons, that threat exists, and it is bound to increase with the proliferation of nuclear weapons. While the availability of nuclear weapons has radically transformed the international environment and the very structure of international relations, we still think and act in terms which belong to an age that has passed.

The same is true of our economic thinking and policies. The enormous concentrations of economic power, amounting to private governments competing with the public one, have called into being a new feudalism, as threatening to the integrity and effectiveness of the public power as was the feudalism of old. The conjunction of ever-increasing productivity with large-scale obsolescence of human labor creates economic and social problems unaccounted for by traditional theory and practice. Our traditional concepts as to what the relations between government and the economic sphere ought to be are inadequate to cope with these new problems.

The assimilation into our society of ten percent of the population, racially distinct and underprivileged socially, economically, and educationally, poses problems which cannot be solved by liberal good will and legislative enactments alone. It raises problems with regard to the assimilation of our Negro population into American society as well as with regard to the adjustment of large masses of our white population to the Negroes. It conjures up the possibility of large-scale social disturbances, unmanageable with the traditional methods which our Constitution and political practices have established.

Both the economic and the racial problems pose acutely the issue of education. The equalitarian concept of a uniform mass education has been a dubious instrument of civilization from the beginning. Institutions which have been fashioned in the image of that concept are helpless in the face of large masses of underprivileged children, white and black, of the requirements of new technologies, and of the opportunities of expanded leisure.

Finally, the concentration of unprecedented power in the hands of the executive branch of the government has posed the age-old problem of democratic government in a new setting. Democratic government faces a dual paradox. On the one hand, the concentration of unprecedented powers in the hands of the government coincides with the government's inability to govern effectively; this is the paradox of thwarted government. On the other hand, the dependence of the government upon the will of the majority, in the form of an extended and equalized franchise and public-opinion polls, is greater than it was ever before. Yet this ascendancy of majority rule coincides with a marked decline of both popular participation in public affairs and popular control over the actions of the government. This is the paradox of the thwarted majority. How can we restore the ability of the government to govern effectively and the ability of the people to control the government? [1]

These are momentous issues, and they ought to evoke thoughts and actions commensurate with them. What is striking is the absence not only of political thought commensurate with the issues facing us, but of creative political thought of any kind. It is almost a commonplace to point to the absence of creative political thought as a distinctive characteristic of our epoch. The age has produced no Machiavelli, no Hobbes, no Locke, no Burke, no Marx, not even a Laski. The great political parties of the Western democracies differ not so much in philosophy and policies as in the personalities who present themselves to the electorate. Nor is this intellectual poverty limited to the West. Reading the Marxist literature of the Soviet Union and the Chinese polemics against it, one is impressed with the intellectual bankruptcy of a movement which, if anything, was once too intellectual for its own political good.

The decline of political thought is, then, a universal phenomenon. We have all become, in Acton's phrase, "docile and attentive students of the absorbing Past." We try to know, understand, and improve the past. Yet when it comes to dealing with the great issues of the age, political thought resembles what Tolstoy said modern history has become: " a deaf man answering questions which no one has asked him." Thus while nuclear power threatens us with destruction, while the very success of our economic system and racial conflict threaten society with disintegration, while our educational system produces millions of barbarians, and while government can no longer govern nor the people any more control the government, we debate the relative merits of conservatism and liberalism, a juxtaposition which once had a political function in Europe but which has always been meaningless in America.

[1] I have dealt with these issues at greater length in *The Purpose of American Politics* (Alfred A. Knopf, 1960, and Vintage Books, 1964).

This condition of intellectual fatigue would not be disquieting were we living in an age of consolidation, calling for the pragmatic safeguarding and elaboration of what has been achieved rather than for new ideas in anticipation of, and preparation for, what needs to be done. There have been such ages, but ours is not one of them. What is so disquieting is exactly the contrast between the novelty of the conditions under which we live, on the one hand, and the obsolescence of the modes of thought and action with which we try to cope with these conditions. This age—like the fourth century B.C., the age of Plato and Aristotle; like the fifth century A.D., the age of Saint Augustine; like the sixteenth and seventeenth centuries, the age of Machiavelli, Spinoza, Hobbes, and Locke—cries out for new modes of thought and action, commensurate with the novelty of the conditions which we must master. Yet that cry finds no answer, except for the ritualistic incantations of old ideas that have lost their meaning, and for the routine use of institutions that have lost their purpose.

Throughout history, political life has drawn its vitality from the creative contrast between the political world in which men found themselves and the political world which men thought to be ethically, rationally, or pragmatically necessary. Political philosophy performed the political function of demonstrating either that the actual political world and the necessary one were identical or that another one, imagined once to have existed in the past or susceptible of creation *de novo*, had to replace it. That creative intellectual tension between conservation and innovation has been the lifeblood of politics.

With that creative tension having gone out of politics, all seemingly antagonistic political movements—and this is as true of Germany, France, and Great Britain as it is of the United States—express in different ways a stagnant mood, a hedonism of the status quo that equates what exists with what ought to exist, if not with the ultimate purposes of the universe. Thus we are approaching a moribund state of political life which Karl Mannheim analyzed with prophetic insight in these words thirty-five years ago: "It is possible, therefore, that in the future, in a world in which there is never anything new, in which all is finished and each moment is a repetition of the past, there can exist a condition in which thoughts will be utterly devoid of all ideological and utopian elements. But the complete elimination of reality-transcending elements from our world would lead us to 'matter-of-factness' which ultimately would mean the decay of the human will . . . human nature and human development would take on a totally new character. The disappearance of utopia brings about a static state of affairs in which man himself becomes no more than a thing. We would be faced then with the greatest paradox imaginable, namely, that man, who has achieved the highest degree of rational mastery of existence, left without any ideals, becomes a mere creature of impulses. Thus, after a long, tortuous, but heroic development, just at the highest stage of awareness, when history is ceasing to be blind fate, and is becoming more and more man's creation, with the relinquishment of utopias, man would lose his will to shape history and therewith his ability to understand it."

What, then, accounts for the contrast between the apathy and complacency of the popular mood and the existence and even urgency of the issues before us? Some of these issues transcend in importance, not only for society as a whole but for each individual citizen, most of the issues that in the past have commanded the passionate commitment of the people. Is the nuclear-armaments race, for instance, not more important than a tax on tea or the expansion of slavery to new territories? Objectively, there can of course be no doubt that it is, but it has not aroused the political passions of the American people one way or the other to make it a political issue. Why is this so? Two interrelated answers suggest themselves.

The great unresolved issues, while intellectually recognized by at least a minority, are not experienced by the mass of the people as being of direct concern to, or manageable by, them. A century ago, the legal issue of slavery could be settled by a presidential proclamation emancipating the slaves; yet it takes more than a decision of the Supreme Court to stop the treatment of their descendants as though they were still slaves. It was easier to free the slaves than it is to ensure that their descendants will be dealt with as equals. And a century ago the issue of slavery presented itself in so clear-cut a fashion that a civil war could be fought about it. On the other hand, the contemporary issue of equality in all its practical ramifications is too complex to allow at least thoughtful and responsible people to take so simple a position pro or con.

Admitted that the nuclear-armaments race threatens all of us with destruction, that our public education is inadequate, that our economic system is wasteful and potentially destructive, "I personally," says the man in the street, "have nothing to complain about, I am satisfied. And if I were not, what could I do about it?" The vital link between the intellectual awareness of unresolved issues and the resolution not to leave them unresolved is missing. The man in the street is no longer convinced that public issues will, or even ought to, yield to concerted popular action. They have become remote, unintelligible, and intractable; they are the province of technical experts. And if the experts cannot cope with them, how can he?

This abdication of political will on the part of the electorate is duplicated by the abdication of political leadership. The potential political leaders justify that abdication by citing the political apathy of the electorate. There is no political mileage, they say, for instance, in stopping the nuclear-arms race, in a radical reform of the economic and educational systems. The failure of isolated attempts, such as Adlai Stevenson's in the campaign of 1956, to identify the electorate with the solution of these issues seems to bear out their reluctance. So does the success of Barry Goldwater, who either denies the existence of the great issues of the age or proposes simple and painless solutions for them.

How can the gap be bridged between these great issues and our modes of thought and action? Both the nature of the issues and the American tradition indicate the answer to that question. The novelty and complexity of the issues preclude one comprehensive, systematic solution in the grand manner. What is possible and necessary is what American society has always done when it had to come to terms with a new and vital problem: to carry it toward at least a provisional solution, suggested by some general philosophic principle, through a series of piecemeal pragmatic attacks.

This book was initiated by Americans for Democratic Action, though it presents independent contributions to the solutions of problems of general concern. The purpose of the book is to clarify at least some of these problems and to present for discussion some pragmatic attacks upon them. It seeks out some of the crossroads at which we stand and tries to glimpse some of the roads we must travel. This book can claim no more than to be a modest and uncertain beginning in a task upon whose performance the survival of American society depends. Its faults are in good measure the faults of American society, perplexed in the face of the issues with which it must, but would rather not, deal. Whatever merit it has lies in its call upon American society to stop averting its gaze from these issues, in its attempt to define some of them and explore solutions to them.

Equality and Freedom—the Unfinished Agenda

The Future of the Race Issue

STANLEY H. LOWELL

It has become commonplace to say that the United States today stands at a crossroads. The issue of equality of races, which has tormented us since the introduction of Negro slavery into the colonies, has become the number one domestic and, perhaps, foreign policy issue we face. It has permeated every aspect of our democracy. Nothing more important faces us. We must choose the road that we are to follow in the future and the decision that we make will effect the nature and content of American democracy for generations to come.

It is no longer possible for us to continue to live a lie, to make believe that our image of ourselves as a free society with equal treatment for all is reality; the harsh truths of the Negro revolution have finally stripped away the papier-mâché façade that we have used to mask the built-in inequities of past centuries.

Every American carries somewhere in his heart the image of an America free from human misery and tears, where there is equal opportunity for each individual regardless of race or color, where there is freedom from fear and want, and where simple human decency pervades all relationships between people—the

"Great Society"! Today, if we are honest with ourselves, we must recognize that there is a large blemish in the mirror in which we see ourselves. That blemish mars the picture of a free society; it is now spreading until soon we will not be able to see ourselves at all save as a monstrously distorted and perverse reflection. Unless we find solutions now to the rankling issue of racial equality, we will forfeit our dream image and a certain hope will be forever lost to the world.

Again, if we are honest with ourselves, we must reflect on the impact our true image has abroad. What do the emerging peoples of Africa, Asia, and South America, so many of whom fall into the category we call colored, see? Why should they really trust us until we set our house in order?

It has been left by history to our generation to face this issue, once and for all. It was not faced by the founding fathers; it was not faced squarely in the reconstruction period after the Civil War; nor by the labor movement of the thirties. We have no time to lament these earlier failures or to bemoan the fact that we do not meet this Herculean task in a period of domestic and international tranquility, but rather in the midst of the greatest foreign crisis in our history. There is a kind of self-protective cloud that nations as well as individuals live in—that makes us imagine we will endure forever. Unless the race problems that torment Americans are resolved, our future as a great nation and a great democracy is in question.

The only Americans who have faced the color question squarely so far in our history have been its main victims, our Negro citizens themselves. ("Main victims" because it bears repeating that we are all victims of prejudice.) It is they who have made the most eloquent and effective protests, and the Negro revolution which is now in being is their creation. Responsibility for its success, however, rests with all of us. The mood of militancy which became apparent in the late fifties was there all along; like an iceberg it was mostly submerged. Now that the Negro in our society has exploded into full view, we see that there are many differing views and tendencies operating within that community itself. It has come as a shock to many whites to learn that there is virulent racism also among Negroes. The demagogy expressed by the Black Muslims and other forms of black nationalism has not yet been fully grasped by the liberal community at large. No rational person can endorse violence for its own sake, and the violence and threats of violence exhibited last summer by the nationalists cannot be condoned. In the long run, however, some benefit may arise from the fire. We have at the very least been forced to look at the entirety of the Negro community, instead of the fortunate, particular few at the top.

Yet, no people have been more aware of the limitations of the Negro community than the responsible leaders of that community themselves. They have been telling us all along. Somehow, we were not really listening. White liberals, hysterically hypersensitive about appearing to "lecture" Negroes, let the opportunity for a real dialogue slip away. We must reopen that dialogue without delay.

Initially, we cannot escape the tremendous importance of finding the answer to the question "who speaks for the Negro?" One of the things we must clarify is exactly what we mean by the ubiquitous and oft-used phrase "responsible leadership." We must find out and agree, Negro and white, what and who is a responsible leader. Surely we cannot accept only those who do not "rock the boat," or only those who happen to agree that our own formulas are the ultimate in wisdom. One criterion for measuring responsibility of Negro leadership may well be evidence of the desire to bring their people into, not away from, the full compass of our national life.

Continuing and full communication is essential to the future. All over the United States the greatest progress has been made where the fullest communication has existed. Spokesmen for each community have the obligation to talk, to clarify, to discuss every aspect of the problem as it develops. Every resource, every forum, every medium must be available so that the most complete dialogue may be carried on in the presence of the

American people. Negroes cannot be left to talk only to Negroes, liberals to liberals; the totality of our society must be involved in the meaning of the struggle for equality, its benefits to the full community, and the nature of the solutions proposed. Without communication, leaders, however responsible, will talk only to themselves. Most important, as the major civil rights organizations have said, responsible Negro leadership desperately needs responsive white leadership as it relates to jobs and job advancement, improved housing and educational opportunities. It is the substance, the reality, of our progress in these vital and essential areas that will permit the leadership of the minority community to succeed in its task.

Turning from method to means, we have begun to understand that it is important to alter the social structure by chipping away and ultimately eliminating the underlying economic limitations on the Negro, which have "frozen in" the discriminatory pattern of our American society.

Although the passage of the Civil Rights Act of 1964 has given what was in part a moral issue the strength and backing of the law and made integration the official policy of our national government, it is not enough. Perhaps greater and more important is the passage of the anti-poverty Economic Opportunity Act of 1964, because basic to any progress on the race issue is economic progress. We know that much of the American color psychosis can be traced directly to anxiety about dollars and cents. The Negro, brought here against his will, entered the labor market from beneath the bottom, first as a slave and then, when freed, as a pool of cheap labor threatening the status of the white working man. We know that this is still perhaps the main reason for organized labor's curious inability to mount a real offensive in the civil rights area, an area which would seem logically to be one of the first objectives in terms of its oft-stated aims.

The structure of discrimination, in this country, is in the form of a great pyramid—with economics (jobs) at the base and poor, segregated housing and schools resting in layers respectively above. Experience has shown us that we must make progress at the base of the pyramid to be able to effect more than token changes above. Dollars, jobs, and job advancement are the foundation stones on which change must be based. It will do no good to tell Negroes that they are legally free to move into apartments in non-segregated areas, until they can also afford to pay the rent. It does no good to stress to the Negro the importance of diligent application to the job when he so often sees less-deserving white men promoted over his head. We will never eliminate the ghettos by the passage of fair housing laws *alone*, nor will we abolish the segregated school *solely* by mass transportation of pupils.

If we give the Negro the means—the economic means—to better himself, unfettered by the chains of segregation and discrimination, then he will use these means to seek for himself better housing and fuller educational opportunity. In a real sense the attack on poverty in America, of importance to white and Negro alike, will strike a blow for the egalitarian society that cannot be duplicated by civil rights laws, no matter how stringent.

Verbal acceptance of this premise is not enough. We talk incessantly of creativity; it is time that we showed some. New ideas, new methods to achieve true *equality in our time* must be advanced.

The concept of *special effort* or *affirmative action*, although initially resisted, is gaining greater acceptance as an essential element of a program of equality. In essence it states that the basic definition of equal opportunity must be broadened to include the recognition of the urgent necessity for special effort and action to overcome the inequities resulting from past discrimination. In 1963, the New York City Commission on Human Rights called for this special effort in a statement which stated that "for one hundred years the deliberate color consciousness of a prejudiced and unconcerned white majority has placed the Negro at a competitive disadvantage that cannot be eliminated by old methods and old means." The Commission urged aggressive action in every area to accelerate the minority groups' full participation in the benefits of American freedom. Color consciousness as a concomitant of such an effort, the Commission affirmed, was necessary and appropriate. This special effort cannot be defeated by doctrinaire approaches based upon our so-called color-blind approach to society. Certainly our civil rights laws say that each one must be treated "without regard to race or color." Yet it would be a tragedy and a strange paradox if this language were used to prevent the achievement of integration in jobs, housing, and education. But this is what some so-called experts propose. They would adhere strictly to the letter of the law and refuse to permit any action in behalf of a group which has been discriminated against because of its color, which action in their behalf takes into account that same color!

In the field of education, this approach has met comparatively little resistance. One education board after another throughout the nation is prepared to spend additional funds in minority-group areas to make up for the inadequate and second-class education offered to Negroes in the past. More resistance has developed to the action of Federal, State and City agencies in the housing field to eliminate discrimination by private realtors, while simultaneously developing direct government housing and urban renewal programs to remove the Negro from his traditional slum.

But, most important of all, in the area of jobs and job advancement, our entire society has begun to accept the need for specialized efforts, creative action, a compensatory approach. There has been worked out by the Federal government under President Kennedy's and President Johnson's direction a program known as "Affirmative Action," specifically set up by Presidential Executive Order No. 18925. This program has received little publicity, but it has been hailed as a new concept in contract management.

Under this Executive Order, for example, Air Force contractors, in pursuance of this "affirmative action," are required to submit employment pattern reviews. The burden is put on the contractor to examine his personnel and to take affirmative action to insure that minority-group applicants are employed on these Federal defense contracts. If a number of minority-group applicants are not applying for a position, the contractor must establish new techniques which will stimulate more applications. The contractor must actively encourage minority-group employees to take advantage of training programs and educational opportunities. The contractor is required to utilize qualified members of minority groups in job assignments, where they are not presently employed. Other minority-group employees are encouraged to seek out and refer qualified minority-group job applicants, and training is urged into administrative positions with recruits from among minority groups.

No matter the language that may be used, the essential element of the Presidents' "affirmative action" program is a *specialized effort*, which brings the Negro into job opportunity and job advancement where he has never had such opportunity before.

In the same fashion the front pages of our newspapers have recently carried story after story of the affirmative efforts taken by business and industry to reassess their policies and their employment practices with respect to the Negro community. The hiring of Negroes for office and other executive positions has jumped substantially. This program, under the jurisdiction of the President's Committee on Equal Opportunity, is an active, aggressive effort to seek out the Negro in our community who is qualified, and give him the chance that society has refused him before.

It is essential to understand that such an equalization program does not represent the advocacy of the violation of our existing laws against discrimination because of race or color. Business after business and industry after industry have found that it is compatible with our existing laws. Nevertheless, to the extent that this special effort meets resistance on the ground that it violates present "color-blind" statutes, then those statutes should be amended to permit progress to be made. Nor does this concept constitute support for the institution of quotas. On the contrary, quotas are a device whose very existence places limitations on progress. Nor does the equalization program propose that any person be fired so that another, a Negro, may replace him. Finally, the program does not propose that persons should be hired who are not qualified for the job. It is not suggested in any way that standards be reduced to resolve the problem of discrimination. What is suggested is that the responsibility exists for the entire community to lift up the group which has been discriminated against, by training and education if necessary, so that it may meet the qualifications required.

It is the Negro as a group which has suffered the wholesale prejudice of the past. It is the group which has been deprived; it is the group which has been discriminated against. Therefore, it is the group for which affirmative steps must be taken by seeking out qualified Negroes for jobs and job advancement, by providing on-the-job training where exclusion has been the pattern, by offering special services in our schools to disadvantaged Negro children and by rooting out the Negro slums and replacing them with adequate housing.

It is heartening that not only the government under the influence of civil rights leaders, but employers, large and small, have begun to accept this color-conscious, special-effort approach to the achievement of *equality in our time*. Affirmative action can be a positive force for solution of the race issue, as Negro color consciousness has been an evil in the past.

Finally, one of the essential targets for the future must be the unification and strengthening of the civil rights movement itself. A new wave of "know-nothingism" seems to be sweeping the land, and it is now apparent that we are faced with a negative political reaction on a scale never before seen in America. It must be obvious that we can no longer afford to flounder along as a loose coalition of the minority ethnic groups, the so-called liberals and a small enlightened group of the labor move-

ment. There is a strong possibility that the civil rights movement and its advocates can be isolated and destroyed, unless we
accept the vital importance of reforming the coalition. We
must think our way out of past confusions that have hobbled us
and resist the temptation to isolated action which may well
mean eventual defeat.

For three decades in America the coalition for progress has
been the labor movement, the minority community and the
liberals. That alliance achieved its unity not through any formal
arrangements, but from an understanding of mutual interest,
joint concerns, and joint support of projects and political leaders. With an understanding of the importance of the elimination of poverty from our American society and of the importance of full employment to all, Negro and white alike, the
beginning of a mutual program may emerge. The slogan which
both labor and the civil rights leaders can adhere to, "full employment, full integration," would seem to fill the prescription
for mutuality that is essential to strength. The civil rights movement should not be in apposition, much less opposition, to
organized labor. Similarly the labor movement must do more
than give lip service to its expressed support for equal opportunity regardless of race or color.

These parallel efforts toward full employment and full integration may well fuse what has become two camps, uncertainly
bridged by the liberals and intellectuals. Liberals, the labor
movement, and the civil rights advocates can and must be
natural allies in achieving social movement. Our mutual concerns demand that we band together.

It is late.

The Supreme Court
and Civil Liberties

JOSEPH L. RAUH, JR.

THE price of liberty, every American learns at school, is eternal vigilance. But who is its guardian, who maintains this constant watch? In recent decades, we have tended to rely almost exclusively on the Supreme Court—whose members, unlike Senators and Congressmen, are insulated by life tenure from the political pressure of the day. Yet is is becoming obvious that the contribution of the Court, although pre-eminent, is far from sufficient, and that the responsibility for guarding—and extending —our liberties needs to be more broadly shared.

Thomas Jefferson could and did say in his First Inaugural Address: "If there be any among us who would wish to dissolve this Union or to change its republican form, let them stand undisturbed as monuments of the safety with which error of opinion may be tolerated where reason is left free to combat it."

But Jefferson spoke a century before the emergence of totalitarian parties—communist and fascist—which systematically exploit democratic liberties in order to destroy them. Nor could he have anticipated that adherents of these parties, during the hot and cold wars since 1939, could prove to be security risks or even traitors.

We have undergone severe tests of our democracy's capacity to tolerate error and it cannot be said that the legislative and executive branches of our Government have passed them with flying colors. Congress quivered with fright every time the late Senator Joseph McCarthy rose to his feet, and his own colleagues in the Senate censured him only after he had substantially destroyed himself. The House of Representatives year after year perpetuates and richly endows the House Un-American Activities Committee.

Nor can we rely with any confidence upon the executive branch of Government, despite the good intentions and honest efforts of recent Presidents. A hangover McCarthyism still pervades many of its personnel procedures. Even today security-screening is so arbitrarily administered that a young sailor can be denied promotion because of an allegedly subversive aunt— and the sailor's family is too frightened of the Navy to carry the fight into the public arena. And the head of the FBI, the all-but-universally accepted arbiter of loyalty and Americanism, is a man who once publicly identified himself as an admirer of Joseph McCarthy and a witness to his honesty.

In default of other guardians, therefore, it is understandable that we have looked to the Supreme Court to maintain those basic liberties reserved to the American people by the First Amendment to the Constitution, which provides that: "Congress shall make no law . . . abridging the freedom of speech, or of the press; or the right of the people peaceably to assemble, and to petition the Government for a redress of grievances."

It was not, in fact, until 1919 that the Supreme Court decided a significant case under the First Amendment. In *Schenck v. U.S.* the Court upheld a conviction under a Federal statute against "criminal syndicalism." But it was in this case that Mr. Justice Holmes in a dissenting opinion enunciated his historic "clear and present danger" doctrine. He held that the Constitutional guarantee of freedom of speech applies unless the utterance presents a "clear and present danger" of disorder.

A number of important decisions protecting basic American freedoms flowed from the Holmes doctrine—particularly after the Court, in 1925, decided that the Constitutional restraints upon Congress applied, through the "due process" clause of the Fourteenth Amendment, to state and local governments as well. In a number of cases, mostly involving local laws, the Court upheld freedom of speech on public streets and in public parks, freedom to preach door-to-door (in a series of Jehovah's Witnesses' cases), and freedom of publication from state censorship.

Both historically and logically, it would seem that constitutional restraints upon Congressional power to interfere with freedom of speech should be applied most stringently when the object of restraint is heretical political opinion or belief. But this has not been the case. The Congress has enacted three sedition acts in its history, and none of them has ever been invalidated on First Amendment grounds.

Indeed, in 1951, in the heyday of McCarthyism, the Court upheld the Smith Act of 1940 by materially adulterating the Holmes doctrine of "clear and present danger" which it had previously applied. In the case of *Dennis v. U.S.*, a divided Court upheld the conviction of leading officials of the American Communist Party for "advocating" the overthrow of the Federal Government. The majority opinions did not altogether mesh with one another, but they seemed to recognize that the Smith Act did apply a direct restraint upon freedom of speech, and therefore had somehow to meet the "clear and present danger" test. The result was the recasting of the Holmes formula, so that "the gravity of the evil [to be prevented] discounted by its probability" became the test of whether Congress unjustifiably encroached upon freedom of speech.

In short, the Court in this decision held that the danger of the overthrow of the prevailing order need no longer be "clear and present" in order to permit Congress to limit freedom of speech and association. Doctrinal niceties aside, the Court in effect decided that advocacy of the forcible overthrow of government, at least in a conspiratorial context, is not the kind of free speech protected by the First Amendment.

After this backward step, the Supreme Court on June 17, 1957, took four giant steps forward.

In *Yates v. U.S.*, the Court all but invalidated the Smith Act. This case concerned the conviction of a number of officials of the California Communist Party. In reversing the convictions, the Court drew a distinction between the advocacy of the forcible overthrow of government "as an abstract doctrine" and the advocacy of "action to that end," only the latter being beyond the sanctuary of protected speech. Although it did not specifically overrule its decision in *Dennis v. U.S.*, it did seem to return to the Holmes doctrine in something like its original form, and hence to cast grave doubt upon the constitutionality of the Smith Act.

In *Watkins v. U.S.*, the Court struck a heavy blow against the House Un-American Activities Committee. Watkins was a labor organizer who declared himself entirely willing to tell the Committee about his own past, but refused to inform on former Communist associates who had repented of their activities and presented no existing danger to the country. The Court reversed his conviction for contempt, on the ground that the Committee's generalized demand for the names of former associates—a demand to which the Committee, as is well known, is much addicted—was unlawful in the absence of a clear explanation of the Committee's need for the names. Although the actual grounds for the decision were narrow, Chief Justice Warren's opinion included a strong (and potentially fatal) indictment of the Committee's loose and undisciplined inquiries and inquisitions.

In *Sweezey v. New Hampshire*, the Court applied similar limitations on the operations of State "subversive activities" investigating committees. Professor Sweezey had declined to inform the State investigators about his past associates and activities in the Progressive Party of New Hampshire. The Court held that this inquiry impaired academic and political freedoms.

In the absence of a clear legislative manifestation of desire for the information sought, it found the inquiry to be unauthorized.

Also on the same day, the Court struck down the dismissal of John Stewart Service by Secretary of State Acheson, after numerous Department hearing panels had found no reason to question Mr. Service's loyalty. In the Service case, the Court ruled that the Secretary had failed to observe his own promulgated regulations in effecting the dismissal action, which was thereby rendered procedurally invalid.

So far as civil liberties are concerned, June 17, 1957, was the Court's finest hour. Both the Smith Act and the House Un-American Activities Committee emerged from these decisions alive, but gravely—and, it appeared, mortally—wounded. The rights of civil servants under Government charges had been reasserted, after years during which they had seemed to dwindle almost to the vanishing point. The decisions seemed to confirm the recovery of the nation from the nightmare years of McCarthyism, and to lay the groundwork for the reassertion in their full vigor of First Amendment freedoms. It was reasonable to expect that the Court would move forward along the new paths it had staked out.

Unfortunately, this has not happened. June 17, 1957, proved to be the high-water mark at the Court for civil liberties, and the tide has receded in subsequent years. The 1957 decisions have largely been shunted aside or limited, so that they have had little practical and continuing effect.

The counterattack upon the Supreme Court's civil libertarian achievements in 1957 was prompt and furious. A group of Senators headed by Messrs. Eastland and Jenner launched an attack upon the Court as a subversive institution. Public hearings were held on Senator Jenner's bill to limit the jurisdiction of the Supreme Court, and it elicited considerable support. A convention of State Supreme Court Justices issued a public attack upon the Court's rulings. Segregationists, blasting away at the school cases, added to the fury of the attack.

The message was heard by the sharply-divided Court. The

balance began to swing. In 1961, the Court sustained the Mc-Carran Act against First Amendment attack, upholding a statutory requirement that the officials of the Communist Party register with the Attorney General, furnishing also the names and addresses of all its members, the addresses of its major offices, financial information, and other details concerning its operation. Registration alone raised serious enough problems with regard to freedom of speech and the right of association; together with the other onerous requirements, the McCarran Act was patently calculated to suppress the Communist Party altogether.

Speaking for the majority of the Court, Mr. Justice Frankfurter observed that, as against the "impediments which particular governmental regulation causes to the entire freedom of individual action, there must be weighed the value to the public of the ends which the regulation may achieve." Paramount in the Court's evaluation of these "ends" were the legislative findings of Congress that the International Communist conspiracy imperiled this country's internal security. These it accepted without examination.

In *Scales v. U.S.*, also decided in 1961, the Court blighted the hopes that it had aroused in its decision in the Yates case. By virtually returning to its 1951 Dennis decision, it revived the Smith Act, upholding its clause that active membership in the Communist Party is illegal if the accused was aware of the Party's objectives when he joined.

The House Un-American Activities Committee also enjoyed a new lease on life. In the case of *Barenblatt v. U.S.*, decided in 1959, the Court affirmed the conviction of an ex-college teacher for refusing to answer almost the same kinds of questions that had been put to Watkins. Here the Court articulated the doctrine by which it has implicitly resolved most of the critical issues spawned by McCarthyism—the "balancing test." In the Barenblatt case, Mr. Justice Harlan declared for the majority of the Court: "Where First Amendment rights are asserted to bar governmental interrogations, resolution of the issue always involves a balancing by the courts of the competing private and public interests at stake in the particular circumstances shown."

Also in 1959, the Court in *Uphaus v. Wyman* took back most of what it had affirmed earlier in *Sweezey v. New Hampshire*. It now upheld the power of the very same state investigating committee to require the organizer of a "World Fellowship" summer camp to produce its guest lists for 1954–1955. Uphaus and his camp were found to have a sufficient connection with "Communist front" activities or allegedly subversive organizations to require wholesale disclosure of the camp's guests to satisfy the supposed security need of the State of New Hampshire for information concerning subversive activities.

Alone among the four historic cases decided on June 17, 1957, the Service case stands undiluted by subsequent decisions. But it has hardly proven itself in practical results; no adequate reforms have since been effected in the loyalty and security procedures for government employees.

Additional encroachments upon freedom of thought and expression, which have been sanctioned by a majority of the Court, include the use of Government test oaths, in the form of non-Communist affirmations, as a condition for union leadership, state employment, admission to the bar, and the like. The Court has also upheld the power of Congress to deport legally resident aliens because of Communist Party membership, even when their membership had terminated before the enactment of the law which authorized such deportation.

A dauntless minority of Justices, spearheaded by Black and Douglas, has battled unremittingly against the "balancing test" and other doctrinal innovations which tend to limit First Amendment freedoms. Justice Black has stated his position in these words: "My belief is that we must have freedom of speech, press and religion for all or we may eventually have it for none. I further believe that the First Amendment grants an absolute right to believe in any governmental system, discuss all governmental affairs, and argue for desired changes in the existing order." But the balancing test is the law, and security has too often outweighed liberty in striking the constitutional balance.

It is the majority which decides. And it is the position of the majority which has led Dean Eugene Rostow of Yale to write: "Civil liberties in the U.S. are in a state of grave crisis, and I venture to hope that some of these decisions of the Supreme Court will not prove to be its lasting position."

Too much, of course should not be expected of the Court alone. Like all agencies of government, it is composed of human beings—its personnel (and changes in its personnel) are matters of considerable consequence. President Johnson may well determine the future of the Court and of civil freedom in America if and when he selects successors for those great civil libertarians, Warren, Black, and Douglas. And, quite apart from the question of personnel, there are institutional obstacles to the attainment of the millennium.

We must remember that, when it makes a decision in defense of civil liberties, the Court is often setting a pioneer standard—a standard which, to have full effect, requires acceptance by the other organs of government and, more importantly, by the people. In a very real sense, as Harold Laski wrote: "Authority . . . is always acting at its peril. It lives not by its power to command but by its power to convince." Moreover, the Supreme Court does not enjoy the same access to public opinion as do Presidents and Congressmen. It communicates to the American people only through its decisions—and it cannot count upon more than a small minority to read them.

The Court is also limited by the judicial method, which requires the formulation of legal doctrine case by case. In the interpretation of the law, both the past and the future must be taken into account; the law draws its force from the traditions of the past, and its present and future utility from its responsiveness to current social needs.

Yet, with all these qualifications, the situation is replete with tragic ironies. The inimitable Mr. Dooley, had he still been giving us the benefit of his trenchant comments, might have observed once more, with respect to the Dennis case in 1951, that the Supreme Court follows the election returns. But what would he have made of the decisions since then, which at least at times seem to run contrary to them?

There are larger ironies than this. There is the irony that, in the course of taking measures intended to protect our freedoms against totalitarian threats from without and within, we have ourselves accepted curtailment of our traditional freedoms. There is the irony that, while we have tolerated the erosion of basic freedoms, a growing number of courageous men and women within the Communist world are reasserting them. To take but one example, Prof. Robert Havemann, a lifelong Communist, said in a series of lectures in East Berlin last year: "Freedom cannot be bought by voluntarily doing what one is asked to do because otherwise one would be thrown into jail." And, in words which echoed Thomas Jefferson, he said: "In the whole of history, reactionary regimes have sought to keep the people in ignorance."

No one, in fact, values freedom so highly as people who have been deprived of it. We have taken our liberties too much for granted. We have relied too much upon the Supreme Court to maintain the "eternal vigilance" which they require, and as a people we have assumed too little of the responsibility ourselves.

We certainly cannot put the whole burden of the preservation of our liberties upon nine men, however learned and estimable. It is a task for the legislative and executive branches of government, no less than the judicial. It is a task for all of us.

There was a time when the First Amendment freedoms were expressed in words which came readily to the lips of Americans. When we thought of saying something that was on our minds, writing something that we wanted others to read, or associating with whomever we liked, we used to say: "Why not? It's a free country."

We should use these words over and over again, until they

once more come naturally. Our basic freedoms are not mere historical relics, to be preserved under glass in our national archives. They are meant to be used—and used vigorously. As we put them to use, we shall depend less upon courts of law and more upon the conscience of the community to make the exercise of freedom a living reality in our national life.

Beyond the Welfare State

Reconstruction

in American Economics

LEON H. KEYSERLING

Ever since the attainment of peace in Korea removed the galvanizing effects of wartime, the United States economy has suffered (with only minor ups and downs) from chronically rising idleness of manpower and plant. More important, despite some recent gains, no really large improvements seem just around the corner.

Unsatisfactory economic performance indicates inadequate national economic policies. I have on various occasions been critical of these policies during the Eisenhower and Kennedy Administrations, and most of these policies still remain. The time which has run since then (as of this writing) has not been long enough, nor the changes in national economic policies extensive enough, to permit further evaluation.

It has become fashionable, at least since early 1961, to attribute the inadequacies of our national economic policies to so-called "political" difficulties in the Congress or among the people. But the real cause is far more fundamental: the trend of the "best" economic thinking, upon which a President and his Administration must rely in policy *formulation* before going to the Congress and the people, has run substantially counter to the real problems and needs of the American economy. Mainly, there has been unwillingness to recognize that *excessively* disparate income distribution is basic to our economic troubles and related social evils: excessive idleness of manpower and plant; low economic growth; and an amount of poverty intolerable in terms of our productive potentials.

The unity of the economic and moral problem in the United States

Recognition of this distributional problem should not be a divisive but rather a unifying force in American life. Indeed, our situation is peculiarly fortunate just because the measures required to bring income distribution more into line with the social conscience (that is, not to achieve a drab equalitarianism, but to avoid the glaring contrasts of luxury and poverty) would be identical with the measures required for improved economic growth and full employment. These measures would yield more to almost everyone in *absolute* terms even though they would involve some altering of the shares to be distributed. And the commonly heard pleas that adequate economic growth in itself would not solve the problems of unemployment or poverty, that full employment in itself would not solve the problems of inadequate economic growth or poverty, and that neither would *per se* strike a proper balance between public needs and private tailfins, misconceive the whole nature of the challenge.

This does not mean that even high economic "growth," regardless of its content, would be tolerable; nor that all of the poor are unemployed or underemployed, although a large percentage of them are; nor that all of the unemployed are poor, although most of them are at least temporarily; nor that the very high rate of poverty among our senior citizens who are too old to work can be cured by giving them jobs. But it does mean emphatically these two things: *First,* adequate economic growth, which when properly understood means the growth rate required to maintain full employment and the content required to serve the priorities of our needs, would on the basis of all experience and reason be the most powerful single weapon toward reduction of poverty; and second, massive direct programs to uplift the poor through raising their levels of living would be the first and foremost lever toward higher economic growth and full employment. This would be true whether these programs took the form of better wages and/or more jobs, or of better housing and health services and education and training mainly through enlarged public outlays, or more helpfully took both forms.

In short, the huge underdeveloped market for goods and services in the United States, resulting from more than 34 million people living in poverty and more than another 32 million living in deprivation between poverty and a barely adequate American standard of living, is the main reason why we are not making full use of our productive resources of manpower and plant and hence not enjoying an adequate rate of economic growth. Living in poverty are about 9 million families with money incomes under $3,000 and 5 million unrelated individuals with money incomes under $1,500. Living in deprivation are about 8½ million families above the poverty level but with money incomes under $5,000 and almost 2 million unattached individuals above the poverty level but with money incomes under $2,500. (The average number of people in the poor families, which include many old couples whose children have left them, is somewhat lower than the average number of people in the deprived families.)

The poor economic and social performance,
1953–mid-1964

According to customarily used official statistics, full-time unemployment rose inexorably (with some ups and downs) from 2.9 percent of the civilian labor force in 1953 to 5.6 percent in

1963 and stood at 5.4 percent in mid-1964, even though a recession began in the middle of 1953, and mid-1964 marked the third full year in an uninterrupted "recovery" movement! We must also take into account the full-time equivalent of part-time unemployment, and the concealed unemployment of those not counted as within the civilian labor force—and therefore not counted as unemployed—whom the scarcity of jobs has discouraged from looking for employment. Thus, the true level of unemployment rose from 4.9 percent in 1953 to 8.5 percent in the first half of 1964 (seasonably adjusted), or from 3.2 million to 6.4 million. Correspondingly, the production "gap," representing the difference between actual production and maximum production, rose (as I estimate it in uniform 1963 dollars) from an only nominal gap in 1953 to 80 billion dollars or 11.7 percent of the maximum production in the first half of 1964 (annual rate). For the whole period from the beginning of 1953 we lost an estimated 529 billion dollars of total national production (measured in 1963 dollars) through the first half of 1964, and about 32 million man-years of employment opportunity.

The consequences have been most severe where needs have been greatest. The past decade has witnessed an average annual reduction of only slightly above one percent in the total number of Americans living in poverty, as against an annual rate of reduction several times higher during long previous periods of reasonably full resource use. Since 1953, it appears that there has been very little reduction in the number of Americans who receive even less than half the amount required to lift them above the poverty level. In the public sector, the poor economic performance since 1953 has in itself reduced tax collections at all levels of government by at least 135 billion dollars. This has added mightily to the growing neglect of those domestic public services which serve very important national needs and play a significant role in reducing poverty—especially in a climate which tends to adjust public outlays to tax receipts instead of adjusting them to the real needs of the nation.

The chronic rise of idle manpower and plant is intimately

associated with a low rate of economic growth. Optimum economic growth is the rate required to utilize fully the growing labor force despite rapidly accelerating automation and other technological advances. From the beginning of 1953 to the middle of 1964, the average annual economic growth rate in real terms was only 2.9 percent, contrasted with an average annual rate of between 4 and 5 percent which examination of all relevant factors indicates would have been optimum. Even during the two years ending with mid-1964, the average annual economic growth rate was only somewhat above 4 percent. This should be contrasted, not with the 5 percent or so (in view of the most recent technological advances) which would be adequate *after* full economic restoration, but rather with the rate of 8–9 percent which would have been needed during these two years for reasonably full economic restoration by mid-1964. This explains why the full-time unemployment rate of 5.4 percent in mid-1964, while somewhat lower than the 5.6 percent rate in 1963 as a whole, was nonetheless *higher*—despite an uninterrupted so-called "recovery" from early 1961 on—than the rates in comparable stages of the "recoveries" from the recessions of 1953–1954 and 1957–1958. This leads me to conclude that the chronic rise of unemployment and other unused resources has not been significantly interrupted and that, without drastic policy and program changes, the next recession will lift the unemployment rate higher than it was during any of the three recessions thus far since the Korean war.

Aggregate demand
and economic equilibrium

"Modern" economic theory expresses a not very useful truism when it observes that excessive idleness of manpower and plant exists because aggregate spending (demand) for goods and services—composed of private business investment, private consumer expenditures, and public outlays—is not sufficient to keep our resources fully in use. For, at least theoretically, a higher or lower volume of dollars spent should affect the price level rather than the volume of production and employment. Thus, it is maladjustments in the *composition* of spending (closely allied with income maldistribution), rather than any serious deficiency in aggregate purchasing power, which have periodically destroyed economic equilibrium and turned the economy from an adequate rate of economic growth toward recurrent recessions or economic stagnation. To illustrate with an extreme case, if all of the spending were for plants and none of it for consumption, no aggregate volume of spending could be high enough to keep the economy in shape for very long.

Based upon my construction of economic equilibrium models, corrected yearly in terms of actual economic developments, it seems abundantly clear that the prime factor in the economic disequilibrium has been the tendency of private business investment—which adds to producers' facilities—to grow more rapidly than the demand for ultimate products (as distinguished from producers' facilities) in the form of private consumer expenditures and public outlays. The inadequate consumer spending has resulted primarily from inadequate consumer incomes. These incomes have been inadequate in part because wage-rate gains have lagged seriously behind productivity increases. The situation has been aggravated by excessive disparities in personal income distribution which have caused too high a rate of personal saving for investment purposes as against immediate consumer spending. The insufficiency of public outlays has been reflected in the downward trend in the Federal Budget, which has declined from 18.66 percent of total national production in fiscal 1954 to an estimated 15.25 percent in the fiscal 1965 Budget. Meanwhile, during each period of economic upturn (including the current period despite the repressive effect of long-enduring excess plant capacities), private investment in plant and equipment, which is a major factor in enlargement of productive capabilities, has grown immensely more rapidly than the demand for ultimate products. This relative excess of investment has been abetted by an actual oversupply of bank funds for business borrowers, by retained earnings growing even faster than actual investment, and by more than ample profits after taxes—refuting the prevalent notion that tax rates even before the recent gigantic tax reduction have borne down oppressively upon investment. The recurrent sharp downturns in investment, which together with the more enduring deficiencies in private consumer expenditures and public outlays have sparked the recurrent recessions, have not resulted from any inadequacy of after-tax profits or other investment funds; they have occurred only where the outlook for demand for ultimate products plus the amount of idle plant capacity prevented adherence to exuberant investment programs.

Under these circumstances, our economic policies should strive to restore economic equilibrium by using every available method to enlarge private consumer expenditures and public outlays; this in itself would generate enough profit and saving and other inducements to call forth a high enough if not too high rate of private investment in producers' facilities. Before describing how our economic policies have moved mainly in the opposite direction, it is desirable to analyze the unemployment problem a little more closely.

Is United States unemployment a "structural" problem?

Possibly with more heat than light, a controversy is now raging between those who stress the need to enlarge aggregate spending (demand), and those who insist that the training and capabilities of the labor force are ill-suited to the new job opportunities resulting from the new technology and automation. While substantial programs of training and education are always necessary, I agree with the Council of Economic Advisers that sufficient aggregate spending (assuming that proper attention is given to the problem of economic equilibrium, that is, the needed balance between private investment in producers' facilities and demand for ultimate products—a problem which the Council seriously neglects) would lead to remarkably prompt adjustments of the labor force to the nature of available jobs and would reduce unemployment to a "frictional" level plus a relatively small number of people still needing personalized help. This view is reinforced by experience during wartime and other periods when the economic climate was sufficiently favorable.

But to generate this sufficient amount of aggregate spending, attention must focus upon the *structure* of this spending in ways which go even beyond customary equilibrium analyses. And it is here that the Council of Economic Advisers and many other analysts fall short. For employment opportunity does not occur in general; it occurs in particular occupations. And the amount of additional spending which can be generated for the goods or services turned out by any particular occupation depends not only upon the availability of purchasing power, but also upon the upper limits of the needs and wants of the American people for these particular goods or services. Further, a given number of dollars of additional spending for particular goods or services will have a higher or lower impact upon the employment entailed in their production, depending upon the rate of advance in productivity (output per man-hour worked) in the particular industries; and, in turn, higher demand in some instances tends to speed up the rate of productivity advance.

To illustrate the significance of this: Using the years 1947–1949 as a base period, it took only 47 people working in agriculture in 1963 to produce as much as 100 produced in the base period. Viewing the still-accelerating advance of farm productivity, it is clear that, even with a growing population, improved nutrition programs for the underprivileged in this country, and Herculean efforts to expand our food and fiber exports, no feasible increases in spending for farm products will interrupt—though it should ameliorate—the long-term trend toward less employment opportunity in American agriculture. In all manufacturing, less than 61 workers were required in 1963 to produce as much as 100 produced in the base period. With a constantly rising standard of living, utilization of our manufactured products can increase much more than utilization of our agricultural products. Consequently, if aggregate private and public spending for ultimate products is sufficiently enlarged, the trend toward a decline in manufacturing employment can be reversed. But even in this area, because of the progress of technological advances and of automation in particular, combined with any foreseeable patterns of private and public demand, expansion of manufacturing employment (even with an optimum rate of over-all economic growth) cannot possibly be large enough to take care of a major portion of the 22½–27½ million jobs needed over the next decade to get unemployment down to minimum levels, to absorb the increases in the civilian labor force, and to provide new types of jobs for those who will continue to be displaced from many occupations.

The meaning of all this is plain: The needed employment expansion must occur very largely in those areas of endeavor where unmet national needs and desires are vast enough to absorb an increase in production so large as to more than counteract the consequences of the rising productivity in these same areas of endeavor. The most significant opportunities are in housing and urban renewal, mass transportation and basic resource development, health and educational facilities and personnel, and expansion of various other welfare services. And to obtain large enough volume in these areas will obviously require very large increases in Federal outlays, combined with new admixtures of private and public efforts sparked by new Federal legislation.

Toward an
American Economic Performance Budget

The first task of our economic policy, therefore, is not to make a mechanistic and misleading calculation of how many additional dollars in purchasing power are necessary to achieve economic restoration without due regard for problems of economic equilibrium, essential changes in the structure of spending, the priorities of our private and public needs, or social justice. The first task, instead, is to develop under the Employment Act what I call a long-range *American Economic Performance Budget*, setting forth balanced quantitative objectives for economic progress which bring all of these factors into play.

The goals for employment and production, which should obviously be correlated, would be based on sustained maximum resource use, and would take account both of diverse technological trends and the evolving patterns of our wants and needs. This table of our real resources and goals would indicate the appropriate objectives for purchasing power and its desirable patterns of distribution. We should bear in mind that our financial (purchasing power) mechanisms can always be influenced so as to bring forth full and reasonably wise utilization of our real resources. This is the task of programmatic decisions geared to the quantitative goals. All of this is within the specific mandate of the Employment Act of 1946, calling for goals for maximum employment, production, and purchasing power, plus needed programs. But this mandate of the Act is not being significantly observed.

My equilibrium model indicates the need for drastic changes in the structure of spending and production. In line with these changes: In 1970, compared with 1962, the structure of employment would shift greatly, ranging from a decline of almost 8 percent in agriculture to increases of almost 29 percent in government, about 39 percent in services, and almost 49 percent in contract construction. The immense increases needed in private consumer spending would require (in addition to the indirect impact of the public spending programs subsequently described) wage increases more in line with productivity gains; improved minimum wage legislation; perhaps some shortening of the work week without reductions in weekly pay; a much more progressive Federal tax policy; a reversal of the high interest-rate policy; a new farm program to lift per capita farm income greatly; and a vast increase in the human welfare programs represented by transfer payments. These payments (including among other objectives the doubling within five years of average old-age insurance benefits for the close to 20 million of our senior citizens, more than half of whom now live in poverty) should rise from the 1963 base by more than 70 percent by 1970. No comparable efforts are now in the offing.

Residential nonfarm construction, responsive to the fact that one-fifth of the nation still lives in substandard housing, and that housing and coordinated urban renewal offer by far the largest single opportunity to expand employment, should be lifted to an average of about 2 million units a year during 1964–1970. A balanced program toward this end would require about 400,000 units a year of new publicly assisted housing for low-income families, contrasted with about 60,000 units of publicly assisted housing contemplated in the 1965 Budget (including substantial use of existing housing). It would also require new Federal efforts, with much lower interest rates and public loans or guarantees, to expand production of homes for middle-income groups.

In line with the priorities of our needs for goods and services and the technological nature of the employment problem, the conventional Federal Budget for fiscal 1965 ought to be about 107 billion dollars instead of the 97.9 billion now intended, and then rise to about 116 billion by calendar 1966 and about 135 billion by calendar 1970 (calendar goals in 1963 dollars). With optimum economic growth, both the Federal Budget and the national debt as a percent of total national production would gradually decrease: This would leave room for still more tax reduction, but of the right sort. For economic and social reasons, the great need in this area is to reduce the tax burden on low- and middle-income people, so as to increase their after-tax incomes and lift their standard of living. While there may not be very much room left to reduce personal-income taxes toward this end, there is much room left to reduce sales taxes.

Through expansion starting at once, with heaviest accent upon the first years for both economic and social reasons, per capita Federal outlays for education, comparing calendar 1970 with fiscal 1965, should be increased almost 4 times; for health services and research, more than 2½ times; for public assistance, and for labor and manpower and other welfare services, more than 50 percent; for housing and community development, from a negative figure of $1.57 in fiscal 1965 (when the government took in more than it laid out on its housing programs) to $15.61; and for all domestic programs and services, from $180.96 to $250.71 (all measured in 1963 dollars). Such programs, reconciled with all of the other quantitative objectives set forth in my model American Economic Performance Budget, would by 1970 reduce to nominal numbers those who fall below a genuinely adequate American standard of opportunity and enjoyment. Further, these programs allow for considerable increases in Federal outlays for national defense (if needed), space technology, and international purposes.

The American Economic Performance Budget represents neither top-heavy concentration of responsibility nor excessive "planning" alien to our institutions and values. It does not envisage governmental encroachment upon the traditional functioning of our private economic groups. It does not even propose any major additional types of public functions although it proposes quantitative increases in many of these functions. It does, however, embrace the idea of more planning, but only in the sense of steering more effectively between the Scylla of doctrinaire statism and the Charybdis of doctrinaire laissez faire. According to it, national economic policies would be guided by the same managerial integration and purposefulness which mark large business enterprises; and one of its important by-products would be that the Government could slough off or reduce many of its rapidly proliferating activities by doing a few essential things better. And while the Performance Budget does not improperly mingle private and public responsibilities, the general goals embodied in it would offer voluntary guidelines to the private sector of the economy. The goals for employment, production, and purchasing power, accompanied by meaningful analysis of our potentials and needs, would be helpful to private enterprise in somewhat the same manner as were the "Postwar Market" surveys made by the Government and others toward the end of World War II. Moreover, by providing a better rationale for recommended public policies, the Performance Budget would enlarge private understanding of needed public action. This in itself would tend to reduce greatly the ultimate determination of public policies by a compromise of competing group pressures, because it would bring to the fore the long-range mutuality of real interests which should override the short-range or superficial conflicts. Developed through consultation and cooperation between private economic leadership and the Government, the Performance Budget would help toward that larger degree of unity under freedom which is the fundamental answer to the totalitarian challenge. In many respects, the Performance Budget—though adjusted to our own institutions—would be similar to the "indicative planning" which has sparked the remarkable performance of some countries in Western Europe during the past decade. Nothing short of this can meet our own needs in the second half of the Twentieth Century.

How the war against poverty
fits into the Performance Budget

The foregoing proposals demonstrate in detail the thesis set forth at the outset: A sufficiently comprehensive effort toward optimum economic growth and maximum employment, and a sufficiently massive effort to liquidate poverty at a speed compatible with our economic potentials and social conscience are actually identical. To achieve any of the main objectives, the allocation of available resources must take all objectives into account, determine relative magnitudes, and apply policies accordingly.

Theoretically, we might allocate so much of resources to reduction of poverty that we sacrificed other vital objectives. For example, we could immediately cut our defense outlays to zero, or starve the growth of technology which underpins all economic progress, or move toward a stultifying share-the-wealth program. But none of these is within the realm of possibility. The real danger is entirely in the opposite direction: that an anti-poverty program not thoroughly integrated with treatment of the other great problems of our economic life would be lamentably small in terms of its objective, fail to make its proper contribution to treatment of these other great problems, and concentrate far too much upon a purely "casework" or "welfare" approach which sought to make the poor a bit more comfortable, or lose itself in a few highly dramatic situations, instead of building an economic society in which extensive poverty ceases to exist. Across the whole domestic field, there can be only one *successful* war, fought on many fronts, using both general and specific weapons, but nonetheless guided by a single strategy and never degenerating into random battles by disconnected task forces with only limited awareness of the full significance of their assignments.

Where current national economic policies
fall short

The most important national economic policies in this context are probably (not in the order of their importance) spending, social security, housing, taxation, and monetary management. I have already set forth the inadequacies in current approaches to the first three. The tax concessions to corporations in 1962 and the huge tax reductions in 1964 amount to total tax cuts of an annual value of about 13.1 billion dollars when fully effective. Of this amount, about 6.7 billion (according to my estimates) is allocated to stimulation of private investment, counting both corporate tax cuts and that portion of personal tax cuts for high-income people which they are likely to save and attempt to invest. About 6.4 billion is allocated to stimulation of consumption. The first of these two allocations is almost entirely wasteful, because there is already a surfeit rather than a shortage of available investment funds. And if a substantial portion of this allocation should actually flow into investment, it would tend to incite (as similar policies did prior to the 1957 recession) an unhealthy "boomlet" in the short run, and intensify the economic disequilibrium in the longer run. The allocation to consumption is woefully inadequate.

Further, the distribution of the total personal tax cuts is seriously regressive. About 40 percent of these cuts go to the 12½ percent of taxpayers at the top of the income structure. The disposable or after-tax incomes of families with incomes below $3,000 (the poverty group, according to the Administration's estimates) are increased by only 2 percent, and about the same would apply to all families with incomes below $10,000; meanwhile, families with incomes above $200,000 would receive at least a 16 percent increase in their disposable incomes.

In exchange for the tax cuts already enacted, the Federal Budget for fiscal 1965 is somewhat lower than during the previous year, and almost 6 billion dollars lower than would have resulted from continuation of the average annual rate of increase during the four immediately preceding years. A very large part of the tax cuts is an unwise priority choice in terms of economic stimulation, as each dollar of increased Federal spending has a higher "multiplier" effect than each dollar of tax cuts. Hence, the reversal of the trend toward an expansionary Federal spending policy will probably cancel out much of the shorter-range stimulative effects of the tax cuts (which I think have been greatly overestimated), aside from the unbalancing effects in the longer run and the neglect of the great urgencies of our national needs. As already indicated, I do not expect the level of unemployment by the end of 1964 to represent even a tolerable movement toward maximum employment after almost four years of widely heralded efforts. And I expect unemployment to be much higher when the next recession comes—which seems to me inevitable without drastic policy changes.

To be sure, the reversal of the trend toward an expansionary Federal spending policy has been due in part to large cutbacks in defense spending. To the extent justified by the international situation, such cutbacks are always welcome because of the wasteful nature of the armaments race in a purely economic sense. But it is important to note that, contrary to the nation-wide clamor about the neglected needs in the public sector for several years following the first Sputnik, the trend in Federal *domestic* public spending is now downward by the two most important measurements. Total domestic spending (stated in 1963 dollars) of $182.40 per capita and 5.71 percent of total national production (estimated) in the fiscal 1965 Budget contrasts with $185.67 and 6.01 percent (estimated) in fiscal 1964. It is true that the new Budget adds about a billion dollars to those programs included in the new anti-poverty program, although only about half of this is marked for actual expenditure (as distinguished from commitments) in fiscal 1965. But the adverse trend in total domestic spending is nonetheless inimical to the war against poverty, because many Federal programs outside of the new anti-poverty program but inside the Federal Budget as a whole have a direct bearing upon poverty. Indeed, most Federal domestic spending (including even payments to veterans and certainly farm outlays, but excluding interest payments on the national debt) tends in the main both to improve income distribution and to stimulate economic performance.

The setting of the anti-poverty program in an over-all fiscal and economic policy that is highly unlikely to meet adequately the problems of low economic growth and high unemployment means that this program is highly unlikely to make substantial inroads upon poverty even in the long run. Adequate revision of the program itself would in fact depend upon a very much altered over-all fiscal and economic policy. The rationale advanced by the originators of the anti-poverty program is that the tax reduction will open the doors to adequate economic growth and full employment; and that the anti-poverty program is basically designed to help those whose personal characteristics would otherwise prevent them from moving through these doors. I simply disagree that the tax reduction will open the doors. I do agree that the anti-poverty program is immensely valuable in that it focuses nationwide attention and efforts upon the poverty problem.

Moreover, the program's emphasis upon the training and education of young people assumes, in my view erroneously, that a catalogue of the characteristics of the poor explains why so many people are poor, and that once these characteristics are modified most of them will no longer be poor. This seems to me essentially the same error as that which assumes that excessive unemployment is caused mainly by the deficiencies of training and education of the unemployed. And it seems to me rather strange that the Council of Economic Advisers, which has fought so valiantly against major emphasis upon the retraining approach to unemployment, seems so fully committed to the retraining approach to poverty—even though the preponderant focus of the poverty program is upon *training and educating people for jobs*.

Actually, the explanation of the absolute and relative amount of poverty in almost any country is to be found primarily in the average *per capita* output of the country, and secondarily in how this output is distributed. If the average *per capita* output is such that, under any pattern of income distribution which is feasible in view of the institutions and ideologies of the country, a large number of people must be poor, revealing the special characteristics of the poor does less to explain why so many people are poor than to explain why the poverty has hit the particular people suffering from it. Granted the need for improved income distribution in the United States, the central reason why so many people are still poor today (as distinguished from which people have been hit) is that for a decade or longer our over-all economic growth rate or average per capita growth in output has been abysmally low when measured against our capabilities. This is the case, even though it is true that whatever amount of poverty exists will be concentrated among those who are most vulnerable in personal terms.

This point is so vital that it needs further explanation. If people are poor because a deficiently functioning economy deprives them of jobs, or because they earn low wages for the same reason, it is to be expected that on the average those hurt first and most will be those below others in training or education or other personal characteristics, or those discriminated against because of race or some other irrational reason. Yet obviously a large part of these people would be employed and/or would receive better wages if the over-all economic environment were favorable—as wartime experience so clearly illustrated. Similarly, it is to be expected that when jobs are scarce men are more likely to be able to get jobs than women, and when aggregate wages are too low, to receive better wages—either because of discrimination or differentiated experience or abilities. Yet again, if there were enough jobs to go around and if aggregate wages were sufficiently high, more women would be employed (and at better wages) if they wanted to work, and consequently fewer families headed by women would be poor.

The farm population receives a much lower share of national income per family than others, and hence is much poorer. But this is not because of the characteristics of farmers; it is rather because agriculture in general, in almost all industrial countries, has suffered from relatively weak bargaining power, and is always particularly vulnerable to unfavorable over-all economic conditions. The excessive poverty among old people could not be cured by rejuvenation—to engage in an exercise in science fiction; making them younger, under current economic conditions, would merely mean more unemployment; there is too much poverty among our senior citizens because our social security system has treated them inequitably, but even if it treated them better, this would still be at the expense of others—unless the whole economy were performing better.

If all those with less than eight years of education suddenly blossomed forth with college degrees, they would have a better chance of being less poor by taking jobs away from employed people (or if already employed, by taking better jobs away from other employed people); but this would be the only way most of them could improve their lot, so long as the total number of jobs throughout the nation remained millions lower than it ought to be. If all the Negroes could change the color of their skins (which I would not want to do if I were a Negro), the distribution of poverty and unemployment according to color would change; but the totals would not change much, except by virtue of improved over-all economic performance. When the *Titanic* sank, the men did not drown because they were men; they drowned because there were not enough lifeboats to take care of all the people on the ship. If the people in the South, where poverty is so high, moved to the North or the West, most of them would have to go on relief. And only a higher rate of over-all economic growth can reduce the excessive poverty in the South—or in the depressed areas—unless we are merely to export the problem of poverty and/or unemployment from one area of the country to another.

It may be urged, in opposition to what I have said, that if those with inadequate education were better educated they would become more productive; that this would add to the per capita productive potentials of the economy as a whole; and that, with such higher productive potentials, there would be less poverty. But this misses the main point. We have made so little progress in reducing poverty during the past decade not because the *potentials* for production *per capita* have not developed rapidly; under the new technology and automation, they have advanced more rapidly than in the past. The trouble has been that the chronically rising tide of idle manpower and plant has *wasted* this increase in productive potentials instead of *using* it. Further, while education and training help, the main way to make people more productive is to give them a chance to have a job, to receive training on the job, and to advance to better jobs. The number of people whose personal characteristics render them ineligible for this process is relatively small; the number denied the opportunity to participate in this process is immense and growing. It is putting the cart before the horse to say that people must be improved personally to qualify for opportunity; most personal improvement occurs through enjoyment of opportunity.

To sum up: placing appropriate emphasis upon the characteristics of the poor is helpful. But exaggerating these characteristics as the major cause of their poverty tends to "blame" individuals rather than the malfunctioning of the economy in which they live, and leads to misdirection of programmatic efforts toward "case work" instead of toward all-pervasive remedies. The whole notion that we have so much poverty and unemployment because great masses of our people are still seriously deficient in their personal capabilities describes a situation relevant to the underdeveloped countries rather than to the United States. This mistaken diagnosis tends in one sense to dull rather than to sharpen the national conscience, by implying that the poor and unemployed are basically at fault. It tends to create the delusion that the war against poverty and unemployment can be fought cheaply; it costs a lot less to train and educate a few hundred thousand people a year than to undertake the programs really needed. Essentially, the only way to reduce poverty is to lift the incomes of the poor. About two-thirds of the poor in the United States now can be helped best by *earning* more income. The main highway toward this is to restore optimum economic growth and sustained full employment, toward which the re-education and training of individuals is a supplementary rather than a major weapon. About one-third of the poor in the United States, comprised mainly of old people but including several million others, need to have their unearned incomes raised through allocating to them a larger share of the national product even though they cannot or should not be brought into the labor force. For this third, training and education programs have almost no relevance. It has already been made clear that this suggested line of approach does not negate the need for programs—as part of the very process of economic restoration—which focus directly upon the liabilities peculiar to the poor, such as bad housing, lack of educational opportunity, inadequate medical care, etc.

An additional word is desirable as to where the money would come from to pay for the most-needed programs, aside from the fact that in an economic sense they would be paid for by bringing into use productive resources which are now idle. In a purely money sense, we are now formally committed to continuation of the tight-money policy which represses economic growth and aggravates unemployment, and which, through its gradual pushing up of private and public interest rates, is extremely regressive in its income-distribution effects (many better ways of dealing with the balance of payments and gold problem are available). By fiscal 1965, interest payments on the national debt will be about 5 billion dollars higher than they would have been if a more salutary monetary policy had been maintained. Adding the almost 7 billion dollar annual value of the wasteful portions of the tax cuts, about 12 billion dollars annually would now be available, in better-conceived tax reduction and increased public spending, for a war against poverty which in its very nature would be fused with the war against unemployment and low economic growth, if only our tax and monetary policies had not gone so far astray. This 12 billion dollars annually is about 24 times the size of the fiscal 1965 additions to the anti-poverty program.

Those among the "modern" economists who tend to admit much of the substance of what I say argue nonetheless that enactment of the 1964 tax measure represents a great triumph for the "principle" that we should deliberately run a big Federal deficit to restore the economy. This is sometimes advertised as Keynesian economics. But Lord Keynes, quite aside from whether he would urge now what he urged a generation ago, was a distributional economist with profoundly progressive leanings. Despite the passage of time since he wrote, his diagnosis and remedy were quite similar to those set forth in this article. Viewing the unsatisfactory distribution of income which encouraged periodically an excessive rate of private saving and private investment in producers' facilities relative to the demand for ultimate goods and services, Keynes noted this as the central cause of the high unemployment of manpower and plant which came when these relative excesses were followed by sharp investment cutbacks. He therefore urged vast increases in public outlays, financed by public deficits. He followed the conventional terminology of calling these increases in public outlays "investment" rather than "consumption," but nonetheless he was urging an increase in the public demand for ultimate products to compensate for the periodic tendency toward private overinvestment in producers' goods. In other words, Keynes urged that increased public outlays, financed by public deficits, would help to absorb the excessive private saving and to maintain total demand at levels high enough to restore and maintain full employment. Further, he insisted that, even with an optimum public investment program, he very much doubted whether full employment could be restored or maintained without vast efforts to improve the distribution of private incomes and thus encourage the propensity to consume. The great Englishman would turn over in his grave at the nationwide programs, adopted in his name, which add to the already excessive private saving, give impetus to further excesses in private investment, neglect the ultimate needs which public investment serves, and aggravate the maldistribution of income and the economic disequilibrium. Sadly, the recent tax reduction does not represent a triumph for truly modern economics; it represents a triumph for those powerful private interests who have been agitating for decades in favor of their own pocketbooks.

The "politics" of the problem

Many of the "modern" economists attempt to excuse all this on grounds of "political" necessity. I expressed at the outset my belief that, even allowing for "political" difficulties, the economic policies initiated by the President could be much improved if the economic advice made available to him by his experts (who run far beyond the Council of Economic Advisers) were much improved. Granted, the President has to strike a balance between the "political" risks of asking for too much, and the economic risks of asking for too little. But he can make this calculation effectively only if his economic experts are not behind the times, and do not in addition attempt on their own to adjust excessively to real or fancied "political" difficulties. This calls for much reconstruction in economic thought and education, beginning at the university level. It also calls for economists in the public service who, even at the possible risk of losing their jobs, speak their own minds instead of attempting to be too pleasant. There is sharp contrast, in this matter, between recent times and the early New Deal. The New Deal, with all its defects, was enriched by economists within its ranks who had a deep commitment to its causes. The same was true during World War II.

Turning from the economists to the responsibilities of top political leadership, there is an inescapable distinction between (a) attempting programs which are so arduous (however much needed) that they risk destruction of the effectiveness of the political leadership itself, and (b) pushing for those lesser but moderately adequate programs which political leadership should undertake even though this risks considerable loss of political popularity and involves what Walter Lippmann has called "getting one's nose bloodied." The essence of our greatest political leadership has always been its capacity to stop short of (a) while pressing forward with (b).

The need for this (b) type of political leadership has become especially urgent in recent years, when those most seriously hurt by the inadequate economic performance are not yet sufficiently hurt in sufficiently large numbers to overcome their relative inarticulateness and lack of effective power, while the defenders of the *status quo* are always articulate and strong out of all proportion to their numbers. In such times, those programs on the necessarily thorny economic and social front which seem to be the least controversial, and blessed with the widest "consensus," are almost inevitably very different from those which the nation urgently needs. Under such circumstances, it is the highest duty of top political leadership not merely to follow the ostensible "consensus," but to help form that new consensus which will prevent the ceiling of "political" feasibility from sinking below the floor of what we need to do, to prosper and advance.

The consummation of this political task is by no means unattainable for the very reason that, in our democracy, the views of the majority of voting citizens when properly informed and articulated are likely to coincide broadly with the interests of the nation. And this is especially true because of the real identity of our moral, social, and economic purposes when fully understood. Recognition of this identity—a recognition essential if the American society is to move forward in accord with its great potentials—seemed to me a heartening aspect of the anti-poverty program initiated by President Johnson in 1964, even though the start proposed by this program was a small one.

Yet in the final analysis, the problems of action in a democracy impose responsibilities not only upon top political leadership, but also upon those leaders throughout the land who speak for the real interests of the people. This type of nation-wide leadership is now reasonably well-informed and highly dedicated. But it has not yet struck a balance between its wholesome desire to support the policies of a top political leadership which it properly prefers to the opposition, and the need to press hard beyond the programs of this preferred leadership when these programs are still not adequate. While I am as committed today as ever before to the top political leadership of the party to which I belong in contrast with the opposition, and while I reject any idea of a Third Party movement, I nonetheless believe it essential that some way be found to strike a balance between these alternatives. Perhaps "courage," as applied to our nationwide liberal and progressive leadership, best indicates what is needed. In the challenging times ahead, much depends upon the strength and vision of all those who are the trustees of the liberal tradition in the United States—a tradition which is fairly immutable in its basic directions despite constantly needed changes in the particulars of policy and program.

The Government
and Your Income

ROBERT R. NATHAN

During and since World War II, the economy of the United States has demonstrated a capacity to produce beyond anything ever seen or even contemplated in this or any other country. The combination of an exploding technology, a highly competent labor force, skilled management, and an abundance of capital for investment has brought to the United States, for the first time in the history of man, the ability not only to abolish poverty but to replace a social and economic order based on the specter of scarcity with one based on the prospect of plenty.

With such magnificent prospects, it would be absurd to continue to resign ourselves to the anomalies of underemployment and unmet needs, of widespread poverty and recurring idle capacities. The central question of economic policy in our time is how to use existing institutions both to produce the plenty of which the economy is capable and to distribute it more widely and more equitably.

This will require planned, determined pursuit of economic policies well advanced over the standards of the past. But there is no magic in planning or in economic policy to solve for us the hardest question: whether we have the will to seize the opportunities for abundance which our economy and our technology offer. The answer is political, though the issue is economic.

The road to full employment

In charting the road to full employment, we must recognize some fundamental facts. It is obvious that we can produce more than we have been producing. It is equally obvious that, despite our so-called affluence, most of our people want and need to buy and consume far more goods and services, publicly and privately, than we have had available or have used. There is still far too much poverty—public and private—to accept as normal the excessive levels of involuntary unemployment of men and machines in recent years. To achieve and maintain full employment, it will be essential to achieve and maintain a level of demand for goods and services sufficient to empty the market of all we can produce.

Production generates income that is then available for spending or saving by those individuals and corporations who receive the income. Spending stimulates production by providing markets for what is produced, capital goods as well as consumer goods. A sufficient level of spending (demand) is dependent in considerable measure on the division of our country's total income between personal income and business income, and between higher and lower income classes.

The greater the share of total income that goes to business, the higher will be the portion of total income that is saved for investment and the lower the portion that is spent directly for consumption. Similarly, the higher the portion of total personal income that is received by the higher-income brackets, the larger will be the level of personal savings and the lower the level of direct consumer spending.

Savings are an important and essential ingredient in the functioning of any successful economy. They are the source of funds for investment in plants, equipment, dwellings and other productive facilities which make it possible to produce more and more goods and services. There must be more and more investment spending—not only to increase the nation's capacity to produce but also to activate and use savings. If savers try to save more than investors are prepared to invest, then there tends to be oversaving, and total demand is inadequate to support full employment and to stimulate more production and more investment.

Private investment expenditures are influenced or determined by a wide range of factors that go to make up the investment climate or the investment environment. The most important single factor is that of the current and prospective market for the goods or services that will ultimately flow from the investment. Investors do not invest their own savings and the savings of others just for the pure joy of it. They invest to earn profits. Favorable market opportunities are essential for profitability. If individuals and corporations seek to save so much of their income that their direct expenditures are inadequate to support the level of investment essential to use this high level of savings, then total demand will not be enough and inventories will pile up, or losses will replace profits, or further investment will be discouraged and we shall fall further below levels of full employment.

While it is clear that income distribution affects the use of income, it is less apparent what all the consequences will be of seeking to shift this distribution. Some uncertainties should not deter us from seeking progress, but we should be aware of the problems. A greater contribution toward full employment would appear to be attainable in the distribution of income between business and personal income than within the area of personal income distribution.

The degree of concentration in the distribution of personal income in the United States is far less than it was a generation ago, due largely to the progressive nature of the personal-income tax. As the general level of personal incomes rises, the tendency to save directly or through mortgage payments, insurance policies, pension systems, and the like, involves more and more of the middle-income groups as well as the higher-income recipients, where the savings-to-income ratios are naturally highest. Federal tax revisions in the post-World War II period, plus the great increase in state and local taxes relative to Federal taxes, have reversed the progress toward a more equitable and more expansionist distribution of personal income. Still, shifts in the distribution of personal income would make only a modest contribution to solving problems associated with tendencies toward excess savings.

More important is the distribution of income between individuals and business. Savings generated internally by corporations (undistributed profits plus depreciation charges) are the most important source of funds for investment. At the same time, capital expenditures by corporations are the most important single influence in determining the level of total investment expenditures. It is desirable to achieve the highest sustainable level of business investment, and this requires favorable profit prospects. But if, in seeking to make the prospects for profits more favorable through investment credits and accelerated depreciation schedules and lower corporate profit tax rates, there is a shift in income to business from individuals which in turn results in too little consumer spending and too much savings, then there is likely to be less rather than more investment over a period of time, and the goal of full employment will be more elusive.

Too great an emphasis on enlarging the incentives to invest can and will be self-defeating. That is why, in addition to considerations of equity, we must resist the pressures to move from income taxes to sales taxes and to introduce more and more tax-incentive gimmicks to stimulate more business investment. Such measures could bring less growth and less stability to our private economy rather than more.

An important relationship which influences the distribution of income as between business and individuals is that of prices, wages, and profits. To the extent that labor income increases relative to profits, there will tend to be a larger level of consumer spending relative to savings. Put another way, higher wages relative to profits will make the level of economic activities somewhat less dependent on a higher level of investment and this, in turn, may lend greater stability to the economy. It may even bring more rapid growth, since the higher level of consumer spending will support a higher sustainable level of investment spending. Of course, the level of profits at full employment must be adequate to stimulate and encourage businessmen to invest and also sufficient to help provide the level of savings needed for growth in productive capacity.

One of the serious problems associated with the role of wages, prices, and profits in determining the distribution of income between business and individuals is that of possible inflation. Our economy is not as competitive as it once was, nor as competitive as some would have us believe. Administered pricing is practiced in many industries, and higher wages too often are passed on in the form of higher prices, whether or not warranted by unit costs. Labor-management negotiations can make a significant contribution to a more stable and expansionist income distribution, but new techniques and devices for fighting inflation are needed.

All these objectives of income distribution and of relationships between consumer expenditures and savings and investment should not lead us to conclude that little or nothing can be done to influence the distribution and use of income with the purpose of making the private economy function with greater stability and greater growth. Rather, through tax policies, wage-price-profit policies, income transfers, anti-monopoly measures and the like, we should seek to bring about those relationships and those balances which will assure a more satisfactory performance. To the extent that such measures affecting the private sector are inadequate, the role of public economic policy must provide the combination of diverse and complementary economic methods which will achieve (a) compatibility of consumption, saving, and investment, (b) a socially and politically desirable division of functions between the private and the public sector, and (c) a workable balance between the dynamic use of the profit motive and the goal of social justice.

The principal means is "fiscal policy." This requires that, when aggregate demand falls short of full employment, either taxes be reduced to enlarge private demand or public expenditures be increased to enlarge public demand, or both measures be combined. It requires, moreover, that the configuration of taxes and public expenditures be such as to strengthen consumer purchasing power, especially at the low end of the income scale; and at the same time to offer the right pattern and level of incentives needed to bring forth the volume of saving and to encourage the corresponding amount of private investment sufficient to expand productive capacity. Apart from persistent and mounting government deficits, full employment can be maintained only by tax policies which bear more heavily on profits and high personal incomes, by wage-price-profit mechanisms which assure rising labor income without inflation and by income transfers and other related policies.

The Federal fiscal system has been designed to bring about government deficits automatically when private incomes and private spending lag. When incomes fall, income-tax revenues fall even faster because taxpayers have less income to be taxed and it is taxed at lower rates. Moreover, public expenditures like those for unemployment insurance and relief increase as the private economy recedes. The resulting deficits provide a "compensatory" stimulus to the demand for goods and services. Instead of being welcomed as safeguards against depression—which they are—these automatic compensatory deficits have been bewailed as calamitous aberrations by those whose notions of public policy have never progressed beyond the rudiments of elementary bookkeeping. The *deliberate* use of fiscal policy to incur deficits for the sake of strengthening total demand— the most effective instrument of economic expansion—has been viewed with horror as "fiscal irresponsibility." The tax reduction enacted this year was the first significant step taken by the

Government in the use of discretionary (as opposed to automatic) fiscal policy. But even this deliberate step toward solving the growing problem of chronic unemployment was accompanied by a tightening of public expenditures which in part negated the expansionary effect of the tax cut and which resulted in continuing serious deficiencies in the supply of needed public services and facilities.

Full employment policies

There are too many undernourished public sectors of our economy. The level of non-military public expenditures must rise sharply and must keep on rising as our population and affluence grow. We who originated free public education now seem to find it difficult to decide to support it adequately. We who created TVA for all the world to admire and imitate now seem unwilling to repeat this spectacular success in regional development of people and resources. We have used self-financing public "authorities" and corporations to build dams and sell power, to operate the Panama Canal, to build bridges and waterways, to buy and sell mortgages, to insure bank deposits, even to launch satellite communications. But we have not used this versatile device ("with the power of government, but possessed of the flexibility and initiative of a private enterprise," as Franklin D. Roosevelt said of TVA) to build enough housing, public schools, hospitals, high-speed surface transportation and other essential facilities in short supply.

Increased expenditures for public facilities and services need not wait for reduced defense spending. Existing needs dictate that such expenditures take priority over tax reductions. Apart from the great deficiencies in food, shelter, clothing, and essential services among the lower-income groups, there are many public needs which should take priority over increased consumption. Increased public outlays, efficiently undertaken, are in the best interest of most Americans and make good economic sense.

Tax policy for full employment requires four departures from present policy. First, the burden on consumption by low-income groups should be lightened by easing Federal taxes at the bottom, and by shifting part of the burden of state and local taxes from regressive sales and property taxes that bear heavily on low-income consumers to progressive income taxes. One simple and direct device for doing this would be to allow individuals to deduct from their Federal tax bill a substantial part of *income* taxes paid to states, thereby encouraging states to rely more on progressive income taxes. Or, part of the receipts from the Federal income tax could be distributed to states or even to localities. This would permit state and local governments to provide the more and better public facilities and services that are desperately needed at these levels of government.

Second, taxes should be designed not only generally to encourage consumption but specifically and selectively to encourage needed shifts in the allocation and use of manpower and money. Up to now, tax policy has been designed mainly to sharpen the incentives for investment, largely indiscriminately, in attempts to stimulate the economy. But we have not fully explored and exploited the use of tax incentives to achieve *specific* economic policy objectives, such as investment in depressed areas and undercapitalized backward industries or investment in middle and low-income housing, or financing benefits to cushion technological displacement of workers.

Third, the Federal tax loopholes should be closed to catch billions of income, almost all of it at the top, which now escape taxation. The ways of accomplishing this, and its economic advantages, are well documented; only the political convictions have been lacking. The massacre of the proposed (and very modest) tax reforms of the 1963–64 tax bill is a sordid and shameful case history. Elimination of loopholes would ensure greater fairness and make taxation a more effective vehicle for economic policy. Lower rates effectively applied are preferable to higher rates with greater avoidance and evasion.

Fourth, in order to permit prompt action to compensate for occasional deficiencies or excesses in economic activity, the President should be given the authority (which the late President Kennedy requested) to lower or raise tax rates temporarily under specified conditions and within specified limits. We need such a device to respond promptly to short-term changes: for example, the need to reduce taxes to stimulate the economy was clear in 1961 (or earlier), but the reduction was debated in 1962, proposed in 1963 and enacted in 1964. Each year's delay increased the amount needed for effective action.

As stated earlier, the relationships among consumption, saving, and investment are powerfully influenced by the relation between wages and profits. Wages are the main source of consumption, profits the main source of funds for investment. As long as wages per man-hour do not rise faster than output per man-hour, wage increases do not encroach on profits; and this amount of wage increase is often tolerated without an increase in price. This has given rise to the well-known guidepost, "wage increases should equal average productivity increases," which now has official sanction. But such a concept is valid only if profits were high enough (but not higher than necessary) to serve their only economic function—namely, to attract a sufficient flow of capital into investment. The tendency of the economy to oversave, plus the recent phenomenal rise in gross profits (including depreciation reserves), suggest that expansion will not be sustained, because the huge corporate savings will have to be offset by a higher level of investment than we can count on sustaining. Many of our most profitable corporations are flooded with more cash than they are prepared to invest.

The high level of "administered" prices is itself both a cause and a result of underemployment of the economy. Important industries (steel, conspicuously) have arbitrarily set prices high enough to make a profit at a rate of operations far below capacity. As a result, when volume picks up, profits rise sharply, faster than they can be invested. Such pricing policies tend to cut off economic recovery long before relatively full employment is achieved. National policy commitments to maintain the economy at a high level and assure production at near capacity should result in lower levels of prices, because business can continue to make good earnings on high volume at a low profit per unit.

Trends toward increases in administered prices and profits have frightened those timid policy-makers who, for most of the past decade, have chosen underemployment as the safeguard of price stability. Underemployment is not the proper weapon against inflation. The essence of sound price policy is not economic slack but the pursuit of price competition and expansionist, though not inflationary, fiscal and monetary policies. Dynamic price competition is essential for full employment.

Since the earliest days of the industrial revolution, competitive enterprise and technological change have been the two dynamic elements of the Western economy. Competition is the midwife of technological development and the means of bringing its economic benefits to consumers and investors in the market place.

Rising efficiency in competitive markets pushes down costs and prices, while pulling up wages. Together, they have created a growing mass market and new jobs. The Council of Economic Advisers reminds us that if demand per person were no greater now than in the "boom" year of 1929, with output per worker at today's levels, nearly half our labor force (instead of 5 or 6 percent) would be unemployed. Rising demand is both a requirement and a benefit of a fully employed, technologically advancing economy. To have full employment, total demand in the next decade must rise by something of the order of 60 percent, instead of the 30 or 35 percent increase recorded from 1953 to 1963. Impossible? Not at all. The needs are evident; the capacity can be provided; the skills are available. To achieve it, breakthroughs in economic policy affecting total demand, price competition, and innovation must be as daring as those which resulted in creating a wartime economy that overwhelmed the Axis powers.

Blessings or disasters?

In spite of many important and puzzling economic imponderables, the majority of economists favor more steps toward full employment than the majority of politicians are willing to take. Legislators and executives in the United States recoil from what, in other countries, is considered a rather conventional modern view of fiscal policy and, especially, of public expenditures. Worse, they pander to public prejudices and reinforce them in the process. The brainwashed public, for its part, is only too eager to be convinced of the virtues of low taxes, restraints on public debt, and sharp pruning of public expenditures, and to be blinded to the costs of accumulated neglect of public services and facilities. Stockholders will glow with pride at the announcement of their companies' huge borrowings (up $200 billion in the past decade, and nearly half again larger than the national debt) but will vote a "spender" out of public office and applaud the kind of "pay as you go" policy which has left the state of Virginia debt-free—and backward.

A venturesome and imaginative application of economic policies would permit this country to reach and maintain full employment. It would require, first of all, a massive liberation of our political leaders—and the voters—from myths and stereotypes and their re-education to the realities of modern economic policy. The need is urgent. It has been estimated that we need to add two million new jobs each year to offset rising productivity at the present rate of technological change. We need to add another one and one-quarter or one and one-half million because of the growth of the labor force. These changes alone require the annual production of goods and services to increase by about 5 percent each year just to avoid a rise in unemployment. That is far above the growth rate of the best decade. And productivity may speed up even more.

Another challenge (and another opportunity) may come if—

as we pray—there is a breakthrough in disarmament negotiations which permits us to taper down spending on national defense. This would release more resources of manpower, productive capacity, and technology for the pursuits of peace. A reduction of one-third in defense spending, for example, would by itself fully finance the war on poverty proclaimed by President Johnson.

Will these be blessings—or disasters?

This depends mainly on how we are prepared to regard them and act on them. If the economy continues to grow only as fast as it grew during the 1950's, it will be not expand nearly fast enough to fill our needs and occupy our labor force. The country would then be divided between an affluent majority and an impoverished (and growing) minority—between the well-paid, comfortably employed and the excluded, embittered unemployed. Conflict between "haves" and "have nots" could threaten the economic, social, and political stability of the country.

If we choose, we can grasp our great technological changes as an opportunity to employ the economy fully for those things that up to now we "could not afford"—to feed, clothe, house, heal, and educate our entire population; to rehabilitate our cities, to rebuild ourselves out of the slums; to educate our children properly; to attack poverty with an intensity and on a scale that will win the "all-out war"—and bring within the reach of everyone the comforts and pleasures now enjoyed by 20 percent of us. In addition, we could double or triple, instead of scraping and paring, the resources we offer to underdeveloped countries to support their struggle to modernize and develop.

To do this, we must invoke bold ideas and new and imaginative practices to assure adequate incomes for all Americans— including adequate wages for the employed, supported by continually higher statutory minimums and rising at least as fast as productivity rises; compensation for the temporarily unemployed, replacing far more of their wage loss than is now provided; comprehensive health insurance to cover medical and hospital expenses, as well as wage losses; pensions for retired workers high enough to permit them to approach their pre-retirement level of living; and a system of income payments for families without working members sufficient to provide a decent standard of living.

The demand generated by such income maintenance would call for an output in line with the rising capacity of our economy and our technology. It would require far more than the present output of goods and services for private consumption and for investment. It would both require and support vastly improved services for education, health, transport, recreation, and conservation. It would require and permit building an adequate supply of housing and community facilities. It would make possible the waging of Walter Reuther's proposed $20 billion "peace offensive" to speed the progress of developing nations.

Would this provide "jobs for all"—that is, full employment of a labor force growing at the rate of more than a million a year? Indeed so. For a few years, this kind of economy would need all the manpower and other resources we could deploy—so great is the accumulation of poverty and neglect. If the advance of technology and a decline in the defense burden made it possible, at some future time, to meet such needs by the employment of a smaller part of the population than they would require now, we must invent ways to assure that the rest are not penalized or pauperized, but are allowed to share the general affluence in dignity and comfort. If 30 percent of our population well employed can produce all we need, this will make it possible for our young people to extend their education and our older people to retire earlier. Or we might then choose more leisure through a shorter work week. But, in one way or another —whether by scholarships for the young, early pensions for the old, or living allowances for the non-employed—the maintenance of the vigor of our economy and the quality of our society will require assurances of at least a minimum adequate income for all its members.

It would be folly to suppose that such vast transformations of the economy can come about automatically through the workings of the market or that they can be improvised in response to immediate political demands and opportunities. On the contrary, they will require a greater degree of national planning than we have ever before been willing to accept. The opportunities presented by advancing technology and by progress toward arms control are in reality opportunities for the reallocation of resources. The problem is to use the liberated resources of manpower, capital, and know-how to meet needs which we now neglect or cannot afford to satisfy. How and where can manpower released by more efficient manufacturing be turned to the purposes of housing, health, or education? How can research and development groups be converted from the design and production of missile guidance systems to the problems of teaching machines, low-cost housing, or oceanography? The answers to such questions will require painstaking research and inventive planning, which cannot be left to the operation of market forces.

Planning, far from subverting our enterprise economy, is increasingly needed to preserve it. Planning in the United States does not mean bureaucratic direction of private enterprise or general regimentation. It means systematic and consistent efforts to use economic policy to provide an environment in which enterprise can function effectively to supply the needs of the society. Far from being incompatible with freedom, planning is necessary to give effect to decisions of goals and priorities democratically arrived at. We must prove ourselves equal to those decisions.

The Economics
of Disarmament

EMILE BENOIT

THE economic problems of disarmament are less important than the political ones. Compared to the dangers of an atomic war, the temporary inconveniences and deprivations—as well as the possible long-term benefits—resulting from shifting a fraction of our resources from defense to nondefense uses appear trivial indeed. However, fears of the short-term economic difficulties of disarming may significantly affect political attitudes toward disarmament. Hence the topic cannot be ignored. Moreover, the potential waste involved in an unsuccessful transition to a less defense-oriented economy would be no minor tragedy.

The political problems of achieving disarmament are the primary ones, and they are still very great. We are, nevertheless, beginning to take some small and tentative steps in the general direction of disarmament. The Washington-Moscow hot-line broke the ice. The limited nuclear test ban and the United States-Soviet understanding not to develop orbited nuclear weapons generated momentum. Now the United States government seeks to negotiate a freeze on strategic nuclear weapons and delivery systems as the next practicable step. Already substantial cuts have been announced unilaterally.

The weapons-freeze proposal reflects a fundamental change which is shaping up in the strategic situation: as the Russians move toward an invulnerable deterrent, there is less and less reason for us to increase our already fantastically large stockpile of nuclear weapons. Secretary of Defense McNamara has now pointed out that owing to the Soviet shift to hardened missile sites and submarines "even if we were to double or triple our forces . . . our calculations show that fatalities would still run into tens of millions." [1] The reduced vulnerability of the Russian strategic forces to a United States pre-emptive strike should also result in a lessened Russian reliance on concealment for protection, and thereby weaken a major obstacle to disarmament, namely an unwillingness to be inspected.

A freeze on strategic weapons and delivery systems would probably involve a cutback in annual defense expenditure of upwards of $5 billion. We were, in 1964, spending $4¼ billion on strategic weapons and delivery systems, and, even with a freeze, would presumably be permitted to replace missiles that are test-fired, etc. On the other hand, some cuts in our nearly $7 billion of Research, Development, Testing, and Evaluation, and in our $2.8 billion of expenditure by the Atomic Energy Commission would be likely to accompany any weapons freeze. Presumably a *full* weapons freeze (including tactical and continental defense weapons and delivery systems) would involve cuts in defense expenditures of $15 billion or more. After his resignation, Roswell L. Gilpatric, Undersecretary of Defense 1960–64, predicted a $13 billion cut in the defense budget by 1970 if the *detente* continues.[2] These cuts, it should be noted, could occur without in the least reducing our present awesome military capabilities.

With general and complete disarmament along the lines of the official United States proposal (*General and Complete Dis-*

---

[1] Statement of Secretary Defense Robert S. McNamara before the House Armed Services Committee on the Fiscal Year 1965–69 Defense Program and 1965 Defense Budget, April, 1964.
[2] "Our Defense Needs: The Long View," *Foreign Affairs*, April 1964.

armament in a Peaceful World, Blueprint for a Peace Race)
cutbacks could be larger, of course, but not as much larger as
might be thought. The net cutback involved has been estimated
at $32 billion starting from the 1965 budget total of $60.2 billion for Defense, Atomic Energy Commission, and National
Aeronautics and Space Administration.[3] This reflects an estimated cutback in annual United States defense expenditures of
about $48 billion, partly offset by $7 billion contributed to an
international inspection and peace-keeping organization, plus
an extra $7 billion for space and atomic energy programs. Be-
cause of the political, military, and administrative problems
involved—not for economic reasons—the disarmament program
would probably require at least a dozen years to complete. But
nearly half of the total cuts, including the bulk of procurement,
would probably fall within the first three years. Thus while
general and complete disarmament would have a more prolonged economic impact than a general weapons freeze, the
difference in the first few years might not be great, especially for
defense industry. However, we will consider the more extreme
case of general and complete disarmament as a measure of how
severe the economic disruptions might become.

General disarmament might involve the elimination of about
6¼ million defense-dependent jobs—close to 3½ million from
the Armed Forces and defense agencies, and 2.8 million from
industry. As would be expected, aircraft and missiles, ships and
boats, ordnance, radio and communications, instruments, primary metals, fuel and power, would be most directly affected—though substantial numbers would be indirectly affected in services and trade. Up to one-fifth of the 6¼ million
jobs might be replaced by the assumed expansion in civilian
space and atomic energy work and by the United States contribution to international peacekeeping activities. In any case, the

[3] Emile Benoit, "The Disarmament Model," Chapter 2 in Emile Benoit
and Kenneth Boulding (Eds.), Disarmament and the Economy, New York,
Harper & Rowe, 1963. By a coincidence the projected total in the model
for calendar year 1965 is identical with the amount budgeted for the fiscal
year 1965.

number of cuts in defense-dependent jobs gives no indication of the number of people who would actually become unemployed. This would depend on the speed of the cutback and the adequacy of the adjustment programs adopted.

The impact would be particularly heavy in certain areas— such as Kansas, Washington, New Mexico, California, Connecticut, Arizona, and Utah—where defense production accounts for from 20 to 30 percent of total manufacturing employment, or certain other states such as Alaska, Hawaii, Washington, D.C., and Virginia, where from a tenth to a quarter of incomes derive from defense-agency payrolls.

Much reassurance has been drawn from our success in handling the large defense cutbacks after World War II and the Korean War. These adjustments were not, however, quite as successful as often assumed. Moreover, they occurred under much more favorable circumstances than now prevail. Unemployment after World War II was unexpectedly low, partly because of a rapid decline in the total labor force and hours of work, which had been raised abnormally in the war years. The changeover, furthermore, involved a sharp decline in industrial production. Such declines in labor supply and in output would not be welcome today. Adjustments in 1945–47 were also eased by the $157 billion of liquid financial savings of individuals which had been accumulated during the war, reflecting the enormous amount of Federal deficit financing. The situation was one of hyperliquidity and inflationary pressure; with the money supply equal to 47 percent of Gross National Product in 1945, as compared with only 26 percent in 1963.

Even at the end of the Korean War, the economy was still highly resistant to deflation, with recent experiences of full employment, labor and materials shortages, rapid rises in commodity and real-estate prices, and a relatively low level of consumer debt. Even so, the relatively moderate defense cuts, totaling 5 percent of GNP in real terms from 1953 to 1960, precipitated a marked industrial slowdown, with a growth of only 18 percent in the index of industrial production over this period, compared to 54 percent in the previous seven years—and with a rise in unemployment from 2.9 percent to 5.6 percent.

The relation between the way we handled the defense cuts and the economic slowdown seems to have been more than incidental. There was little recognition at the time that offsets to the defense cuts would be required. Federal non-defense purchases were sharply reduced by about 30 percent, instead of being raised as an offset, and the tax cut of 1954, while helpful, was far too small to check the rapid increase in Federal revenue. The Federal Government thus ran large surpluses of $11.5 billion for the years 1955 to 1957 and another $3.5 billion in 1960. These estimates are measured by national income data that give a truer picture of economic effects than the Administrative Budget. Thus the government taxed away substantially more spending power from individuals and businesses than it restored to them through its own purchases and other income payments. Such deflationary surpluses choked off economic revivals before full employment and full utilization of industrial capacity had been achieved, and substantially slowed down the average rate of growth. Average industrial output from 1956 through 1958 remained below the end-of-1955 level.

Conditions in the mid-sixties render us much more vulnerable to deflationary pressures than we were in 1945 or 1953. We now suffer from persistent excess unemployment, much unutilized capacity, high consumer debt, a far lower supply of money in relation to Gross National Product, a much higher level of securities prices in relation to earnings; a looming problem of automation, and a rapid built-in growth of the labor force which will intensify the problem of creating enough jobs.

The possible effects of various tax and expenditure measures and budgetary policies for adjusting the economy to disarmament—involving an assumed $32 billion of defense cuts—were computed by means of an econometric model in the study done under the Program of Research on Economic Adjustments to

Disarmament.[4] The results, while only a first approximation, are of interest. It appears that a laissez-faire policy which provided no tax cuts or offsetting expansion of government non-defense programs could easily produce a major downturn (a 4–8 million increase in the number of unemployed and a decline of $37—74 billion in Gross National Product). A program which sought to achieve a budget surplus of $10 billion for national debt reduction, with similar amounts of tax cuts and of new government programs, would seem to imply at least a serious recession. Attempts merely to balance the budget, with some tax cuts and new government programs, would appear to produce at least moderate recessions and slowdowns of growth. Efforts to stabilize production or employment solely by means of tax cuts were found to require impractically large tax cuts and budget deficits. The most satisfactory solution in my view is one of "balanced offsets" consisting of approximately equal amounts of tax cuts and of new government programs, the total of the two being slightly larger than the net defense cuts. This would require a small deficit.

There seem to be three major political obstacles to the use of a "balanced offsets" program: (1) opposition to expansion of Federal non-defense programs; (2) desire to reduce the national debt; and (3) problems of coordination and timing. Resistance to expansion of Federal non-defense expenditures is probably the most basic of these political difficulties.

Such resistance stems, in part at least, from deeply-rooted popular delusions about their alarming rate of growth. In point of fact, per capita Federal expenditures for non-defense goods and services, expressed in 1963 prices, were $83 back in 1939, $75 in 1953, and only $56 in 1963. And non-defense purchases of all government units—including state and local—have declined from 17 percent of GNP to 12 percent of GNP over the same period. Clearly there are major backlogs in government

[4] Emile Benoit, "The Role of Monetary and Fiscal Policies in Disarmament Adjustments," *Journal of Finance*, May 1963.

services to be made up as soon as the insistent claims of national defense are relaxed. Merely a restoration of the 1939 per capita expenditures in Federal non-defense goods and services would involve an increase in such expenditures by $5 billion over present levels; a restoration to their 1939 percent of GNP would increase them by $18 billion—about all that would be called for on the "balanced offsets" formula. There is no lack of high-priority government projects to absorb two or three times that volume of resources during the 1960's, in such fields as health, education, housing, urban renewal, water and other natural-resources conservation, support of Research and Development and programs to alleviate serious poverty in the United States and promote economic development abroad. It should be kept in mind, moreover, that the "balanced offsets" proposal presented here involved a *decline* in total Federal expenditure, with only a part of the cuts in defense expenditure being offset by new government programs. It should be easier to obtain Congressional approval of an expansion in public-welfare programs in the context of a shrinking total budget.

As for public hostility to budget deficits and anxiety to reduce the national debt, this could undoubtedly become a serious danger to a successful disarmament adjustment. A public-opinion poll has shown the use of defense savings for debt reduction to be as popular as tax cuts and particularly popular among the college-educated, reflecting, presumably, a more responsible attitude on their part in personal monetary matters. However, the analogy that people often draw between public debt and the personal consumer debt of an individual is unsound. (For a good simple exposition of why, see *A Primer on Government Spending* by Peter L. Bernstein and Robert L. Heilbroner, Vintage Books, 1963.) Public debt is more like the long-term bonded debt of large corporations which ordinarily is never paid off but regularly renewed, and the national total of which keeps growing—and indeed has to grow if prosperity is to be maintained.

Ideally, offsetting measures should be announced concur-

rently with defense cuts and actually carried out at the time
defense spending drops. This would best be achieved by giving
the President more discretionary power in fiscal matters—
subject to broad criteria established by Congress. Such discretion would, however, conflict with Congressional prerogatives—
as one Congressman once put it me quite frankly: "When
there's a tax cut, we want to get the credit for it, not the
President." In that case, Congress should revise its own procedures to provide more flexibility in changing tax rates and expenditures, as required for economic stabilization.

Professor Paul Samuelson, of Massachusetts Institute of
Technology, once asked me how the government, which has
failed in recent years to keep unemployment below 5 percent
even with the economic stimulus of a large defense program,
can be expected to maintain full employment in the event of
disarmament. This is a sobering question, but there are at least
partial answers. First, one can take hope from the improved
public understanding of fiscal policy, evidenced by the recent
passage of the deficit-financed tax cuts during a period of rising
business activity—which creates a most important precedent.
Second, the somewhat exaggerated fear of the impact of disarmament makes it likely that much attention would be given
to allaying the ill effects. This was not the case with the post-
Korean defense cuts, which were not viewed as economically
upsetting. In any case, disarmament will obviously not itself
create full employment. Even the best disarmament adjustment
program is no substitute for a good general program for full
employment and rapid growth.

I have so far emphasized matters that are often ignored in
popular discussion of disarmament adjustments because I think
the usual emphasis on reconversion, retraining, relocation, etc.,
puts the cart before the horse. Unless we maintain adequate
demand by balanced offsets, it makes little difference whether
we provide retraining, redeployment, reconversion, redevelopment, and other adjustment for the structural problems of defense cuts. It does little good to retrain or relocate a disem-

ployed defense worker if there is no job for him to go to, or if, in getting a new job, he merely replaces and forces into unemployment another job candidate. Similarly, it won't do much good to help defense contractors to convert to civilian products if civilian markets are not expanding.

However, even if aggregate demand is successfully maintained and expanded, there will still be difficult problems of conversion to overcome—in several respects considerably more difficult than such problems were in 1945 or 1953. Moreover, these problems will be bothersome even if we have a weapons freeze without disarmament, since even a weapons freeze would knock out a good bit of defense production. These structural difficulties arise from the increasingly specialized, permanent, and geographically concentrated character of defense production. As is well known, the manpower employed in the defense industry has a much higher average level of skill and much more Research and Development talent than in non-defense industry. Such people are above average in intelligence, mobility, and adaptability—which would facilitate job shifts—but they are also more demanding in their requirements, not only with respect to salary, but even more with respect to the job's payoffs in terms of status, intrinsic interest, and opportunities for creativity—all of which may make them a lot harder to place satisfactorily. Moreover, quite unlike the war workers of 1941–45, who thought of themselves as having enlisted only "for the duration," workers in defense industry today view their jobs as permanent, and have increasingly bought their homes in the locality and formed close neighborhood ties.

Since 1945, defense industry has become more and more specialized. The essential economic characteristic of the industry is that it specializes in bidding for and performing large-scale government contracts requiring advanced and large-scale Research and Development, engineering, and systems analysis and management. It is innovation-oriented to a high degree and geared to meeting exacting technical standards, but is correspondingly weak in marketing and distribution.

Defense firms have had relatively poor success at diversifying into civilian industry, even when the products were as much alike as military and civilian aircraft, though they have been highly successful in changing over to new types of defense products. If new markets of a comparable type do not appear, the defense companies will in many cases have to abandon their relatively specialized defense facilities and staffs and, in order to protect the interests of their stockholders, shift their capital into more routine industries. This may be done by acquisitions, mergers, or new ventures—but in any case the existing people and communities in defense work will often be left high and dry. Moreover, the defense companies will have to act fast: they have enormous overheads, and they work on very slim operating margins. A delay of only a few weeks in taking disagreeable steps may be enough to run a good year's profit into a loss.

Defense industry constitutes today one of the major concentrations of truly creative and innovational brainpower in American life. It obtains great dynamism by being operated for private profit by private management, yet is almost wholly dependent on non-private markets. It is important that we understand why this public financing is necessary. Most of the benefits of its activities are too long-range, too fundamental, or too diffuse to be captured by market processes. Hence it could not offer tangible, timely and reliable returns to the private investor unless the government as trustee of the long-term interests of the nation stepped in and created a market for such activities. National defense is one field where the futility of expecting to meet the need by spontaneously emerging private demand is obvious.

It is important to recognize, however, that there is nothing specific to national defense that makes this pattern of organizing and financing economic activities desirable and feasible. Here is where our semantics could create a serious barrier to sensible solutions. There is not, in principle, any reason why such activities organized on a similar private-enterprise basis could not be directed to other broad national objectives, such as basic resource conservation and development, including particularly our dwindling water supply, general improvements in productivity, planning and implementing urban redevelopment, commuter and other transport systems, weather control, improved aviation facilities and traffic control, industrial development of the oceans, establishment of world-wide communications networks, large-scale production of teaching machines and programs for the eradication of illiteracy, and for instruction in various skills essential for rapid economic development, etc. If these tasks were performed by the companies now holding defense contracts, this would be no more "socialistic" than the defense program is now.

Such programs would also have a secondary function of essential importance, closely related to their original goal of national defense. They would provide what might be called "standby-capacity in defense research and development and production capability." This function would be especially important in the event of a weapons freeze which might at some stage break down, as did the moratorium on nuclear testing. It would be extremely important to preserve the nation's capabilities for resuming the weapons race, if necessary—and the retention of such capability might help to prevent it from becoming necessary. Even in the event of a properly enforced agreement on general and complete disarmament, it is likely that for a good many years the nation would wish to maintain its capability to rebuild a well-rounded national defense system in the event of some breakdown in the treaty's implementation.

Such capability would be best preserved by the mounting of bold new programs of the type here advocated, which would not only provide continuing opportunity for the talents and the organizations now employed in defense industry but would also maintain a continuing pressure on our educational institutions to develop a large number of able and highly motivated people with the necessary aptitudes and expertise. In appreciation of the indirect defense contribution of such programs, it would be reasonable for the defense budget to subsidize part of their cost.

It is hard to imagine the vast benefits that the nation and the world might derive from a policy such as suggested here, even if only $5 billion a year were involved. The qualitative aspect here is more important than the quantitative one. There is enormous potential for progress in applying advanced systems analysis and utilizing the fantastic skills of the modern computer to apply the best of modern technology to the problems of our daily life. In effect, we would be having a second space program, but one tied firmly to earth. If I see this century aright, it is upon mounting such great and ambitious programs—which exhibit and continually amplify our capabilities to apply science to the achievement of men's goals—that our nation's prestige and influence, as well as its economic progress, will increasingly depend. Such programs should also serve to eliminate persistent technological obstacles to world economic development, and thereby contribute substantially to our ability to help the developing nations. Moreover, the advance preparation of such programs, by opening vast new perspectives for the use of precious human and organizational resources now heavily clustered in defense industry, would do more than anything else could to eliminate residual fears about disarmament impacts.

The Future
of Education

CHRISTOPHER JENCKS

AMERICAN education stands today where Europe stood in the late middle ages. The localists still hold enormous power, and the nationalists still tread gingerly, uncertain whether they are yet strong enough to assert their growing power—uncertain, indeed, whether they even have power, or what form it takes. Yet just as gunpowder made the feudal castle militarily useless and socially unworkable, so the scientific revolution has made the localism of America's schools and colleges intellectually ineffectual and socially obstructionist. For the moment the forces opposing change still seem overwhelmingly strong, and those who support it are afraid even to articulate the implications of their struggle. Anarchy and controversy remain the outward reality, even while a new order is built backstage.

What is the shape of the emerging educational system? We seem to be entering an era when education will be primarily a national rather than a local responsibility, when a large bureaucratic civil service will supplant the small lay school board, when the old intimacies based on shared experience and personal compatibility will be replaced by impersonal relationships based on shared knowledge and administrative consensus. Education is likely to become outwardly more monolithic and homogeneous, more dominated by the manpower needs of a national economy and the intellectual demands of the leading universities, more exclusively the province of insiders rather than outsiders. At the same time, however, this very creation of an increasingly unified and coordinated over-all system may make room for more genuine diversity, encouraging more experimentation and differentiation, more internal autonomy and less external pressure for conformity.

Such changes are, of course, fundamentally political. The question is who will have power. Is the choice of research problems a job for the scientists who do the work or the laymen who pay the bill? Is the granting of tenure to a school teacher a choice for the other teachers with whom she will work, or for administrators who must in some sense answer for her performance? Is the allocation of funds to buildings rather than salaries a choice for Congress, state legislatures, local school boards, local administrators, or who? Questions like these are not being decided by the same people today as a generation ago, and they will not be decided by the same people a generation hence as today. Yet the shifts in power implied by such changes tend to go unnoticed, for day-to-day controversies usually focus on the merits of particular issues, not the machinery by which they are settled. By temperament, most citizens are lobbyists, not political philosophers. If they dislike a particular decision they attack the judgments of those in power, not the system which places power in their hands.

The most conspicuous exception to this general habit of mind has been the debate about Federal aid to education. Here many critics have seen clearly the connection between creating a new kind of decision-making apparatus and reaching new sorts of conclusions. Even so, the debate has been conducted in such misleading terms that the real issues are largely obscured in daily discussion.

The advocates of higher education expenditures have felt compelled to pretend that Federal aid can be rendered without any increase in Federal control over education. On the face of it, this is silly. The avowed purpose of federal aid is to force the American people to spend a larger share of their incomes on education. This may be a laudable purpose, but it is either naive or disingenuous to pretend that this would not reduce local autonomy. The right not to spend one's money on other people's children (or even one's own) is not perhaps inalienable, but it is certainly highly valued by many Americans.

Nor is that the only right which Congress would limit if it assumed a major role in financing education. The very liberals who proclaim the possibility of "Federal aid without Federal control" also urge that Federal aid be used as a lever to enforce racial integration in the South. Furthermore, just as state aid has led state legislatures to establish "minimal standards" for local schools, so too Federal aid will mean certain Federal standards of equity and efficiency. Not even the recent Higher Education Facilities Act, permissive as it is, gives the states complete freedom in spending federal funds.

Perhaps most important of all, increasing Federal aid will mean that Congress joins with state legislatures and local authorities in setting the over-all educational priorities of the country. This effort is already self-conscious and deliberate. A century ago the Morrill Act established colleges of "Agriculture and Mechanic Arts" because Congress thought existing colleges too preoccupied with the classics. Half a century ago it began aiding vocational secondary education for similar reasons. In 1958, under the National Defense Education Act, Congress backed science and languages, subjects which it felt, after hearing expert testimony, that the secondary schools had been neglecting.

Looking back at the history of Federal education legislation, two points are clear. First, with the early exception of the Northwest Ordinance, the main aim of Federal legislation has been to bring the educational system into closer harmony with the manpower requirements of a technologically changing society. Second, these requirements are fundamentally national rather than local, and when innovation has been left to local authorities, whether in schools or colleges, they have done an inadequate job. It therefore seems reasonable to predict that if the rate of technological change increases, the role of the Federal government in shaping educational priorities will also increase. Congress will, however, act only when the existing feudal system has shown itself hopelessly inadequate; it will not in the foreseeable future admit that the *primary* responsibility for many kinds of education is Federal rather than state or local. Nevertheless, that fact seems likely to be increasingly understood by other Americans, although not widely proclaimed.

Just as power is likely to shift from state to Federal authorities so it is also likely to shift from local to state hands. As a matter of law, of course, primary responsibility for education has always fallen on the states rather than local communities. The state education codes have established the ground rules for education, and have for many years limited the freedom of local boards of education within very narrow boundaries. The local board may not reduce salaries or other expenditures below a certain level without losing state aid. It may only hire teachers and administrators certified by the state. It must build buildings with a certain number of square feet for various functions, provide a certain number of teachers and jungle gyms and toilets for each child, and so on. Even the curriculum is regulated by the state in many cases, with state legislators approving a limited number of textbooks, adopting curricula with required courses in everything from patriotism to the dangers of alcohol, and banning instruction in things as diverse as Darwinism and contraception.

This kind of power is so widely taken for granted that it is seldom even discussed. Few people want to turn back the clock (though the question of teacher certification has aroused some such sentiments). State control arose because local schools were being used for political patronage, firetraps were being constructed with the taxpayer's money, children were being denied an adequate education by parents too niggardly to pay for good teachers. It is hard to avoid the conclusion that an extension of Federal power would, over the years, produce a similar pattern of Federal standards.

All of the foregoing issues are fundamentally of the same kind: which groups of laymen make certain choices about the schools. A second and related issue which has received far less attention, is which *professionals* will have the dominant voice. Here the trend is towards giving university scholars and scientists a greater voice, and everyone else less.

The meaning of what is popularly called "progressivism" in America was, in "political" terms, that for two generations the schools became largely independent of colleges and universities. Only a small minority of the students were going on to college, and in many cases only a small minority of the teachers had any familiarity with a scholarly or scientific discipline. Conversely, university scholars and scientists knew little about the elementary and secondary schools, and cared less. Progressivism was in this sense a revolt against the intellectual demands of the academics. (I should emphasize that this kind of progressivism has only the most distant connection with the kind preached by John Dewey or the practices of the handful of progressive schools, mostly private, which sought to prepare their pupils for further education rather than for "life.")

That era is over. More and more secondary students are going to college. The proportion will, indeed, soon be as high as it was in the nineteenth century. Once again, secondary schooling will be defined primarily as preparation for college. The curriculum is already reverting to a more collegiate model. More teachers have been through a liberal arts college, more have studied an academic specialty. The ties between schools and colleges are tightening in a dozen ways, of which the most conspicuous is perhaps the development of "Advanced Placement" courses in many high schools, offering "college level" work in various subjects. These courses attract a kind of teacher, and set a standard of both academic excellence and intellectual relevance, which slowly permeates the rest of the school. A related phenomenon is the current curriculum-reform movement, which has involved university scientists and scholars in developing detailed curriculum plans for the secondary schools, training teachers to use them, and even occasionally doing some elementary or secondary teaching themselves.

Similar forces are at work in the colleges. More undergraduates are going on to graduate school. More colleges are establishing their own graduate schools. The result is that the standards of the graduate school are more widely accepted as applying to undergraduate programs. The professor who is primarily interested in undergraduates is either an eccentric or an incompetent, and the program which offers something distinctive to undergraduates is on the wane.

The net result is an increasing consensus about what should be taught, running from the primary through the graduate school. This does not mean, however, that the structure of education is becoming *administratively* more monolithic. On the contrary.

At the college level, professors are becoming more like doctors or lawyers—independent professionals with their own constituencies and their own incomes. When a professor was primarily a teacher, supported by a student tuition and alumni endowment, he needed an institution to support him. Few individual teachers could reach enough students to make a national reputation, and even if they did, they could seldom make a living by teaching independently (though the public lecturer in effect did this). The research professor, on the other hand, often acquires a national reputation, and then finds that grants and consultantships can support him. He needs a university only as an office and for facilities. If one university does not suit him, he can move to another. His grants and his graduate assistants will follow. This kind of mobility has become characteristic even of disciplines with limited research funds. In this context the university administrator stops being the director of the academic play and becomes merely the producer, making technical arrangements for the display of stars. If there is direction it comes from the collective wisdom of the legislators and philanthropists who put up the money, and from the committees of scholars and scientists which make the grants.

At the elementary and secondary level there are also signs, especially in big cities, that the teachers are beginning to seek an independent voice, rather than speaking only through administrators responsible to laymen.

If these trends persist, two predictions seem justified. First, no major reforms will be possible in American education which do not begin at the graduate level and filter down through the system. (Indeed, the major "reforms" of the current period consist precisely of filtering ideas and ideals down from the graduate schools to lower levels.) Second, the increasing autonomy of the graduate-school professor will make major institutional reforms even more difficult in the next generation than the last. The era of the great educational leader seems to be over. Innovation, as Clark Kerr indicates in *The Uses of the University*, is something that an administrator no longer plans or even initiates, but rather something that he presides over, keeping the peace as best he can. The autonomous fiefdoms of a great university go their own way, and individual professors run their own realms independently. This is less true in public school systems today, but it may become more so as teachers assert their power.

Yet to say that no individual leader can impress his dreams or nightmares upon the educational system is not to say that educators as a group may not do so, perhaps at the expense of laymen.

The key issue in education today, both public and private, is probably the extent to which teachers at all levels will be allowed to become a self-regulating profession, controlling their own affairs without lay interference. This is the question of "academic freedom," in the broadest sense of that phrase, or as I would prefer to say, professional freedom. It implies freedom not merely to read and write whatever books one thinks best or to teach whatever version of one's subject one thinks best, but freedom to select one's colleagues, to organize research, develop curricula and choose among students as one sees fit.

Until very recently only a small proportion of American teachers even aspired to this "right." These men were found in substantial numbers only in a handful of eminent universities, public and private, in a small number of private liberal arts colleges, and in an even smaller number of private schools. The great majority of teachers accepted, with varying degrees of resentment, the right of boards of trustees, boards of education, tuition-payers and tax-payers to dictate the choice of colleagues, of subject-matter, of research topics, of admissions requirements, and of much else besides. This was (and often still is) true in teachers' colleges, sectarian colleges, technical and vocational colleges—and of course in the public schools. It was not that the rights of the staff in these institutions were violated or ignored. The possibility that they had "rights" was not even imagined.

Today there are signs that this is changing. The men who preside over many American schools and colleges are increasingly intimidated by the intellectual claims of academicians and are more inclined than in the past to bow to expert opinion. This is especially obvious in their dealings with scientists. But school consultants are also in vogue, and when they suggest that the board of education keep out of certain areas, they are often heeded. State boards of education have often made state aid contingent on similar grants of autonomy by local boards to "professionals." More recently, teachers' organizations have begun to assert the right of the staff to a voice in school affairs. Indeed, as Superintendent Calvin Gross said, the issue in the New York strike threats in past years has really been whether the teachers or the Board should decide certain matters of policy. To date, the teachers have done very little to assert their potential power. But there seems a good chance that they will show more solidarity and better organization in the next few years.

This may or may not be a good thing. European education is controlled by educators to a much greater extent than American education, and the results are a mixed blessing. There is certainly more intellectual freedom. But European academicians have also shown a bias in favor of haste. They cover more material each year than their American counterparts, and as a consequence they leave a larger proportion of their students behind. This does not bother them much, however, because their main interest is in children like themselves—the academically talented. Judging by the kinds of pressures now being exerted on American education by leading scientists and scholars in the better universities, a similar kind of speed-up, combined with earlier selection, seems in the making for America. In itself this might not be too serious. But both in Europe and in America academicians tend to take less interest than laymen in providing second chances for those who are rejected—wisely or foolishly—at some point in the educational cycle. Where the academics lead, teachers will increasingly follow.

"Professional versus lay control" is not, of course, an either/or issue. There will always be a mixture. A realistic debate can only be conducted in terms of fairly specific issues. Who should decide whether the high school should spend money on a library or a gymnasium? Who should decide whether to inaugurate an honors program? Who should decide between heterogeneous and homogeneous grouping? Who should decide who gets into college and who doesn't? Who should decide whether space research is of top scientific priority?

As I indicated at the outset, it seems to me clear that the trend for the next generation will be centralized decision-making, and the emphasis will be on technical expertise, either among the decision-makers or their staffs. Laymen will count for less, on boards of all kinds, and even laymen in Congress will rely more on bureaucratic guidance. On paper, this bodes ill for democracy. Yet those who have watched the local Boards of Education in action may doubt that such "democracy" was worth saving. Nor is the Board of Trustees which throws its weight around likely to seem a symbol worth preserving.

There are, moreover, other ways to "democratize" education

than through official representatives of the public. Perhaps the most important would be to give students real choice among institutions at all levels. Then if a parent or child did not like one school, he could enroll (without facing bankruptcy) in another. Likewise if he did not like one college he could get a scholarship at another. The present system of allocating funds encourages precisely the opposite result. Governments give money to particular institutions, and then open these institutions to particular students at artificial rates. Perhaps what education needs is a return to the free market economy. Perhaps instead of trying to tell schools and universities how to run their affairs, laymen ought to consider leaving institutions to their own devices, allowing them to do whatever students and research-clients will pay for. Then scholarships could be granted to all—regardless of ability.

There are enormous difficulties in any such approach. The consequences of freedom are not all appealing to liberals. Such a system might, for example, lead to the elimination of the few existing "comprehensive" institutions—those which now cater to both the very bright and the very stupid. It would also probably lead to more segregation along religious lines—and along racial lines, if that were permitted. Yet if the aim is to restore popular control over education, a system in which the public "votes with its feet" seems more likely to work satisfactorily than one in which laymen try to control a complex profession they only half understand. Education itself, by encouraging professional expertise and exclusiveness, has made the effective exercise of lay power almost impossible.

Art and
the Affluent Society

ERIC LARRABEE

THE late John F. Kennedy was the first American President in this century to exhibit a serious interest in the arts and their role in the life of the nation. True, his personal taste in the arts and letters was relatively undemanding and his natural bent, when it came to the point of action, was on the side of the feasible and the productive. He liked projects to be realistic and to lead somewhere, which is why we will always wonder what he conceived the ultimate role of his own Special Consultant on the Arts to be, and why the report of August Heckscher—when he stepped down as the first occupant of that post—is such an interesting document.

Consideration of the arts and government in the next decade would have to start with Mr. Heckscher's report in any case. It is a blueprint of the presently available devices by which government affects the arts, and of the areas in which that effect might profitably be expanded. It is enchantingly open-ended; it takes the position that there is something called the "national well-being"—or what Mr. Heckscher has named, in another context, the Public Happiness—and that this is profoundly influenced by what government does, or does not, do. The language may be bureaucratic but the message is clear: "A long-standing weakness in what might be called the cultural infrastructure has led to institutions inadequately supported and managed and, as in the theater, to a lack of the stability and continuity which provide the grounds where talent can develop and mature. Often, inadvertently, government has imposed obstacles to the growth of the arts and to the well-being of the artist." In short, this is a society organized to make art difficult, and government participates in the process.

When the office of the Special Consultant on the Arts was created, Mr. Heckscher writes, "it was understood that he would be concerned with the progress of the arts primarily as they affect, not our international posture, but the well-being, the happiness, and the personal fulfillment of the citizens of our democracy." Here the Presidential commitment is distinctly indicated, and it has the Kennedy mark on it. He would go Jefferson one better, not the "pursuit of happiness" but "personal fulfillment." It is a conception characteristic of a man trying to cope with some of the problems of an Affluent Society before they got completely out of hand. The notion of a Public Happiness is somewhat akin to J. K. Galbraith's division of the economy into the public and the private sector. The assumption of cultural laissez faire behind Jefferson's phrase was that happiness not only ought to be pursued privately but that the national happiness, if there was such a thing, was merely the product of such personal pursuits indefinitely multiplied. Mr. Galbraith's contribution has been to show that we have long since passed the point where any assumption of the kind is justified and now find ourselves, indeed, in a world where personal fulfillment—whether economic or artistic—is continually frustrated by the lack of public (as Mr. Heckscher put it) "infrastructure."

Cultural laissez faire has its attractions and its eloquent advocates. For one thing, it is evident that art thrives on a certain amount of discouragement and that much of the energy of artists ought to be expended in attacks on the existing order whether that order is friendly, unfriendly, or buoyantly indifferent. The American tradition of private support theoretically works against the emergence—in contrast to the European pattern—of a single artistic Establishment. The tradition is also a healthy one in that it disowns art with a capital A or culture with a capital C; that is, it rejects received opinions as to which is a proper medium for creative self-expression and thus allows for the flowering of vernacular arts like jazz and the motion picture. So defined, American culture is not something government ought to be involved in, and not something government could do very much about even in the unwelcome event that it should try.

This system worked well enough in a society of scarcity where everyone had to scrabble, since the artist could scrabble along with the rest. But the Affluent Society is something else. It is presently organized to favor certain forms of activity over others, since some are either better suited to Affluence or else they attracted the attention of Affluence's early pioneers, like the national superhighway system or the vast machinery of the expense-account style of life. Affluence is highly selective, as we are beginning to realize; it permits poverty in the midst of plenty. Where it bestows its blessing is in no way determined by society's need or even by a conscious act of public choice. Someone is always turning up a new and unexploited possibility, such as selling vending machines to defense contractors, and already there are affluent individuals in nearly every sector, including even affluent writers and abstract expressionists. But it is still safe to say of the arts in general that compared to industry or the armed services they are Affluence's underdeveloped area, a last refuge of the Protestant Ethic.

The artist, regrettably, ventures out into the harsh world of cost-plus contracts and tax write-offs from behind a private system of lean, pared-down values. The coin he trades in with himself, the terms of his art, is very hard money. Either the line is well-drawn, the phrase well-turned, the chord well-struck, or it is not. Affluence leans on the side of the ephemeral and the expendable; art is perennially tempted toward the exact and the enduring. One can imagine an Art of Affluence: we will get to it eventually and it will be very oriental, seizing the evanescent instant for its own sake. Prince Genji trying to decide what color of notepaper and what style of calligraphy with which to write his momentary lady-love is a work of affluent art. But that time is not yet. For us aesthetic aims are still priced in the deflated currency of permanence. What causes us all the trouble is forcing the arts to compete in the same market with necessities, and on disadvantageous terms. What art needs is not an artificial subsidy but an even break.

"The problem," as Mr. Galbraith writes, "is not the discipline imposed by economic organization but the effort of economic organization to accommodate society to its needs and, given the priority we accord to economic goals, the concessions that these needs are assumed to require of society." One of those concessions is that art be treated as unnecessary. Economic activity is assumed to be benign as long as it is directed to personal gain, but if it is directed to an aesthetic goal it is regarded as superfluous and self-indulgent. If I take a man to the opera because I am hoping to sell him something, the government subsidizes me in this action; if I go merely for the sake of the opera and the cultivation of my own sensibility I am considered to be serving no useful purpose. Art fights for economic life with one hand tied behind it.

At the same time, the opera has to pay its own employees as though they were engaged in a legitimate economic enterprise, and they have to be maintained up to the standards of a consumer economy paced by highly productive industries. Under the circumstances it is miraculous that any cultural activities whatever manage to survive. The musicians have understandably organized to maintain themselves at a level which might support a Pontiac and a split-level in Queens, with the result that there are fewer and fewer jobs, moonlighting is endemic, and all the symphony orchestras run deficits. The composers, who are not organized as well, fare worse. Henry Cowell has been candid enough to put on record the total earnings from his music (over a thousand compositions) for the year 1961: they came to $5,500, of which $3,500 was from radio and television performances and $2,000 from record sales. "I could live on what I make from music," Mr. Cowell remarked, "but not as I care to live—and so I am a professor."

The priority of the economic motive in the private sphere, as Galbraith indicates, creates in the public sphere a whole series of demands it cannot satisfy—for all our elementary social equipment, for schools, for parks, for habitable cities, for fresh air and clear water. Something similar happens in the cultural economy: the devices for processing art tend to prosper at the expense of those which create it. Perhaps these are the growing pains of a great civilization. Mr. Justice Goldberg, when he was Secretary of Labor, made a speech calling on government to subsidize the arts in which he took this view. "The problems of the performing arts in America today," he said, "are not the problems of decline. They are the problems of growth: a growth so rapid, so tumultuous, so eventful as to be almost universally described as an explosion. . . . One could hardly hope for a climate more receptive to the creative artist. An era of unequaled achievement may well be upon us." Unfortunately, as Mr. Goldberg went on to say, this explosion (or what others have called a "cultural revolution") has not progressed so far that the average artist can make a decent living, or an exceptional one like Henry Cowell afford to practice his art full-time.

"Cultural revolution" is a singularly misleading phrase, anyhow. There has been a revolution in several techniques of diffusion, and these have had a profound effect on the range of choice open to the consumer. The paperback and the long-playing record have enlarged the quality audience, for example, and increased the quality and diversity accessible to it, by a factor so large that the adjective "revolutionary" is deserved. But the change has come about primarily through increased efficiencies of manufacture or distribution in the limited areas where innovation was overdue. Mail-order marketing of books has had revolutionary possibilities in recent years because the bookstore system of reaching customers is so inefficient (it misses 90 percent of the population). Where technical innovation is clumsy or inappropriate, however, as in painting or the live performance of music, the signs of any startling improvement are less easy to descry. The visual arts as yet have no hi-fi, so that visually the audience remains relatively poorly serviced; and in music, where hi-fi does exist, the ordinary performing artist has yet to profit from it to the degree that the audience has.

Hence the curious artistic and literary situation we are located in, where a lot seems to be going on but to no great avail. The consequences of the LP and the paperback, if any, will be long-term. Surely it is bound to make a difference, in the long run, that so many more millions will actually have listened to Berlioz or Haydn, or as many more thousands will have read Carl Becker's *The Heavenly City of the 18th Century Philosophers* than might otherwise have done so. But the immediate impact on the arts or on the individual artist is virtually invisible, and the implications for the over-all muscularity and skin-tone of the culture, though vast, are so subjective that they can be debated endlessly—as they nearly have been. The arrival of a new mass audience, as in television, is culturally a potential fact rather than a negotiable one. It is neutral in regard to art insofar as it has not proved innately antipathetic. Television's genuflections in the direction of culture are on a par with radio's, and about equally portentous.

The distinction therefore must be made between kinds of art and kinds of audience before any judgment on the national performance can be passed. Showing Shakespeare on television and showing Shakespeare free in Central Park are both in their way admirable but they should be sharply differentiated as to the scope and location of their cultural impact. The former uses the going contemporary medium, with all the gains in penetration and power that this implies; but the latter affects social structure: it builds an institution and sets patterns of behavior. It gives actors longer and more consistent employment and training; it establishes habits in its audiences—like the little girls from Spanish Harlem who turned out to have seen *Romeo and Juliet* five times. Structural change is self-perpetuating and irreversible; it changes, not the odds, but the rules of the game.

It is a mistake to suppose that this country is a cultural mess simply because it has been left alone to be messy. It has been made into a mess, and the mess can be unmade by the same instruments used to make it. Most of them are legal, and laws can be amended. The laws which sustain the vulgarity of café-society expenditure, while punishing creativity and intellect, are obnoxious and demeaning laws. Yet the slightest effort made to ameliorate them this past year produced such tantrums of self-pity on the part of restaurant and nightclub owners that it was soon abandoned. When will the arts speak with as loud a voice? We have passed far beyond the time for indulgent joking about loopholes and lawyers, or worldly-wise head-shaking about the impossibility of tax reform. Our system cannot continue, in decency and self-respect, to tolerate a depletion allowance for petroleum but not for poetry.

The ugliness of visual America is similarly man-made, and can be re-made. We are not a tidy people, as D. W. Brogan once observed; we go away and leave things. Much of the country looks like what Peter Blake has aptly called "God's own junkyard." But much of it also has been shaped by law, by governmental regulations, and by the availability of credit. The phenomenon of postwar urban sprawl was not an accident; it was built into the arrangements for veterans' housing, the legislated assumption that the natural habitat of Americans is the individual, detached dwelling. The downtown of American cities was at the same time made increasingly unfit to live in by tax practices which encourage real-estate manipulation and speculative building, but discourage anything else. The high point was undoubtedly reached when New York City proposed to tax the Seagram building at a higher rate than usual on the grounds that its good design was a luxury. We have allowed government to become an instrument for enforcing—not merely tolerating—squalid mediocrity.

Actually the shabby impermanence of the American landscape might turn out to be an advantage. Since we are going to have to tear most of it down anyway, there may be a chance to undo the worst of the damage. Fortunately the opportunity—and the incentive, since Affluence requires ever-larger outlets for our surplus energies—comes at a time when the profession of visual design is potentially equal to it. Design in the sense that the present generation of architects and other visual professionals understand it is a crusading faith; its converts are all carriers of the doctrine, and they have been multiplying at a remarkable rate. They are unique among practicing intellectuals in retaining a touch of utopian fantasy; the job of redesigning the entire country would strike them as not in the least illogical, and there will soon be enough of them to set about it at a high level of style, aspiration, and three-dimensional imagination.

If only the defenders of culture were similarly daring and impassioned! The next few years' agenda for government and the arts is filled with proposals, all worthy and no doubt deserving to be put into effect tomorrow, but all palliative. There will be more culture centers, and maybe some more arts councils, and perhaps the twenty-percent-of-income limit on gifts for cultural purposes will be lifted, and it is even possible that the Kennedy Center may raise the money it needs. But all these gestures of patronage are precisely that and no more, and it is not surprising that such presidential appointments as there have been in this area draw heavily on persons properly described as "patrons of the arts." The less charitable term is "fund raisers," and fund-raising is charity in one of its least charitable forms. It is the curse of American cultural enterprise; it is the institutionalizing of deficit, an outlet for energies far more likely to be social than aesthetic, and a permanent source of friction and ill will. It perpetuates an archaic system for supporting arts like opera, symphony, and the ballet which were originally created for an aristocratic clientele whose economic ability to afford them has long since vanished. The fund-raising system, and the fund-raising attitude, is wholly inappropriate today. None of the remedies it offers are truly structural; none of them change the rules of the game.

The game was set up in the days when necessities came first and amenities of any kind were costly. Unhappily, the attitudes it nurtured have carried over into a time in which these conditions no longer apply—a time, in fact, in which they have been reversed. The ethics of scarcity are no longer binding, and the needs of Affluence are for precisely those "luxuries" we used to think we couldn't afford: livable cities, a clean and harmonious landscape, open access for all to the arts of leisure. What Mr. Galbraith has been trying for so many years now to convince his fellow-countrymen is that unswerving pursuit of the economic goals has become self-defeating. When public needs are sacrificed to private ones, the private ones now suffer as well. There is no justification any more for treating art as a luxury and it has, indeed, ceased to be one. In an era of automation men will hunger less for material welfare than for something to do, less for bread than for meaning.

Subsidies are no good, if only because they put too much power in the hands—and the ideologies—of those who grant them. Tax reform is logical and desirable; writers should not be penalized as they now are, for example, merely for living in New York City, which taxes them as independent business enterprises. But we find ourselves in a new world, one whose shape is so strange and incongruent with the old that no familiar remedy is likely to be effective. We have come to the point where real estate based on the rights of property is no longer able to organize the environment rationally and the question has to be raised (as did *Architectural Forum* before its lamentable demise) whether a way must not be found to regard land legally as a common resource. We have come to the point where commodities are so much easier to create than jobs that one can reasonably argue (as does the Ad Hoc Committee on the Triple Revolution) in favor of paying everyone an annual wage merely to exist, and go on consuming, in the topsy-turvy universe of automation and abundance.

Art is its own justification. There is no merit or future in arguing for it as social therapy, or as the ornament of a more efficacious foreign policy. Either it is at the heart of civilized life, and of the human mystery, or our confidence in its preoccupying power has been misplaced. All that is asked of us now is the willing suspension of disbelief in the impossibility of art's coming into its own, the willingness to imagine a world in which the priority of economic goals has literally been replaced by aesthetic ones. It is a prospect so alien and unimaginable that no one knows what it would look like, let alone how to go about building it. Somehow we are going to have to find out.

The Future
of the Metropolis

NORTON E. LONG

The United States, already an overwhelmingly urban country, is now becoming a well-nigh equally overwhelmingly metropolitan country. A few score metropolitan areas account for more than 60 percent of the population. By 1980 this percentage is expected to climb to nearly 70 percent. The future of metropolis is the future of most of us. The quality of the life that is lived in it is the quality of American life. Its capacity to structure itself—or be structured—as a significant, self-governing political community will determine the future of local self-government in the United States. Our capacity to maintain and develop vital institutions of local self-government may well decide the fate of grass-roots democracy. In so doing, it may ultimately determine the fate of constitutional democracy nationally.

The metropolitan problem has been depicted as a crisis of traffic and sewage, of slums and bad housing, of declining central business districts, of central cities fiscally eroded and fast becoming ethnic ghettos of poverty, unemployment, and crime, of fragmented governments incompetent to solve pressing common problems and of a fleeing citizenry dedicated to the motto "every man and every splinter government for himself or itself." It is true that some or all of these ills afflict almost every major metropolitan area in the United States.

Central cities are for the most part largely built up. New building and new patterns of land use consonant with modern tastes in residence and modern demands in industry and commerce are therefore largely confined to the suburbs. This means that central city properties are inevitably obsolescent and face the same fate as aging motor cars. In the sociologists' language, they are downward mobile. They have uses, but (like used cars) aging housing, stores, and factories must accept lower returns, even in the face of rising maintenance costs. The circumstance which in the past has prevented structural obsolescence from having this effect has been enduring high locational value. But the locational value derived its stability from the stability and peculiarity of transport technology—the technology of ship and wagon, modified and intensified by the effect of rail transport and in particular rail terminals. This transport technology has been shattered by the advent and diffusion of the motor car and the truck. Locational values that compensated for structural obsolescence have now, in the face of the new transport technology, begun to obsolesce. The land use appropriate to the older transport technology is now being revolutionized, and the changes, like all massive social and economic change, are painful and costly to many.

The central city, with declining property values and stationary population, is confronted with a change in the character of its people that increases its costs, at the very time that its capacity to meet these costs is being reduced. The aging housing of the central city and the slipping suburbs is all that the lower-paid members of the working class, the marginally employed, the elderly, those on relief and the ethnically segregated can afford. This population occasions high welfare and other service costs, while producing minimal amounts of revenue. Frequently the plants or homes where these people are employed (if they are employed) are located beyond the city's boundaries. In escaping the city's taxes, they escape a good part of their labor costs, that is, the costs of providing schools for their employees' children, etc.

What is true of the central city's housing tends, with the exception of a few cities such as New York and a few places within other cities, to be true of the central city's commercial and industrial properties. Obsolescent structurally and locationally, they must accept lower returns while facing rising maintenance costs. Therefore, the owners of these properties must strive to reduce the burden of their taxes at the very time when the city's needs make such a reduction well-nigh impossible.

What is happening to the central city in the metropolitan area is, indeed, no more than what in the past has happened to neighborhoods within the central city itself. But, whereas in the past the decay of one area in the city was compensated for by the growth of another, now the growth occurs almost exclusively outside the corporate limits of the central city and thus escapes sharing the burden of the decay. The ecology of growth and of decay, of rich and of poor, that had previously been contained within the corporate limits of the central city, is now severed by political boundaries. In addition, the revolution in transport technology has destroyed the foundation of permanent locational values on which all hopes of so-called natural renewal depend. All this is made even more unmanageable by the explosive process of urbanization and suburbanization.

The central city is not the only victim of the pell-mell pace of social change in which we are involved. Well-nigh 100 percent of the population increase over that of 1960 that is anticipated by 1985 (approximately 106 million) will occur in present and future metropolitan areas. Given our present pattern of suburban land use, a doubling of metropolitan population will mean a tripling or quadrupling of the areas covered. If past experience is any guide, this enormous territorial spread will be balkanized into a patchwork of jealous and competing local governments. Some of these will be rich in tax resources. Others will have to provide schools and services with little or no tax sources beyond the lower-middle-class homes of suburbanites strapped by mortgage payments. There is no reason to expect that industrial and commercial establishments, providing sources of tax revenue, will locate in any evenly distributed pattern among the patchwork of municipalities that have spawned (and are now spawning) in metropolitan areas. This can only mean that, along with the central city, there will be suburban poor relations, frequently in even worse state—governments incapable of providing a standard budget of public services. It also means, unless there is a revolutionary change in local government behavior, that this ecology of fiscal wealth and poverty will produce (as it has in the past) a dog-eat-dog and devil-take-the-hindmost competition for a place in the fiscal sun—a scramble to secure valuable assets and a ruthless struggle to escape liabilities.

The obvious metropolis-wide problems that cut across local government boundaries and transcend the power of individual jurisdictions have not escaped the notice of the press, politicians, civic leaders and scholars. The metropolitan problem has been vigorously discussed from the 1920's and before. In fact, the creation of New York City might be regarded as the most successful political effort in this area to date. Boston's Metropolitan District Commission also achieved at an early date, has been so successful that it has blunted the urge for further action. Up to now, despite widespread agitation under impressive civic and business auspices and with the benefit of well-supported Ford Foundation studies, the cause of metropolitan government reform has not prospered. Miami-Dade County, a special case, has achieved a limited degree of metropolitan government. More recently, Nashville-Davidson County has joined it in the short list of success stories. Elsewhere, attempts at metropolitan reform have met with unremitting and increasingly bleak failure. Indeed, the most striking metropolitan success on the continent—Toronto—is not in the United States but in Canada. There, the absence of our stubborn home-rule shibboleths and the willingness and power of the provincial legislature to impose a political settlement made possible the creation of a truly significant metropolitan experiment. Toronto is in many ways reminiscent of what was done by the New York legislature at an earlier date in creating New York City—an achievement that today would be beyond its will or power.

The agitation for metropolitan government reform has been largely conducted by municipal leaguers, the metropolitan press, civic leaders and businessmen—some with a financial stake, such as the downtown stores and the utilities, others out of a vague feeling that this was a worthwhile cause. Their efforts have succeeded only in mobilizing the latent majority for the status quo, a majority composed of its office-holding beneficiaries and of all the people, whether in the suburbs or in the central city, who fear change as threatening either their local public good or their share of local political power. It is, for instance, an ominous portent for metropolitan reform that the Negro communities in Cleveland and St. Louis, previously favorable to reform, now see it as jeopardizing their power and influence in the central city.

While the advocates of metropolitan government reform have painted a grim picture of the evil results of "fractionated government," to use Luther Gulick's phrase, the evidence for what most concerns business protagonists of reform—the harmful effects on the local economy—seems inconclusive. The massive Vernon studies of Greater New York yield the impression that, barring incredibly poor government performance, its economy will be molded by national and international economic forces largely beyond the power of any likely local efforts to affect it for good or ill.

The most probable response to the problems presented by metropolitan life seems to be the continuance of piecemeal, ad hoc improvisations to remedy specific ills. This means in practice the creation of special districts and authorities to handle specific problems and to by-pass fiscal limitations. It means an ever greater reliance on state and Federal governments as sources of revenue and therefore as sources of leadership for innovation. This may not bring the big city all the way to a palsied, penurious state of inactivity and clientship, but it will inevitably tend that way. Indeed, even now the fiscal strait-jackets of local governments are forcing them into a dependence that is only relieved by the Federal bureaucracy's overwhelming need of local initiative for the creation of a demand for their funds and services.

At first sight, it seems extraordinary that the central cities and many of their suburbs are in straitened circumstances and must seek aid from the state and the nation. After all, the wealth of the nation is produced in the metropolitan areas, not in the capitals. The two-hundred-odd metropolitan areas of the nation produce the bulk of the country's wealth and provide the bulk of the tax resources of the state and Federal governments. But, while they are the source of most of the revenues of higher levels of government, they are neither legally nor administratively capable of mobilizing their own resources to meet their own needs and are compelled to beg for a fractional return of the dollars they have sent to state capitals and to Washington. Fiscal anemia in the midst of plenty afflicts central cities and suburbs alike. For this reason, their officials are severely handicapped in exercising the leadership that their collective resources should make possible and that meeting their most pressing needs would seem to require. The fragmentation of fiscal resources and political leadership in the metropolitan areas insures their incapacity to translate their potential influence into effective action.

The size, the wealth, the talent, and the problems and possibilities confronting the emerging metropolitan areas demand —and should inspire—a veritable flowering of local civic initiative. Unfortunately, this seems most unlikely at present. The impoverished and declining central cities are increasingly the home of the poor, the alienated, and the incompetent. They are surrounded by the balkanized trivialities of a self-centered suburbia. There is no focus or fulcrum for effective metropolitan leadership. To the extent that limited, piecemeal solutions to problems of traffic, sewerage, sanitation, and water supply succeed in meeting immediate needs, they blunt the impulse to seek comprehensive solutions. Handouts from state and national governments take the edge off the pressing concerns of schools and welfare, but fail to come to grips with local problems locally, and freeze bureaucratic patterns that palliate evils while insuring their continuance.

The Federal Government has spent $3 million on its urban renewal program—only to reduce substantially the housing available to the poor. It has done this without studies and without research, so that we are unable either to analyze the experience or to learn from it. The Department of Health, Education and Welfare, along with the states, gives millions of dollars to welfare recipients, and through them to slum landlords, while the Housing and Home Finance Agency spends millions to ameliorate these same slums and check their growth. Neither agency seems in effective communication with the other. The Bureau of Public Roads and the Department of Defense exert colossal (though unplanned and therefore irresponsible) pressures, with hardly anyone in Washington to raise even a feeble voice on behalf of cities or metropolitan areas. Given the lack of adequate area-wide leadership to formulate an area-wide public interest, to defend it and to mobilize the local resources needed to implement it, power is sucked upward. Local government is enfeebled and the kinds of talent and ability always difficult to enlist for civic service in our business-oriented society are not forthcoming. The present drift may well portend a permanent decline in local self-government, with a growing tendency to substitute higher-level administration for it. Indeed, why should we trouble to govern ourselves if we can substitute the benevolent efficiency of, say, the Port of New York Authority for this painful and burdensome chore?

If all we were presently concerned with were traffic and sewage and smog and nuisances, we might well continue to drift along with piecemeal ad hoc solutions, letting nature take its course. Those who hold to the ancient liberal faith of Jefferson, de Tocqueville, and John Stuart Mill and believe that true local self-government is not a luxury but a vital necessity to a liberal society might well take alarm. But in these latter days of a liberalism that (with Rousseau) sees no merit in any mediation between the individual and the nation, this view may seem old-fashioned, if not downright conservative. In its fear for the consequences to the country of the destruction of local leadership and its attendant pluralism, it may appear actually alarmist.

What will ultimately force us to face the problem of metropolitan government is neither nuisances nor economics. It is politics: political problems of a kind that can not in our kind of society be solved by paratroops in Little Rock; political problems that are shrieking from every headline about school boycotts. The central cities of the largest metropolitan areas of this country have a darkening core and an impermeable white ring. The American Negro in an amazingly short period of time has migrated from farm to city and from the South to the North. Meanwhile, American industry, whose insatiable demand for unskilled labor has incorporated every past minority in the world of work, has begun inexorably to close its doors to the unskilled and the uneducated. Underemployed, unemployed, and embittered, the American Negro is realizing his political power, particularly in the central cities of the North. Increasingly, the flight of white families to the suburbs is resulting in de facto school segregation. The situation in Washington D.C., whose public schools are now over 80 percent Negro, is the nightmare that haunts most Northern cities.

As now constituted, our central cities and our suburbs lack a leadership of sufficient prestige, ability, and dedication to mobilize support for the measures necessary to bridge the menacing gulf between core and outer ring. As devices for absorbing people and acculturating them to the norms and standards of middle-class life, our metropolitan areas are failing badly. A hard core of alienated and embittered poverty is developing and reproducing itself at an alarming rate. The decay of the kind of local loyalties that have made "fellow-citizen" more than an empty word has left us ill-prepared to cope with present conflicts. A business leadership made up of "birds of passage," winging their way from branch plant to national office in the pursuit of their corporation careers, with little more than a public-relations concern for their civic responsibilities, is a poor substitute for a locally committed elite. What local political leadership exists is systematically downgraded by the press (too often with reason) and is powerless to mobilize community support. It concerns itself largely with keeping afloat rather than breasting the tide.

Increasingly, we will face in central cities a powerful and embittered Negro population and a growing number of the aged, the unemployed, and the dependent. Business assets of declining but still immense value will be at the mercy of the growing political power of this population. It is inconceivable that those interested in these assets will fail to urge sympathetic state legislatures to protect their possessions. While for the most part these legislatures have cared little enough for central cities, this will be an appeal, especially if it be preceded by outbreaks of violence, to which they will lend a considerate ear.

It would be a pity if metropolitan government had to come to the United States under the lash of this kind of fear. It will be a sad day when it does. However, in the absence of competent, courageous, dedicated local metropolitan leadership it seems not unlikely that this is the direction in which we are drifting.

To halt the present state of drift, to provide a program of action, and to hearten and enlist citizens of good will is even now not an impossible task. The country does not—though both in war and peace it usually has—have to wait until disaster is upon it before rousing itself to action. Individual local efforts are heartening as showing that there is still life at the grass roots. But the problem we face is nation-wide, of massive scope, and beyond any likely spontaneous efforts of the disorganized, leaderless populations of metropolitan areas to cope with. The hardening class lines between central cities and suburbs, the growing and increasingly bitter color line make effective action urgently necessary before mounting antagonisms become fixed patterns of our political culture.

But what is involved is no less than the whole future of responsible local self-government in the United States. The question at issue is whether we have the wit, the courage, the good sense and the good will to transform the two-hundred-odd metropolitan areas in which the overwhelming bulk of us live into responsibly self-governing communities. As they are now constituted they defy any efforts to achieve their responsible government at the local level. As the states and the Federal government are now constituted, they can assist, they can interfere with, but they can not substitute for local leadership and local self-government. Despite good will, such as it is, in state capitals and in Washington, it must be recognized that the emergence of some two hundred new sources of effective political power would be a major threat to the *status quo*. The restructuring of American local government to take account of new needs and new facts amounts to a revolution. Can those who stand to lose from this change be expected to lead it?

The most hopeful source of leadership in an effort to revitalize local government in the United States is the Presidency. The metropolitan areas of the country are his prime constituency. In fact though not in law, they are the United States. Their state, good or bad, is the state of the union. The inability to mobilize their abundant leadership and fiscal resources to keep their own house in order is the single most important governmental problem in the country. The peril to the American federal system of the growing bankruptcy of our local government was recognized by the Kestenbaum Commission. The question of revitalizing local government by making it competent to shoulder the problems that now confront it is beyond partisan considerations. Its successful answer will determine our ability to conserve our political heritage by renewing it.

There are several things that the national government can do that would be of immense help in starting an effective movement to provide the nation's metropolitan areas with effective capacity for self-government. First and foremost would be the devotion of top-level attention to transforming Washington and the Washington Metropolitan Area into a model for imitation rather than what it now is, the nightmare of those who fear it as their own likely fate. Unless we can mobilize the leadership and resources to solve the problems of schools and government in the District and its surrounding metropolitan area, it is idle to expect that our chances will prove better elsewhere. If we cannot make the nation's capital something we all can be proud of, how can we expect to rally people elsewhere? The leadership in Congress and the Executive branch, those who believe in what they say, can provide the most effective propaganda, that of the deed, by venturing their families in the task of building quality integrated schools. The President can put the spotlight on Washington and in doing so give the lead to the nation. He has vast resources for turning our capital into an embodied program for action that will pioneer the road for others.

The President can check out the efforts of his departments in Washington and its metropolitan area and evaluate their effectiveness and coordination. The reality control of checking these results in Washington would be salutary for President, Congress, and public. If it works in Washington it may not work elsewhere, but if it isn't working in Washington it probably isn't working anywhere. While the President needs a Secretary for Urban Affairs to have a man positioned high enough to speak with a voice of authority and with a single mission to see that the various programs of the Federal government make some over-all sense in their impact on our metropolitan areas, it may be some time before he can persuade Congress to enact the necessary legislation. Lack of such legislation does not have to stop him from moving. In Washington he has the best demonstration project in the country. It is for now his home town and he is, or ought to be, its first citizen. Washington is not a parochial sideshow for petty-patronage politics. It can be the place from which the whole effort of metropolitan reform can get its lead.

In a halfhearted way the Federal government has been inching toward using its fiscal powers to encourage broader areal considerations in the programs with which it is concerned. The time is fast becoming ripe for us to realize that there is a national interest in the effective responsible self-government of the two-hundred-odd metropolitan areas in which the nation lives. A major reason for the political ineffectiveness of these areas is not just their lack of governmental organization but their lack of fiscal ability. The Federal government could make a major contribution to advancing the cause of effective metropolitan self-government by proposing to share revenues with metropolitan governments meeting certain standards and by devolving certain present Federal functions to these governments to the extent they are prepared to meet certain standards. The Federal carrot has been a main source of governmental innovation. It would be a happy use of this device to use the growing fiscal power of the Federal government to strengthen rather than weaken local government and to devolve rather than centralize functions.

There seems little doubt that the centralization of revenue-raising capacity is a major danger to strong local and state government. Given the nature of the national economy and the competition of local units for industry it is doubtful if courageous local tax policies will or can be adopted. If we are to strengthen the local government function, shared revenues seem the most promising way to do it. Sharing revenues does not have to be done in such a way as to deprive local government of meaningful independence. It can, of course, and this has to be resisted.

The states will obviously be more threatened by the rise of responsible self-governing metropolitan areas than the federal government. If these areas become fiscally competent and politically effective they will radically alter the balance of political

power. There is no way, however, to change the present fragmented, leaderless state of these areas without producing such a
result. The carrot of Federal funds can be used to persuade
states to pass permissive legislation that would facilitate the
achievement of metropolitan-area governments. Both by lessen-
ing state revenue requirements through Federal sharing of
funds with metropolitan areas and by devolving powers the
change may be made more palatable. Indeed, careful consideration, as there must be, of a more appropriate division of functions and responsibilities between Federal, state, and metropolitan governments might well lead to a pattern in which the role
of the states would not suffer at all.

In any event, if the general analysis suggested here is correct,
the future of most of us and the future of local self-government
is the future of our metropolitan areas. The future of these
areas is clearly of major national concern. In the light of past
experience there seems no better source of national leadership
than the Presidency and the leaders of Congress. We urgently
need such leadership. Liberal and conservative alike have a
stake in vigorous local self-government and must do everything
to preserve and enlarge it.

The International Future

Peace
and Disarmament

HUBERT H. HUMPHREY

IN DEALING with disarmament, I believe it wise to begin with
the known before proceeding to the unknown. Briefly, I would
like to review where we have been and where we are now. Then
I wish to speculate on where we might hope to be ten to fifteen
years hence.

I believe we have come to the end of one epoch in the
postwar history of arms-control and/or disarmament negotiations. The past eighteen years have largely been years of im-
passe, frustration, and instead of control, an acceleration of the
arms race. Yet in 1963 there were signs that perhaps Russia as
well as the United States was less than satisfied with this. The
situation today appears more fluid than at any time since World
War II.

Nevertheless, many of the conditions which have inhibited
progress in the past are still with us. I shall summarize first the
unfavorable factors affecting disarmament, and then list the
favorable factors, mostly recent or new. Finally I shall project
the hopes for progress that these factors may sustain.

There are three conditions which still work against effective
arms control or disarmament:

1. The deep political and ideological schism between the Free World and the Communist world.
2. The built-in tendencies of the arms race toward self-perpetuation.
3. The technical problems of disarmament.

First, although there have been some signs of mild thaw in the Cold War, no real *detente* has been achieved. The ideological chasm seems to be as deep as it ever was. The Soviet Union may not regard nuclear war as a feasible means of achieving its objectives. But "all other means" including "wars of national liberation" appear to be normal instruments of its policy.

There is a deep rift, to be sure, between the Soviet Union and China, but this dispute has apparently not led to any abandonment of the expressed Soviet desire to bury the West.

Secondly, there is great momentum in an arms race to perpetuate itself. It is the relative, not the absolute quantities and qualities of weapons which become important. Any country feeling inferior will strive to get at least equal with others of comparable standing. Any increase in quantity, or a qualitative improvement on any side, often triggers renewed effort on the other. I do not believe, however, that there is a determinism operating here which makes the process irreversible. There are balanced and safeguarded arms-control measures possible which could slow down or halt the arms race.

The third factor inhibiting progress in arms control or disarmament is really the decisive one at the moment. This embraces the technical, social, and economic problems involved in any attempt to alter complex weapons systems in an equally complex military establishment in a highly organized society. Any given measure may have far-reaching effects on our defense system, our relations with allies, the distribution of bases, strategic concepts, military balance of power, and future technology. All of these must be examined to weigh the effect of a disarmament measure on national security.

After a disarmament measure is agreed on, there may be

required an elaborate system for dismantling armaments inspection and verification machinery, and other tasks. These need thorough, careful, prolonged study.

Timely action must also be taken to reduce the economic and social dislocations that may result from a disarmament measure. Recently I introduced a bill (S.2427) to establish a Hoover-type commission on automation, technology, and employment. One of the duties of the commission would be to plan for possible changes in defense spending. Senator George McGovern has introduced a bill (S.2274) to establish a national economic conversion commission within the Executive branch, and Senator Philip Hart has introduced a bill (S.2623) to establish a national commission on automation and technological progress. Both of these measures provide for study of reduction in defense spending, and how to absorb the resources and the people released. It is imperative that we do this planning broadly, that we develop some "contingency plans"—alternatives to defense spending. The existence of such planning would make our own arms-control proposals more credible, would make it easier for us to accept good plans proposed by others, and considerably ease any domestic political problems on disarmament.

Most of the favorable factors leading toward the accomplishment of arms control and disarmament objectives are of rather recent development. It is these which are precipitating us into a "new era" of hope. Again I would list three main factors:

1. The establishment by the United States of the Arms Control and Disarmament Agency, and outside the government, the growth of a highly qualified professional peace-research community.
2. A deeper realization of the irrationality and dangers of nuclear confrontation by the major powers.
3. The apparent growth in receptivity of the Soviet Union to the discussion of practical, immediate steps.

In September 1961, President Kennedy signed the Act providing for an Arms Control and Disarmament Agency. The Act states the national policy goal of the United States to be a world "in which the use of force has been subordinated to the rule of law and in which international adjustments to a changing world are achieved peacefully." It requires that this goal be approached by means consistent with our security.

Before the establishment of this agency we suffered from too much turnover in personnel in negotiations, from inadequate staff and planning work in this complex field, and therefore from inadequate development of detailed plans and policies.

I am proud to have had a part in the agency's creation. It has gathered a skilled and experienced staff. It is engaged in research, in the formulation and coordination of policy recommendations, and the conduct of international negotiations under the direction of the Secretary of State. It sees to it that problems will be explored continuously, will not be pushed aside for exigencies of the moment, and that disarmament considerations will always have a hearing in the consideration of foreign and national security policy.

I believe its achievements are already making themselves felt. Disarmament negotiations are no longer propaganda forums for the Soviet Union. We have presented detailed, concrete, negotiable plans. They cannot easily be blown away or ignored. We have begun to gain the initiative.

A second favorable item for progress is the growth on both sides in the cold war of the realization of the dangers in nuclear confrontation. The risks involved are seen to be irrational. There has been a fantastic development in weapons since World War II. The atom bomb of Hiroshima is now a "Model-T" type. Intercontinental ballistic missiles delivering those bombs at more than 17,000 miles per hour—nearly thirty times the speed of sound—can reach targets in 15 to 20 minutes. No one is safe, and at present there is no defense against these missiles.

The United States now has the most awesome array of military power ever assembled. The Soviet Union does not have as much, but what it has is very formidable. Even though we could absorb a "first strike" and still retaliate with destruction of an enemy society, it leaves us to suffer tremendous damage. As President Johnson said: "General war is impossible and some alternatives are essential."

The whole idea of nuclear war is irrational. No one can win. But in a "balance of terror," irrationality cannot be ruled out. This is creating a new pressure to seek a way to climb back down the atomic mountain.

The third favorable reason is that partly because of this, partly because of the economic strain of keeping up the weapons competition, the rift with China, and perhaps for still other reasons—the Soviet Union has recently appeared more inclined to take limited measures of control. In 1963, the Soviet Union rather suddenly agreed to three measures previously proposed by us, but until then ignored by them. First was the agreement for a direct communications link or "hot line" between Washington and Moscow. Then came the limited nuclear test ban treaty. Finally, there was the UN resolution against nuclear bombs in orbit. In other areas: space cooperation, trade, cessation of jamming the Voice of America broadcasts, the Soviet Union also showed signs of a "thaw."

Of course, limits have been set to this. Among other things, the Russians still seem to be reluctant about inspection on Communist territory. The Soviets charge that it is an excuse for espionage. We insist on inspection because we do not trust the Soviets to disarm without it.

The limited measures achieved in 1963 were all capable of sufficient verification to protect our security without inspections on Soviet soil. The proposals advanced by the President through the United States delegation at the Geneva Disarmament Conference last year were designed to reduce the scope of inspection as far as we can while still protecting our security. Briefly, these proposals include:

1. A freeze on the numbers and characteristics of strategic missiles and planes.

2. A cutoff in the production of fissionable material for nuclear weapons.
3. Mutual destruction of armaments such as the United States B-47's and Soviet TU-16's.
4. Observation posts to provide advance information concerning an attack by troops, planes or ships; and
5. Measures to inhibit the spread of nuclear weapons to countries which do not now have them.

The scope of inspection can be reduced, for example, by limiting the geographical area of observation, as in the case of the observation post proposal. It can also be done by limiting the kinds of weapons and weapons plants that must be regularly observed, as in the case of the freeze on strategic planes and missiles. In addition, where we have sufficient information about existing strengths on both sides, it can be done by inspecting only the actual destruction of armaments at one depot without checking further on those retained after destruction. This is the situation with the B-47/TU-16 proposal. And there are other methods under study which may open the door to Soviet acceptance of the principle of inspection.

During President Johnson's first months in office, two more steps have been taken which seem to improve the atmosphere for meaningful agreement. At the beginning of 1964, both the United States and the USSR announced reductions in their military budgets, both of which total, by coincidence, about 4 percent. More recently, both Johnson and the Soviets have announced planned cutbacks in production of fissionable material for use in nuclear weapons.

The general philosophy behind these actions is unquestionably sound. President Johnson succinctly expounded the philosophy in his State of the Union message of January 8, 1964, when he said: "Even in the absence of agreement we must not stockpile arms beyond our needs or seek an excess of military power that could be provocative as well as wasteful."

Actions of this sort slow down the senseless, spiraling momentum of the arms race. They were achieved in large part by the exchange of correspondence between heads of state and by talks between representatives of the two countries in Washington and Moscow. This is a method of diplomacy which President Kennedy used successfully during the Cuban missile crisis. President Johnson also put it to good use.

Except for these limited steps, no progress has been made toward agreement so far this year. This does not disturb me. In the first place, the discussions have been much more friendly than usual. Soviet propaganda blasts have been cut down considerably. Obviously, proposals such as ours of a freeze on atomic weapons and delivery systems take considerable time to be talked about and studied. Russia may also have special problems in timing any "conciliatory" moves because of her struggle with China for the allegiance of the various Communist parties of the world.

Outside of the disarmament negotiations, there are other avenues in which progress can be demonstrated toward a "thaw." For example, the matter of paying up United Nations assessments cannot be ignored beyond this year, and will be indicative of Soviet intentions. She has pursued trade negotiations with Western Europe and might be amenable to expand trade with us, too.

I believe the year 1963 was a turning point, although this does not mean that progress will come suddenly or quickly. I emphasize this word of caution in turning toward a longer look ahead.

It has not been too difficult to say where we are on peace and disarmament. However, we want to know where we may expect or hope to be in ten to fifteen years. Prophecy is dubious in any field. It is more so than usual here.

The basic problem is that we are caught between the excessive hopes and excessive fears that plague the present situation. If one does not look forward to a peaceful world, disarmed and living under world law, he may be accused of pessimism or worse. By innuendo he may be charged with not really believing in these things or not working hard enough for them. On the other hand, anyone looking forward to the attainment of lasting peace is expected—fairly enough—to explain the means of achieving it. He must indicate how he proposes to surmount certain of the log-jams currently obstructing progress.

Another stumbling block which has impeded us in the past is that far too many deadlines have been set for far too many goals. Ever since Alamogordo in 1945, we have been given successive deadlines, usually of five years, in which we must have world government, international control of atomic energy, destruction of the bomb, etc., or suffer disaster. This apocalyptic mood has ceased to embarrass by proffering precise dates, but the mood is still there. A sophisticated version of this attitude is C. P. Snow's statement that if an accident can occur, there is a statistical certainty that it will. Incidentally, statisticians tell me this is not so, that there is no way to predict, one way or the other, the "unique" event. In any case I do not care to try to think and hope in this context.

Basically I have one assumption: that we are embarked on a gradualist approach to a peaceful and disarmed world, under law. There are many components in the approach. Arms control is urgent. We must first halt and stabilize the arms race as a prelude to the next step of arms reduction. The agreements and inspection procedures necessary for these will have to be lived with for a while before we can anticipate the ultimate goal of general disarmament. We shall have to have a community of trust develop with inspection before we can write the laws of enforcement that general disarmament will demand.

Strategically, the line of development runs from maximum deterrence, through limited deterrence, to control of the peace by international police forces. Politically, the line of progress leads from international organizations that are political but not governmental, to organizations that slowly acquire some governmental powers. Probably these will be regional at first, but they will ultimately affect and at some point accelerate the evolution of the United Nations as the key to international peace-keeping.

Activity in all these areas must go on simultaneously, as indeed it does, although it is impossible to coordinate it as much as one might like. A most important point to keep in mind is that no progress whatsoever is possible without the consensus of the major powers of the world. This is materializing very slowly indeed. But once a certain amount of agreement is reached, one may expect faster progress. For example, a solid arms-reduction agreement might well, after a few years, make for a rapid acceleration on the road to general disarmament. Up to that point however, we are going to learn well the meaning of President Kennedy's phrase "a long twilight journey."

Apart from the apocalyptic mood I have mentioned, which I believe confuses thought and urgency with a mere ventilation of anxiety, I am most concerned with the effort on various sides to drive a wedge between arms control and disarmament. The two are not the same, but to condemn steps towards the former (when they are the only ones we can take) for not being disarmament is an attitude that may lose both. General and complete disarmament is the ultimate, idealistic goal. Frankly, I do not believe it will come in the foreseeable future. Whatever may be its form, operating under whatever sovereignty, for many years there will remain the need for military forces which can defend the right of self-determination of nations, which can come to the rescue of democratic governments threatened by over-the-border aggression or externally guided insurgency, or which can step between two unreasoning antagonists in the interests of peace.

I do believe that the goal of disarmament will be more realistic in ten to fifteen years if solid arms-control agreements can be reached now. Each agreement and the procedures which accompany it will set new conditions for the next step. Within the context of our ultimate goal, politics must be pragmatic. By such means I believe real progress can be made. There are, of course, no guarantees of progress.

The limited test-ban treaty was a single step. The hot line

and the ban on bombs in orbit were also limited steps, and there are a few other signs of thaw between the two superpowers. A number of other little steps can be taken along the lines of the explorations in the 1964 eighteen-nation conference in Geneva. Implementing some more of these in the next several years would be as much as I would expect, and would be a step from which I would take considerable hope. They would be signs of authenticating the "thaw" and would propel us to the point of considering the first significant arms-reduction confrontation. The bipolar world is indeed becoming multipolar, but, for another few years the United States and Russia will remain the superpowers, and these basic initial agreements can be made, for practical purposes, largely between them.

To move beyond this, time is needed for two things: Russia has to accommodate herself to at least a little dip into the waters of inspection, and the NATO powers have to develop coordinated policies concerned with something besides a crisis of defense.

I am hopeful on both counts. The inspection problem is being helped by progress in technology and by the limited proposals previously noted which do not require extensive inspection for verification. Agreements for more cultural exchange have not gone dead. East-West trade, at least between Europe and the East, is opening more and more widely. The Russian people have not been denied knowledge of from whence cometh their wheat. The Soviet leadership will hopefully be getting closer and closer to a situation that will make it politically feasible for them internally to consent to limited inspection procedures that will verify at least some controls on atomic weaponry.

Solving the problems of disarray in NATO appears more formidable at the moment, but that may well be only because we are now forced to look at what we were aware of, but wished would go away. The act of looking is a step forward.

The problems of NATO are political, economic, and military. The United States is apparently at odds with Europe on aspects of all three. France declined to join the nuclear test ban treaty and is bent on achieving an independent nuclear force. President de Gaulle is probably correct in thinking that there is little danger of Russia starting a war in Europe. But if he is right, it is for a reason he does not admit, namely, that Russia finds the United States retaliatory deterrent credible in regard to European defense even if President de Gaulle does not.

There is a problem nevertheless, of political coordination, partnership, and equal participation in basic military decision-making, that has to be met. Our current proposal for a multilateral nuclear force is designed to eliminate at least one addition to the nuclear powers (Germany) and is an experiment in cooperative Allied decision-making in the use of nuclear weapons. The MLF will not, of course, be the final solution to the problem of American and European cooperation; there is indeed sharp disagreement in both the United States and Europe over the MLF proposal. This should not discourage us. Europe and the United States are still united on the Berlin and German problems, which constitute a considerable prop for NATO. There is time for some fresh ideas to be aired while the MLF undergoes intensive study and negotiation.

This whole process will be affected by the evolution taking place in the economic union of Europe. This too is uncertain at the moment. The United States probably cannot influence the Common Market as much as it thought it could a few years ago. But the odds are that the institutions of economic union in Europe will grow, and augment the forces of political coordination in ways that will open new avenues for solving the problem of military coordination.

The one thing on which Europe is agreed is the race to open up East-West trade. For the last several years our allies have been parting company with us on this subject, and now it is a completely open break. So far we have just been sputtering about it. The French do not bother to give any reasons, and this exercise in "grandeur" piques our pride. The British are disingenuous: "A fat Communist is less dangerous than a lean one," they contend, without offering a wholly convincing argument why.

The real reasons are that these countries have to trade. They are on their own feet now, economically (thanks to the Marshall Plan) and want to compete in any market they can get, and in terms of the ethics of good, sharp business practice.

In due course, we shall be mature enough to realize that this imitation of ourselves in business is the sincerest form of flattery of our free enterprise system. We may develop a little zest for the competition, and with leverages gained in it, bargain with our allies to establish mutually acceptable standards regarding strategic goods, patent protections, credit policies, dollar protection, and defense coordination.

This will probably make some "fat Communists." But it will not materially affect their military power. They achieved high atomic capability while they were lean. Meanwhile, as the West gets fatter too, it will have more means with which to carry the competitive struggle to the underdeveloped parts of the world.

In three to five years, I would hope for a resumption of greatly increased Western coordination on a new and higher plane than the post-World War II necessities of self-defense. We have far fewer internal stresses in the West than does the Communist world since the Sino-Soviet rift.

The tide has already started to turn in the newly developed independent countries, from a virulent reaction against all Western powers who are only to be denounced or baited as "colonialists," to a knowledge that capital and help must come from us, and to a recognition that the Western powers would really like them to stand on their own feet.

The West can help the underdeveloped nations as nobody else can. These nations must trade to have any hope of acquiring the capital for independent development and control of their destiny. They have vast markets which the West ultimately needs. Both of us need peace for it. Much uphill work and cooperation is needed to get them to the economic "take-off" point. However, I am confident that in ten to fifteen years some of them can be brought to the threshold of economic take-off.

Meanwhile, these new nations already constitute the third force in the United Nations. In the last three sessions they have shown a high degree of cohesion and independence from both East and West, with a voting record which on most major points should gratify us. They offer some hope for strengthening the United Nations and making it take its next steps in political evolution. This can be in the direction of developing nuclear-free zones in their parts of the world, supporting adequate financing, and developing an initial police force adequate for effective interposition between the great powers and themselves. The strengthening of the peace-keeping capabilities of the UN can help to create a political environment conducive to progress in disarmament.

In ten to fifteen years I hope to see a more coordinated West, which has won a significant arms-reduction agreement with Russia and thus reduced the danger of an atomic holocaust. From maximum deterrence we will hopefully have moved on to limited deterrence, and be willing to go further. But we will go no further unless and until the Chinese mainland government is included. Perhaps some progress will have been made toward the beginning of a limited world authority to implement genuine disarmament, but the door is locked until China is part of a world consensus, and until the Soviet Union accepts the existence of the Western world in its non-Communist form.

We have the power to influence the direction which arms-control efforts will take in the immediate future by our choice of military strategies. From public discussion, it appears that the Pentagon has recently been debating the choice between the so-called Gilpatric view, which permits a gradual but substantial reduction of defense expenditures over the next five years, and a "damage-limiting" strategy, which would involve expenditures of large sums for an anti-ballistic missile system and a large-scale civil-defense program. Although I will not attempt to assess the merits of these two alternatives, I would like to emphasize that the decision made will have important consequences for future developments in the field of arms control. If we believe that limited arms control is in our national interest, we should not dismiss the first alternative lightly. Certainly we must make either a choice between, or some synthesis of, the two views, rather than permit the situation to drift.

By present projections, China may in ten to fifteen years arrive at the threshold of power Russia achieved eighteen years ago, and this power may be accompanied by a Stalinist type of virulence. That is advancing the worst conjecture. In that case, a developed "third world" of newly emerging nations would be the best neutralizing force.

On the other hand, if so much could be developed elsewhere in ten to fifteen years, it might be possible to put effective political brakes on military power.

I repeat that I am hoping, not predicting. If we hope either too much or too little, we lose the ball game. And if our hopes are not geared to practical politics, they will go awry.

In conclusion, one might say that we live dangerously, but not without hope. Twenty-five years elapsed between 1914 and 1939. Another twenty-five years elapsed between 1939 and 1964. Each year we are able to extend the peace, whether under the conditions of a cold war or not, we have that much more time to approach a peace created by the rule of law among the nations. I pin my hopes on cutting the problem down to one step at a time, on proceeding along a reasonable path, toward broadly feasible objectives, allowing for the new conditions that may emerge from time to time to permit new appraisals. The important thing is the nerve, the patience, and the will. In the rhetoric President Kennedy drew from the Bible, we must be "patient in hope, rejoicing in tribulations."

America and
the Communist Challenge

PAUL SEABURY

W<small>ARS</small> which are not wars in the classical sense bedevil our minds and our times. Men with hearts and consciences pray that this limited yet limitless conflict known as the cold war will not lead to all-out war. But the rational mind remembers past wars which had known beginnings and known ends. The rational mind also remembers that the principal wars of the recent past accomplished very important things—for better or worse. No matter how horrible they were, they involved clear contests, and they achieved definitive solutions: the defeat of Nazi Germany, for instance. They also had their known ends— in a railroad car, a chandeliered hall, or on a battleship deck. The prospect of their impending conclusion made it possible for men to plan for futures in which these specific conflicts no longer existed. Such futures often were called—and sometimes too optimistically—the "post-war world."

Because it has been difficult for Americans to agree among themselves about the nature of the present cold war, it also has been difficult to agree when it began; hazardous to conclude that it has, or has not, abated; and certainly impossible to say that, thus far, our actions in it have definitively "solved" anything. For these reasons, it is extremely difficult to talk about the desirable features of a "post-cold war world." Since we must assume that thermonuclear weapons will indefinitely remain in the hands of the great powers, including Russia, "no-win" policies do have something to recommend them. "No-settle" policies may also be necessary; if war can no longer be the ultimate arbiter, many conflicts will not be definitively settled in our own time. Conflict may be moderated, contained, or tinkered with by diplomacy and by provisional understandings, but not "solved." In time, perhaps, some of these conflicts may gradually disappear, like Lewis Carroll's Cheshire cat; though one might be hard-pressed to identify the moment at which the smile (or the grimace) actually could no longer be seen or no longer mattered very much.

Whether we contine to describe the relationship between America and Russia, between the West and the Communist bloc, as a cold war, it is clear that since the 1962 Cuban crisis the original structure of that cold war has been very much changed. The "grand structure" of American policy has certainly not been abandoned, but developments such as the increasingly strained relations with de Gaulle's France have modified it very substantially; and, as in the case of Southeast Asia, its fundamental assumptions have been seriously questioned. Since 1962, the crisis points of policy (such as Vietnam, Cyprus, and South Asia) may still be described in cold-war language; they may still be dressed in cold-war pyjamas and sent upstairs to the same Procrustean bed. But they have recently had a way of throwing off the sheets and climbing out.

How different is this present climate of thought about American foreign policy from that of a decade ago. In the 1950's, a foreign diplomat once described John Foster Dulles' policy as having the architectonic clarity of a Gothic cathedral. One might not have liked it very much, especially its Calvinist gargoyles, but at least one knew what it was and had some understanding of why it was. This also remained true of policy in the early Kennedy Administration. For in 1961, also, there were clear outlines of an emerging design, attuned to the crisis as it then existed. But Cuba in 1962 seems to have been a very important watershed. Its swift terrors, its brief shock were as psychologically immense as those of a full-fledged war. To stand "eyeball to eyeball," as Mr. Rusk then put it, was to become suddenly aware both of an obliterable humanity commonly shared with an opponent and of a boundless common predicament. Perhaps this was the Third World War, acted in terrifying charade, and the test-ban treaty its provisional armistice.

I

To discuss the future problems and opportunities of American relations with the Soviet Union and the Communist bloc, we must engage in two kinds of thinking: first, we must re-examine the principal characteristics of Soviet and Communist conduct which from the late 1940's were repugnant to us and which constituted a threat to ourselves and to the broader Western community of which America is a part. We must, secondly, attempt to distinguish among our various "policy aspirations" concerning these characteristics. For while it is unhappily true that American policy can only marginally affect most of these, it is the better part of wisdom to acknowledge that, even if our influence were greater, we would still be at a loss to face with candor the question of what kind of Russia and what kind of Communist bloc (or post-Communist bloc) world it is that we would wish, and that might be a "sign" to us that our Cold War with them had indeed no further purpose to serve.

We must distinguish among four aspects of Soviet-Communist society and behavior which have provoked America and the West to fear them and to undertake countermeasures of containment. Since the late 1940's, there have been the troublesome problems of the growth of Soviet power, both absolute and relative; the related matter of Soviet territorial expansion and imperialism; the ideological challenge of Marxist-Leninist (and, more lately Khrushchevian and Maoist) doctrine to American liberal values; and, finally, the behavior and aims of the Communist movement seen in its broadest dimensions. One aspect of our predicament in dealing with the Soviet Union during this Cold War arises from the fact that large numbers of fearful Americans have remained unable or unwilling to make these distinctions, and thus have discerned only an amorphous, yet presumably monolithic threat to our society and its values. The second aspect of this predicament lies in the fact that, for those who were able to distinguish among these features, it was difficult to find agreement about which of them constituted the principal and controlling *causa belli frigidi*, that America and the Western community might wish to see altered, modified or eliminated in the Communist world.

Let us start with the problem of Soviet Russian power, whose relative and absolute enlargement was so poorly anticipated by American policy-makers during World War II. For there certainly can be no doubt that this sudden event, a product of that war, was made all the more disconcerting in the face of a politically prostrate Europe, as well as the disintegration of the great European overseas empires and the collapse of the traditional societies of the non-Western world.

When discussing Soviet Russia's power in the years immediately after Hitler's defeat, we must bear in mind that the power of this empire would probably have been as immense a problem for us even if Russia had never known Karl Marx or his Russian disciples. Just as German unification in 1870 severely strained the European state system, so now on a global stage this constellation of Russian power was bound—irrespective of its special ideological features—to arouse very deep misgivings and fears. This is especially true of those nations in its proximity which had previously experienced Russian domination or the possibility of it. In this respect, an authoritarian Tsarist Russia, even one with Kerensky-like features, would have posed problems somewhat similar to those of Stalin's Russia. Had either of these been responsible for establishing the scope of Russian empire, for governing its enormous land mass and diverse peoples, their actions in important ways would surely have resembled those of a Stalin. So also, a post-Stalin or even post-Communist Russia (were this ever to come to pass) would pose similar problems for Russia's neighbors and for the whole system of international politics.

Related to this matter of Russian power were the imperialistic aspects of Russian expansion in the post-Hitler years. Again we must remember that these cannot exclusively be attributed to Soviet ideology or to Soviet totalitarianism. If we were fancifully to assume that, in World War II, for instance, a "generals' plot" had overthrown Stalin and the Communist Party and then led Russia to victory in Europe, many of the difficulties which gave rise to the cold war in Eastern and Central Europe and the Far East would still have obtained: the problem of Poland and Germany, for instance, and the other areas of Eastern Europe which the Red Army "liberated." We speak in ironic tones of Communist imperialism when describing these expansionist tendencies of Soviet Russia. But Europeans with long memories (and, today, Chinese Communists) remember that such tendencies existed long before Karl Marx went to school. They could be aspects of any Russian political system. The most intractable of them would include, in any future time, the question of whether, in Central Europe or in Asia, we wish a roll-back by Russia, whether under Communist rule or not; also, the question of what kind of a roll-back would be consonant with legitimate Russian security interests, with justice to the peoples now experiencing Soviet imperial rule, and with an enduring international tranquility. Certainly, while most Americans profess still to believe in Woodrow Wilson's formula of national self-determination, none of us should insist that such a formula be recklessly waved as a flag, or imposed in doctrinaire manner on the map of Europe or even of Asia without thought for its consequences.

Viewed from a Central European vantage point, the prudence of being aware of this aspect of Soviet expansionism becomes especially clear. Certainly, further Soviet expansion here would be intolerable to us. But whatever the chances of Soviet retrenchment, the West as a whole—and American policy in particular—has today no formula, satisfactory either to all of its Allies or to the peoples of Eastern Europe, to substitute for the present condition of Russian domination. Certainly, we have no formula which could possibly assuage non-German fears about the enlargement of German power and national aspirations which any German reunification would entail. Nor for that matter does the West have any means of assuring East Europeans—including Russians—that future German independent thermonuclear capabilities would make their lives any more placid and secure. In point of fact, one difficulty in coping with the Communist bloc in Europe arises from the fact that Western leaders have not publicly been willing to acknowledge that the shrill protests from Russia and its satellite regimes about German military revival reflect, at least in part, deep and quite legitimate concerns of thoughtful non-Communist Europeans, including some Germans as well.

II

I deal with these matters of Russian power and Soviet imperialism first in order to stress the fact that in important ways they must be distinguished from the ideological issue which has been so prominent in the conflict between America and Russia. Of course, it was from the beginning this ideological element which deeply aggravated Soviet-American tensions and which continues to do so. Certainly, no one could say that the United States started this quarrel; or that it can do much by itself to abate it. The trouble is that it has struck such sensitive neuralgic points in American culture that it has caused many of us to ignore these other equally troublesome features of Russia's position in the society of nations.

It seems strange that it has been in America (where the internal threat of Communism has been least present) that these ideological aspects of the Soviet threat aroused the deepest popular indignation—so much so that all else seemed at times to pale into insignificance. One explanation of this, strangely, is a wholly negative one: at no time before or after 1917 did traditional Russian expansionism directly collide with vital American interests. The cultural incompatibilities between non-Slavic and Russian cultures never directly troubled Americans much; most of us still today understand them very imperfectly.

One should recall that, long before the Russian Revolution, the principal irritants in Russo-American relations were already ideological. What most aggravated Americans about Tsarist Russia was that is seemed to represent the worst that the Old World had to offer. Its very existence seemed to confirm America's claim to newness, progressivism, and social modernity. Whether, after the Bolsheviks seized power, one took seriously their incantations about the dismal failures of American capitalism, the most aggravating feature of the litany was not its tone of hostility. Nor were the absurd falseness and irrelevance of the charges and prophecies the explanation for the American reaction. What perhaps caused our emotional response to them to be so strong was that they presented a serious philosophical challenge to American liberalism.

Their claim to have "leapfrogged" America in the race of historical progress and the quest for utopia was what hurt most. What was also annoying to Americans was that so many other peoples—the European proletariat especially—now turned their attention away from Jefferson's and Horace Greeley's America to watch a newer social experiment. Had it really succeeded, it would have robbed American culture of its most precious pretension—its claim to a monopoly of social perfection.

This ideological aspect of the cold war accounts in large measure for a serious ambivalence in American thought about what kind of a future Soviet society and Communist bloc we would be willing to co-exist with. If it were merely a matter of Russian power and Russian expansion—or "Communist imperialism"—which troubled us, the remedies would be a bit simpler to find. But it is also the symbolic character of the system which has boggled us.

Our ideological concern with the symbolic character of Soviet Russia presents us with this dilemma: would we really want to see significant improvements in the quality of Soviet life—more civic freedom, higher living standards, greater permissiveness in relations between Russia and other bloc countries—if these were obtained *within* a Communist world? It could be argued, for instance, that (if the Soviet system were actually to begin to fulfill its proclaimed norms) it would be more attractive ideologically and a more plausible threat to the claims and promises of the "American way of life." Changes such as these have been occurring in some parts of the Communist bloc—and in Yugoslavia also. Yet, because of this very ambivalence in American attitudes, we have done precious little cheering as they took place. Our capacities to derive benefit from such changes have been very small indeed, even though the emergence of a polycentric Communist bloc composed of consumer-oriented economies might greatly reduce the threat of Russian power to us. Some observers, furthermore, have argued that Soviet successes in fulfilling its "Socialist norms" might result in conservatizing its leadership. Fat Communists may be preferable to lean and hungry ones, if one has to make the choice.

Americans have not been able to make up their minds which of two alternative expectations they should welcome—Soviet internal successes (with attendant conservatization of Soviet purposes) or Soviet internal failures (with prospects of Communist collapse). This fact may, of course, have only a marginal effect on the outcome of the Soviet experiment. But surely one cannot forever be torn between regarding Soviet society as provisional, or even doomed to some cataclysmic fate, and regarding it as being capable of gradual accommodation to the habits and practices of a civilized world. It is clear that, if a Western window is to open in the Iron Curtain, this will happen because of a conscious decision by the Soviet elites. But it certainly will not take place as a consequence of prison riots in the Communist world. The warmth of a Western sun, rather than the puffing of Congressional resolutions about "captive nations," could cause the coat of totalitarianism to be shed.

III

The present disarray within both the Western alliance and the Communist bloc, whatever its various causes, heightens our awareness of the distinction among these various aspects of the Soviet problem. Is an increasingly powerful Russia to be feared and opposed simply because it happens to be powerful, and regardless of improvements in the quality of its internal life or its external behavior? If, as some Westerners have held, the cold war arose primarily because of a power disequilibrium between the Communist world and the West, would a perceptible redressing of this imbalance be the occasion to say that our principal aims have been attained? One remembers the laconic expression of Dean Acheson a decade or more ago: what was necessary, before significant negotiations to end the cold war, was a "comfortable surplus of power" in the Western world.

Even if one assumes that the West has today in fact recouped its power vis-à-vis Russia, one must see that this recovery severely inhibits any important solely bilateral détente between America and Russia. The recovery of Western power since the 1950's has meant also its diffusion within the West; one now faces the ironic fact that Russia and America today have far less leverage to accomplish together major settlements in Europe or elsewhere, were they jointly to decide to do so. Even "good Yaltas" will no longer be possible.

Ironically, also, one inhibiting feature of this new situation is that significant direct Soviet-American contacts risk tarnishing America's reputation as leader of a Western coalition and weakening the credibility of American promises to its European allies. The dilemma is that bilateral attempts to reduce tensions between America and Russia aggravate tensions within the Western alliance. While one might take comfort from the fact that this dilemma exists for them as well, the point is that the broad diplomatic opportunities which once existed in a tight bipolar world of Moscow and Washington no longer exist. One may welcome the relaxation of tensions and the waning of ideological warfare, but the possibilities of directly treating the *objective* zones of cold-war danger—Germany and East Europe especially—seem no nearer in this new situation than they were when the West was weaker and more vulnerable politically.

IV

One might welcome polycentrism in world politics on both sides of the Iron Curtain. One should remember that, in the 1940's and 1950's, it was a principal American objective to restore power and influence among nations in the non-Communist world, and thereby to reduce their dependence on us. The classic concept of the free world held by American statesmen has been one of plurality and diversity. As blocs lose their cohesiveness, opportunities for new contacts arise. As ideological politics ceases to have the cementlike function of binding the world in two camps, America may have to face the fact that it is no longer the sole custodian of Western civilization. This may be bad for the *amour propre* of American statesmen and utopian idealists, but it follows from our own stated aspirations.

But to return to the central theme—our expectations about the Soviet future. It would be fascinating if, as some have wished, the styles and character of Soviet and American life would converge. Thereby, it has been argued by some, the antagonisms arising from real sociocultural differences between us might subside. Yet much naive and wishful thinking has gone into this "convergence-reconciliation" thesis. The Appomattox

Courthouse of such a reconciliation would be a miracle kitchen like the one Nixon showed Khrushchev; some followers of Erich Fromm would place it in a psychiatric clinic. Yet it remains to be proved that such a convergence is either necessary or sufficient to effect a reduction in cold-war tensions. Likeness does not necessarily make for friendship among nations any more than it does among individuals.

It might be the better part of wisdom to search out the conditions for reconciliation with the Soviet world in more mundane quarters. It may have occurred to important decision-makers on both sides during the Cuban crisis that, if they had blown each other to smithereens, many people in other parts of the world might have jumped in fright, yawned or sighed—but not wept. The principal zones of conflict between us and the Communist world now lie in areas of revolutionary upheaval far removed from the centers of our most vital interests and theirs —that is, in the underdeveloped world. Wisdom might consist in seeing that these upheavals do not explode and involve both of us; in assuming a common responsibility for a more orderly assimilation of these revolutionary societies into a stable yet just world. Neither America nor Russia is predestined to rule the globe; but together they could obliterate it. Together now, irrespective of ideological differences, they might seek to preserve both it and themselves.

The Crisis
of the Western Alliance*

HANS J. MORGENTHAU

THE Western Alliance has ceased to be an instrument for policies to be pursued in common by its members. A *tour d'horizon* of the world scene presents a shocking picture of disintegration. On not a single one of the outstanding issues of world politics do all members of the Alliance see eye to eye. The United States stands alone in its policies vis-à-vis China, South Vietnam, and Cuba. The United States also stands alone in its "strategic trade" policies with the Communist nations. Great Britain, on the one hand, and West Germany and France, on the other, have taken contradictory positions with regard to Berlin. The German question as a whole and the over-all relations between the West and the Soviet Union reveal irreconcilable divergencies of interest and policies which have made abstention from initiative and a passive commitment to the *status quo* the order of the day. Greece and Turkey have been on the brink of war over Cyprus. In Africa, the Allies go their separate ways; Portugal, in particular, proceeds in virtual isolation. The policies of the United States and France toward

* This is the revised version of a paper first presented to The Center for Strategic Studies of Georgetown University.

the United Nations are diametrically opposed. France is similarly divided from the United States and Great Britain in the field of disarmament. The United States is at loggerheads with its major European allies on two basic aspects of military strategy and the policies implementing it: the role of conventional forces and the disposition of nuclear weapons.

The members of the Western Alliance have only one obvious interest in common: protection from Communist aggression and subversion. But such an interest is not a policy; it is an objective requiring common policies for its realization. It is both illuminating and disturbing to note that the Allies come closest to pursuing common policies, of however dubious value in themselves, in the conventional military field (which is least likely to require common action in the foreseeable future) and that they are almost completely lacking in common policies in the political and economic spheres, which the Soviet Union itself has declared to be the arena where the fate of the world will be decided.

What accounts for this decline in the fortunes of an alliance which a decade ago still appeared as the indispensable foundation for the security of the West? The decisive factor in this decline has been the transformation of the American nuclear monopoly, one of the foundation stones of the Western Alliance, into a bipolar nuclear threat. The new "balance of terror" has rendered the Western Alliance, as presently constituted, obsolete.

In the pre-nuclear age, nations who had certain interests in common would try to defend and promote these interests by coordinating or pooling their diplomatic and military resources. Thus a nation would go to war on behalf of the interests of another nation, or vice versa, when it thought that the defense and promotion of the other nation's interests was in its own as well. By thus reasoning, a nation would take a double risk: it could be mistaken about the identity of the interests involved and be drawn into a war without its own interests being sufficiently engaged, or it could miscalculate the distribution of power on either side and allow itself to get involved in a war which it would lose. What a nation had to guard against in its relations with its allies was a diplomatic blunder or a military miscalculation. If it failed to do so, it would as a rule risk at worst defeat in war, with the consequent loss of an army or of territory.

The availability of nuclear weapons has radically transformed these traditional relations among allies and the risks resulting from them. A nuclear nation which enters into an alliance with another nation, nuclear or non-nuclear, runs a double risk different in kind from the risks a member of a traditional alliance must face. In honoring the alliance, this nation (which we will call A) might have to fight a nuclear war against nuclear power C, thereby forfeiting its own existence. Or A's ally B may provoke a war with nuclear power C on behalf of interests other than those contemplated by the alliance and thereby force A's hand, involving it in a nuclear war on behalf of interests other than its own. That latter risk is magnified if B is also a nuclear power, of however small dimensions. If B were to threaten or attack C with nuclear weapons, C might—rightly or wrongly—consider B's military power as a mere extension of A's and anticipate and partly prevent the commitment of A through a first strike against A. Or A, anticipating C's reaction against itself or seeking to save B through nuclear deterrence, will commit its own nuclear arsenal against C. In either case, B, however weak as a nuclear power, has the ability to act as a trigger for a general nuclear war.

B, on the other hand, too, faces a double risk. It may forfeit its existence in a nuclear war fought by A on behalf of A's own interests. Or it may find itself abandoned by A, who refuses to run the risk of its own destruction on behalf of the interests of B.

It is this radical difference in the risks taken by allies in the pre-nuclear and nuclear age which has led to a radical difference in the reliability of alliances. In the pre-nuclear age, ally A could be expected with a very high degree of certainty to come to the aid of ally B at the risk of defeat in war. In the nuclear age, ally A cannot be expected with the same degree of certainty to come to the aid of ally B at the risk of its own destruction. Here we contemplate the reverse side of the mechanics of deterrence. The very same doubt that deters C disheartens B. C cannot be certain that A will not actually forfeit its existence by resorting to nuclear war and, hence, is deterred. B, on the other hand, cannot be certain that A is willing to forfeit its existence by resorting to nuclear war and, hence, is disaffected.

It is ironic that the event which foreshadowed the decline of the Western Alliance virtually coincided with the establishment of that Alliance: the first explosion of a nuclear device by the Soviet Union in September, 1949. While the destructive effects this event was bound to have upon the Western Alliance could be, and actually were, predicted, the policies of the Western Allies for almost a decade took no account of these effects. Three new facts were required to open the eyes of Western statesmen to the ever more acute contrast between the official declarations of unity of purpose and the institutions intended to serve common military action, on the one hand, and the crumbling political and military foundations, on the other. These facts were the new foreign policy of the Soviet Union, the Suez crisis of 1956, and de Gaulle's initiative of January 14, 1963.

The foreign policy of the Soviet Union has fundamentally changed since Stalin's death in 1953. The greatest asset upon which the foreign policies of the nations of Western Europe could bank was the foreign policy of Stalin. Whenever there was a slackening in the Western effort, whenever there appeared cracks in the fabric of the Alliance, Stalin could be counted upon to make a drastic aggressive move demonstrating to the Western powers how necessary for their survival their Alliance was.

The foreign policy of Khrushchev was of a different nature. His was not a policy of direct military aggression or serious military threats. Khrushchev explicitly and emphatically ruled out nuclear war as an instrument of Soviet policy. His policies were aimed not so much, as were Stalin's, at the conquest of territories contiguous to the Soviet empire by diplomatic pressure or military threats as at the subversion of the whole non-Communist world through the impact which Soviet power, derived primarily from its technological and economic accomplishments, makes upon that world.

That policy of "peaceful" or "competitive coexistence" was widely misunderstood as indicating a radical change not only in the tactics but in the goals of Soviet foreign policy as well. We have tended to read into "coexistence" a measure of permanency, which, as Khrushchev reminded us emphatically many times, it cannot have in the philosophy of Communism; it is intended to be an intermediate tactical stage in the inevitable decay of capitalism. Thus we took genuine "coexistence" to be an already accomplished fact rather than a state of affairs to be striven for and to be achieved only if the West has become so strong that the Soviet Union has no choice but to "coexist" with it. In consequence of this misunderstanding, the association with the United States appears to some of our European allies less vital than it once was. Thus the absence of unmistakable pressure, primarily of a military nature, at the confines where the Western Alliance and the Soviet empire meet has contributed to loosening the ties of the Western Alliance.

The intervention of the United States, in conjunction with the Soviet Union, against Great Britain and France during the Suez crisis of 1956 provided what might be called "the moment of truth" of the political vitality of the Western Alliance. It made empirically obvious what before could only be deduced from general principles, that the United States was not willing to risk its own existence on behalf of interests which were peculiar to its allies. The Western Alliance proved to be much less comprehensive, cohesive, and reliable than official ideology and the array of common institutions had indicated.

From the state of affairs thus revealed, de Gaulle drew two alternative conclusions. The Western Alliance, in order to re-

gain its vitality, required a world-wide coordination of the policies of its major members, and to that end he proposed in 1958
a political triumvirate of the United States, France, and Great
Britain. Since that proposal remained stillborn—the United
States did not even dignify it with an adequate answer—de
Gaulle turned to the other alternative: the national nuclear
deterrent. At his press conference of January 14, 1963, and in
subsequent statements, de Gaulle declared traditional alliances
to be, for all practical purposes, obsolete and proposed to replace
them with national nuclear deterrents. In his view nuclear
weapons should be treated like conventional ones in that at
least their deterrent function will be controlled by national governments on behalf of traditional national interests. France
would use its nuclear weapons, as it has used its army, navy, and
air force in the past, for the purpose of exerting pressure upon a
prospective enemy.

   How has the United States reacted to this crisis of the Western Alliance? As long as the crisis was not acute, the United
States proceeded as though the foundations upon which the
Western Alliance had been erected in 1949 were a kind of
immutable datum of nature and as though the factors which
would make the crisis sooner or later inevitable did not exist.
The extraordinary complacency and sterility which characterized the Alliance policy of the United States in the 50's pre-
cluded changes in policy which would take into account the
objective changes that had already occurred, and anticipate
those which were sure to occur in the future. It also caused
American power to be abused, or not to be used at all, for the
purposes of the Alliance.

   Our intervention in the Suez crisis of 1956 is only the most
spectacular and disastrous example of the capricious and devi-
ous disregard of the interests of our Allies which marked that
period of American foreign policy. The other side of this same
medal of complacency and sterility was that the United States
during this period failed to exert within the Alliance that positive political leadership which was its due by dint of its pre-

158 THE CROSSROAD PAPERS

dominance and which its Allies expected of it. Now that the leadership of the Western Alliance has slipped from its hands, it is a cause for melancholy regret to remember how anxious our Allies were then for American leadership to assert itself and how often, during the crises of that period, publications such as the London *Economist* implored the United States to that effect—and did so in vain.

The crisis of the Western Alliance has now become acute, and five possibilities offer themselves to American policy: restoration of the *status quo*, drift, isolation, "Atlantic Union," or pragmatic cooperation with a united Europe. Of these possibilities, only the last two present feasible policies.

In order to do justice to these possibilities, it is necessary to remind oneself that the momentous event which has transformed the objective nature of international relations and undermined the foundations of the Western Alliance is the availability of nuclear weapons to more than one nation. This transformation, while recognized in the abstract, has not affected our traditional modes of thought and action. Hence the dilemma which the Western Alliance faces. On the one hand, the unity of the West is as necessary in the face of Communist subversion as it was in the face of military threats, temporarily shelved. On the other hand, for the reasons mentioned above, that unity of interest can no longer be translated into common policies through the instrumentality of a traditional alliance. Where, then, can a new foundation for Western unity be found?

On rational grounds, there is much to be said in favor of a return to the *status quo ante* January 14, 1963—that is, nuclear bipolarity. The use of nuclear weapons as instruments of national policy by more than two nations greatly increases the risk of nuclear war. Erected into a general principle of statecraft to be followed by any number of nations, it would result in the indiscriminate proliferation of nuclear weapons and thereby destroy the very mechanics of mutual deterrence. These mechanics are based on the bipolarity of nuclear power. Detection systems, such as radar and sonar, are capable of identifying nuclear delivery systems in action, but they cannot identify their national identity, except in a limited way through the calculation of the trajectory of land-based missiles. In consequence, retaliation requires the a priori determination of national identity, which bipolarity provides. Thus an anonymous explosion, caused by a seaborne delivery vehicle and destroying parts of the east coast of the United States, would automatically be attributed to the Soviet Union, calling forth nuclear retaliation. If a multiplicity of nations possessed such devices and the United States had tense relations with more than one of them, such an anonymous explosion could not with certainty be attributed to any one nation, however much suspicion might point to a particular one. And a new nuclear diplomacy would try its best to deflect suspicion and retaliation from the guilty to an innocent nation. In the face of such a contingency, a rational nuclear policy would become impossible.

Yet, however great the risks of nuclear proliferation are and however much nuclear bipolarity is to be preferred to nuclear proliferation, the latter could have been prevented only through nuclear disarmament or at least the enforceable prohibition of nuclear tests. In the absence of either, it is futile to oppose proliferation. What is necessary—and also difficult—is to create political conditions likely to minimize the risks of proliferation and in the end even to deprive proliferation within the Western Alliance of its rational justification.

Yet we have insisted upon trying to restore the *status quo*. As the instrument for that restoration, we have chosen the multilateral sea-borne nuclear force, called MLF, a fleet of surface vessels armed with nuclear missiles and manned by mixed crews recruited from different Allied nations. This force is intended to serve three main purposes: the retention of the ultimate control over the use of nuclear weapons in American hands, the prevention of the proliferation of nuclear weapons by giving the Allies a share in planning and operations, and the satisfaction of the alleged nuclear appetite of Germany without giving her actual control over nuclear weapons. This is not the place to enter into a discussion of the technical, military, and specific political shortcomings of this device and the improbability of its success. It is only necessary here to point to two of its qualities, which shed an illuminating light upon all-pervasive deficiencies of our foreign policy: *the commitment to a status quo which has been bypassed by history, and the attempt to meet a political problem with a military device.*

It is easier, both intellectually and in the short run politically, not to face up to the impossibility of restoring the *status quo ante* January 14, 1963, to keep the legal façade of the Western Alliance intact, and to leave the crucial problems unattended. This policy of drift into which a stymied policy of restoration is likely to degenerate is, of all the possibilities before us, the most dangerous. For it combines in an incompatible amalgam the legal commitments of a traditional alliance with nuclear proliferation. It gives those of our allies who possess nuclear weapons the power to reduce to a minimum our freedom of choice with regard to nuclear war. Both France and Great Britain see the main purpose of the national nuclear deterrent in their ability to use that deterrent as a trigger with which to activate the nuclear deterrent of the United States. As the British White Paper on defense put it on February 13, 1964: "If there were no power in Europe capable of inflicting unacceptable damage on a potential enemy," the enemy might be tempted "to attack in the mistaken belief that the United States would not act unless America herself were attacked." [1] Or as the London *Economist* said in commenting on this White Paper: "The bombers also give Britain the ability to involve the United States in a nuclear war for which the Americans have no stomach, the argument being that the Russians would be led to loose off an attack on the United States if any foreign nuclear bombs went off on their territory, since they would not have time to see the Union Jack painted on its

[1] *The New York Times*, February 14, 1964, p. 1.

warhead." [2] In other words, proliferation combined with traditional alliance commitments turns the obsolescence of the Western Alliance, as presently constituted, against the survival of the United States. Allies of the United States armed with nuclear weapons could virtually decide whether the United States should live or die.

Faced with this unacceptable possibility, the United States can take two alternative courses of action. It can try to escape the risks its present policies vis-à-vis Western Europe entail by severing the ties of the Alliance and retreating into isolation. This alternative is likely to become more tempting as frustrations multiply and awareness of the risks sinks in. Intercontinental nuclear strategy, taken as the sole determinant, would indeed make this alternative feasible. The military security of the United States would not be appreciably affected by whatever course the nations of Western Europe, separated from the United States, would take.

Yet the world-wide conflict in which we are engaged is not primarily of a military nature. It concerns two different conceptions of man and society, and in that conflict the survival of our way of life is at stake. That way of life is an upshot of Western civilization, of which Western Europe is the fountainhead. It is an open question whether our civilization, still unsure of itself, could survive without being able to draw upon the example and the cultural resources of Western Europe. It is even more doubtful whether our civilization could survive in a world which, after the defection of Western Europe, would be either indifferent or hostile to us. It is for this ultimate reason that isolation, however tempting in the short run, is no longer an acceptable alternative for the United States.

The other alternative is presented by the grand design of Atlantic partnership which John F. Kennedy formulated on July 4, 1962 in his "Declaration of Interdependence." That design has remained in the realm of political rhetoric, but it

[2] *The Economist*, February 15, 1964, p. 587.

contains a political concept which alone promises to combine Western unity with nuclear power. In order to understand its import, it is first necessary to remind ourselves again of the political character of the crisis of the Western Alliance.

The Western Alliance is in disarray not because the United States has monopolistic control over the nuclear deterrent, but because the members of the Alliance pursue different and sometimes incompatible policies, on behalf of which they might want to use the nuclear deterrrent. If the policies of the members of the Alliance were in harmony, the issue of the locus of the nuclear decision would lose its present political sting and de Gaulle would have had no need to raise the issue of the national nuclear deterrent. For the nations of Western Europe, either severally or united, would then consider using nuclear weapons for the same purpose as the United States, and vice versa, and the issue of the locus of the decision would be of technical, but no longer of substantive, importance. This is, then, the crucial question: how can the different policies of the members of the Western Alliance be brought into harmony?

Members of alliances have had to face this question since times immemorial, and insofar as they have been successful, they have answered it by a supreme effort of statesmanship. For it is one of the great constructive tasks of the statesman to transform an inchoate and implicit community of interests into the actuality of operating policies. This is the task before us today. However, it must be doubted that we shall be able to perform it. Four facts support that doubt.

Statesmanship—that is, the ability to think and act in the specific terms appropriate to foreign policy—has been at all times and in all places an extremely rare commodity. For reasons which are imbedded in our historic experience and the political folklore stemming from it, it has always been in particularly short supply in Washington. It is unlikely, although not altogether impossible, that of the few among us who possess the intellectual qualities of statesmanship, one will rise to the eminence of political influence and power necessary to equip the foreign policy of the United States for that creative task. The chances for the achievement of that task are further diminished by the unprecedented complexity and diversity of the policies to be harmonized. This task cannot be achieved, as de Gaulle recognized in 1958, through the ordinary processes of diplomacy. It requires a virtual fusion of the foreign policies of the members of the Western Alliance under centralized direction. In the heyday of NATO, we could at least hope for a political "Atlantic Union" to form a permanent political foundation for the military alliance. In the heyday of a revived nationalism, the leading members of the Western Alliance, short of being faced with a direct military threat against them all, are not likely to bring forth simultaneously the political vision, determination, and skill necessary to achieve this rationally required goal.

Two further factors militate against this likelihood: the increase in the political and economic strength of the nations of Western Europe and the corresponding decline of that of the United States. The forging of a political "Atlantic Union" out of several independent political units requires, as de Gaulle has correctly seen, a paramount power which is willing and able to impose its will, if need be, upon a recalcitrant member. In other words, in such an "Atlantic Union" the United States would of necessity be predominant. Yet, when in the 50's the United States had the power and when its allies urged it to play that predominant role, the United States did not have the will to do so. Now, even if it had the will, it would not have the power to make its will prevail.

It is exactly because an "Atlantic Union" would be dominated by the United States that de Gaulle is opposed to it in no uncertain terms. The opposition of the other major European powers has remained implicit. But their desire for emancipation from the United States is obviously incompatible with the pursuit of a political "Atlantic Union."

The United States cannot afford to lose sight of political "Atlantic Union" as the ultimate goal; for nuclear proliferation, inevitable as it is likely to be, can be rendered tolerable only if its centrifugal and anarchic consequences are counterbalanced by the politically unified use of proliferated nuclear weapons. As long as political union is unobtainable and since traditional alliance commitments joined with nuclear proliferation, as pointed out above, are intolerable—the United States must strive for three goals: to mitigate the consequences of proliferation by limiting the number of independent nuclear deterrents, to bring its alliance commitments for the time being into harmony with the interests it has actually or potentially in common with its Allies, and in the end to render proliferation innocuous through unified political control.

The first goal requires of the United States active support for the political unification of Europe. For since proliferation appears to be inevitable and political "Atlantic Union" unattainable, a European nuclear deterrent controlled by a European political authority is the best attainable alternative. Such support implies a radical change in our present policies which, by trying to isolate France, render the political unification of Europe impossible and seek in vain to restore the Western Alliance on foundations which no longer exist.

The second goal requires similarly a radical change from the dogmatic insistence upon the restoration of an unrestorable *status quo* to the pragmatic adaptation to circumstances which, for the time being, are not subject to our control. We must narrow the gap between our comprehensive legal commitments and the limited sphere within which our interests and policies still coincide with those of our Allies. Otherwise we shall run the risk, to which improvident great powers have succumbed in the past, of getting involved in a war not of our making and on behalf of interests not our own.

Finally, we must look beyond these short-term adaptations to the ultimate goal not only of our alliance policy but of our overall foreign policies as well: the minimization of the risk of nuclear war. The substitution of a European nuclear deterrent for a multiplicity of national ones is a step in this direction.

Political "Atlantic Union" would be another step, impossible to achieve at present but to be sought for in a not too distant future.

In the end, we must look for a settlement or at least decontamination of the great political issues—among them a divided Germany, the outward thrust of Red China—which at present divide the world and conjure up the risk of nuclear war. We shall thus deprive the nuclear powers of the incentive to use nuclear weapons as instruments of their national policies. And we shall deal with the present crisis of the Western Alliance with policies seeking, first, to take into account the new circumstances of the crisis and, then, to overcome the crisis itself —not as isolated moves aimed at short-term goals but as steps toward the ultimate goal of banishing nuclear war itself.

The United States
and the Developing Nations

ROBERT E. ASHER*

Rᴀᴘɪᴅ and irrational shifts in public opinion are characteristic of foreign policy discussion in this country. Problems are viewed out of focus at least twice—once too hopefully and once too hopelessly—before they slide into focus. By the time they can be seen in proper perspective, people are weary of them and wish they would disappear entirely.

Proponents of new policies feel impelled to claim the most miraculous powers for them. If adopted, the policies will win friends, benefit business, assist agriculture, give a lift to labor, preserve the peace, roll back Communism, extend democracy, and improve everybody's standard of living. When the miracles fail to follow, disenchantment bordering on revulsion sets in. Investigations must be launched, the culprits ferreted out and punished, the administering agency abolished, reconstituted, or rechristened, and its policies reversed. When common sense at last takes over, the half-deserted battlefield is littered with debris and the legions that should be waging the good fight are

* The views expressed in this chapter are personal views and do not necessarily reflect the views of fellow members of the Brookings staff or of the administrative officers of the Institution.

166

parading elsewhere.

This has been the history of America's postwar relations with the developing countries. Just as we are beginning to know enough to live maturely with them, in a world in which there is no escaping them, we are wondering whether it is really worth the effort.

Which are the developing countries?

Who are these new neighbors? So imprecise has our English language become, in our desire to make it as bland and flattering as possible, that the term "developing nations" includes virtually all the nations that are *not* developing and excludes many that are, such as Japan, Western Europe, Australia, New Zealand, and North America. The Sino-Soviet complex, whether developing or not, is excluded because we abhor Communism and prefer to believe that progress thereunder is impossible.

The term "developing nations" is thus reserved for some eighty countries in the "free world," democratic and authoritarian, progressing and retrogressing, newly-emerged and long-established, whose common characteristic is appallingly low per capita incomes.

The salient facts about these countries are well known. The area they occupy includes all of Africa except perhaps the Republic of South Africa. It includes South and Southeast Asia, the bulk of Latin America, the southern fringes of Europe, and a few other corners of the world. In this broad belt, as Eugene Staley has said, "Poverty is old, but the awareness of poverty and the conviction that something can be done about it are new." [1]

As recently as 1961, more than half the people on earth lived in countries in which gross national product amounted to $100 or less per person per year, and two-thirds of the world—about

[1] Eugene Staley, *The Future of the Underdeveloped Countries*, Harper, 1954, p. 20.

two billion people—lived in countries in which the gross national product amounted to $300 or less per person. These two billion people, most of whom are colored, produced only 15 percent of the world's goods and services while the 750 million inhabitants of the countries enjoying a per capita GNP of $600 or more, most of whom are white, produced over 75 percent of the world's goods and services. In normal times, between three hundred million and five hundred million people in Asia are undernourished. India had more than seventy-five million cases of malaria in 1953. In Nepal, only 5 percent of the people read or write. In the Congo, there were only a dozen college-trained nationals at the time of independence. In the United States, there is one doctor for every 740 inhabitants, but in Yemen the ratio is one per 125,000 inhabitants.

The beginnings of United States involvement

For the first four decades of the twentieth century, the United States had almost nothing to do with the less-developed areas, knew very little about them, and felt no compulsion to increase its knowledge. After Pearl Harbor, the situation changed drastically. The combination of factors that brought the problems of the less-developed countries to the wings of the world stage during the 1940's and onto the center in the 1950's need not be resummarized here.

The first full-fledged American recognition of the special problems of the less-developed countries came in January 1949, only a few months after the launching of the Marshall Plan and less than eighteen months before the Communist invasion of South Korea. President Truman called for "a bold new program" of technical assistance to help the underdeveloped nations of the world. The answer to his call was a very modest program by any standard, but particularly modest in relation to the magnitude of our effort in Europe.

Our eminently successful rescue operation in Europe, moreover, created a climate of public opinion that was unfortunate in certain important respects. It gave rise to a feeling that unless a 100-percent success was achieved elsewhere, too, there must be something seriously wrong with the United States effort. It encouraged totally unrealistic notions about the time required to achieve success in Asia, Africa, and Latin America. It also invited a belief that the development problems posed in these areas, like the reconstruction problem in Europe, might be dealt with primarily by technical and economic means.

The invasion of South Korea emphasized the vulnerability of small nations to Communist aggression and their need for military aid. It provided some rightwing support for American foreign assistance during much of the 1950's. The Communist threat was regularly invoked as a principal justification for aid to underdeveloped countries, and recurrent crises in American-Soviet relations could be counted on to rescue the aid program when faith began to falter.

Liberals sensed from the start that a revolution was brewing in the underdeveloped world and that a program heavily motivated by cold-war considerations would eventually founder. Less-developed countries obviously had other ambitions than to become pawns in a chess game among superpowers—ambitions which the United States would have to recognize if it wished to continue to shape the course of history.

Liberals, however, tended to view the underdeveloped world as a kind of enormous, exotic slum, characterized by appalling poverty, hunger, and disease, but transformable, under a sufficiently massive and vigorous rural and urban slum-clearance program, into decent, respectable living quarters. This humanitarian response, though a good counterweight to the anti-Communist approach, was also inadequate.

The average citizen found himself somewhere in between, favorably disposed toward both good works and military alliances and reasonably hopeful that the combination would win love and respect for the United States. As everyone's illusions about foreign aid were gradually shattered, Congressional support for American efforts to participate in the vitally important job of international development ebbed steadily.

The progressive shattering of illusions

The revolution of rising expectations—alleged to be sweeping relentlessly across Asia, Africa, and Latin America—turned out on closer inspection to be barely perceptible in many parts of the world. The less developed countries were not a homogeneous group, equally ready for independence, equally determined to modernize, equally eager for foreign aid, or equally capable of using it.

They were not uniformly poor. The extremes of wealth and poverty within less-developed countries proved greater than the gap between average income levels in less-developed and highly developed countries. Privileged classes refused to yield up their privileges, pay taxes, and behave responsibly. The new bureaucrats, uncertain of their future and determined to make hay while the sun shone, were not unanimously averse to storing some of the hay in Swiss banks.

Less-developed countries did not see the Soviet threat in the same ominous light that we saw it. Military aid, instead of strengthening the forces of the free world vis-à-vis the Communist world, permitted some of the recipients to gird themselves for attacks on their neighbors. Traditional rivalries were sharpened and, within aided countries, the internal distribution of political power was modified in favor of the military at the expense of civilian authority. Juntas and military dictatorships may thus have been encouraged.

On the civilian side, the mere revelation of more efficient and scientific ways of raising food and producing goods did not lead to their adoption. Technicians became frustrated by deep-rooted social and institutional barriers of which they had been only dimly aware.

The emergence of the Soviet bloc as a source of foreign aid in the mid-1950's increased the bargaining power and orneriness of the less-developed countries. Those that were chafing under Western restrictions could buy leeway by threatening to switch their patronage.

Pioneering in new and complex fields, United States leadership and United States administration were sometimes less than brilliant and not every failure was the fault of the foreigners. Before long, most Americans knew (or thought they knew) of some disastrous project somewhere, some implausible investment, some administrative hanky-panky.

Officially, the standard response was to minimize the defects, to paper over the cracks, and to make fresh investments in order to save those already made. Inability to confess error made it hard to benefit from experience. Almost nowhere could the situation be brought under control and the United States seemed incapable of withdrawing from a country in orderly fashion before getting kicked out. When it tried, as in the Aswan Dam case, it acted so clumsily that the results were worse than letting ill-enough alone.

The United States was necessarily intervening in the affairs of other countries, but seemingly in a misdirected, unbalanced way. It preserved indefensible Maginot lines between aid and trade and between economics and politics. It tended to think of intervention in the domestic political affairs of the countries receiving aid as wrong in principle and unnecessary in practice. Democracy was believed to be a kind of natural state that would be attained in other countries, too, once the obstacles were removed and levels of living began to improve. Democratic governments would pursue peaceful foreign policies and live harmoniously with other self-respecting nations.

Events in Brazil, Cambodia, the Congo, Cyprus, Ghana, Haiti, Indonesia, Korea, Laos, Panama, Pakistan, Peru, Turkey, Vietnam, and elsewhere disillusioned many. The disenchantment came, moreover, during a decade in which the richest country in the world was faced at home with a slow rate of economic growth, a high rate of unemployment, a balance-of-payments crisis, and growing tension over the solution of its own minority problems. Sustained and generous efforts to relieve hardship abroad in the absence of a thriving economy at home, and in the face of repeated rebuffs from recipients, became exceedingly difficult.

The solid achievements
of the postwar years

Failure to achieve in the short run results that are obtainable only in the long run, if at all, should not blind us to the substantial progress made during the turbulent years since 1949, particularly in the promotion of economic growth and development. In the main, we can be fairly proud of our brief involvement in the affairs of the less-developed countries.

The United States was among the first to recognize the emergence of the low-income countries as a force in world affairs. It has been a leader in the effort to channel into the mainstream of world history the latent energies of countless millions of restless, hitherto voiceless men and women. The task has proved complex beyond expectations, costly in absolute terms, frequently frustrating and thankless, but nevertheless not without its successes already and promise for the future.

The struggle is inching toward its climax. As President Kennedy said in reply to a question about mounting resistance to foreign aid at his last press conference (November 14, 1963), "I don't understand why we are suddenly so fatigued. I don't regard the struggle as over and I don't think it's probably going to be over for this century."

Instead of waiting until that never-never day when we would have all the answers, the United States has been learning by doing—an approach that should be thoroughly congenial to our pragmatic society. We have been the true innovators and, as such, have borne a heavy share of what in private industry would be called Research and Development costs—the expensive exploratory work. Our innovations include the technical-assistance concept, the use of surplus agricultural products to promote foreign economic development, the soft loan which makes capital available to needy borrowers on very easy terms, the Alliance for Progress, the Peace Corps, and other inspirations too numerous to mention.

We have also played a leading part in getting other developed countries into the foreign-aid business. The total flow of public funds from the more-developed to the less-developed areas of the world has increased markedly during the last decade; the proportion furnished by the United States has decreased; development assistance has become respectable; and more and more countries are in the aid-giving business. The financial terms on which they give their aid have become less and less onerous to the receivers, but the total burden of foreign debt carried by the receivers is mounting alarmingly.

Most impressive and least appreciated is the actual economic progress that seems to have been made by the low-income countries in the 1950's. Statistical data concerning the developing nations are notoriously unreliable, but less so with respect to broad trends than to specific figures in a series. According to United Nations sources, the gross domestic product of the less-developed countries, measured in constant 1959 prices, increased from $121 billion in 1950 to about $180 billion in 1959, or at an annually compounded rate of 4.65 percent. During the same period, the gross domestic product of the developed countries of the free world (including the spectacular advances made by Western Europe and Japan) increased at an annual rate of only 3.7 percent. Because of the much faster rates of population growth in the underdeveloped areas, however, the rates of improvement per person were more nearly equal. And because of the great difference in starting points, the gap in per capita incomes in the more-developed as compared with the less-developed countries actually widened in dollar terms. (For example, a 2 percent increase would add $20 to an income of $1,000 whereas a 2.5 percent increase would add only $2.50 to a

$100 income, thus widening the gap by $17.50, despite the 25 percent greater rate of improvement at the lower end of the scale.)

Averages conceal as much as they reveal. The impressive over-all performance of the less-developed countries does not indi-cate which countries did better and which did worse than average, whether foreign aid had anything to do with their performance, how equitably the fruits of productivity increases were distributed within the countries that improved their lot, and whether the improvements served or did not serve the national interests of the United States.

The January 1964 *Report of the Council of Economic Ad-visers* contains some interesting data on twenty-six less-devel-oped countries that have received significant amounts of United States economic assistance and in which economic development has been a principal objective of American assistance. (Coun-tries like South Korea, South Vietnam, Laos, Cambodia, and Libya, in which economic development was not the prime objective of United States assistance, are excluded.) More than two-thirds of the underdeveloped countries listed achieved a rate of growth in real gross national product greater than the 3.7 percent average of the so-called developed countries, and more than half achieved a rate of 5 percent or better. On a per capita basis, exactly half registered gains of 2 percent or better in real terms.

The correlation between aid received and improvements registered is quite imperfect, but some of the largest recipients registered some of the best gains. Skillfully combining external resources with those mobilized locally, Israel during the 1950's sustained one of the highest rates of economic growth on record, exceeding even the 9 percent per year rate achieved by Japan and the 7.5 percent rate of the Federal Republic of Ger-many. Taiwan and Greece have also done spectacularly well and, like Israel, should soon be on their own. Mexico, the Phil-ippines, and Iran can take pride in their record. Self-support for India is at least a decade away, but the foreign aid it has received has been well-used, and the economic progress made affords a basis for modest optimism. Though India has received large absolute amounts of aid, the assistance on a per capita basis has been small, averaging only a little more than $1 per person per year during the period 1957–62.

In some other places, we may at best have bought time. But, in a field unmarked by guidelines, the purchase of time while one studies the terrain is itself an accomplishment. It would be hard, moreover, to argue that the aid program has been any great burden on the American economy. On the contrary, it generates jobs for over 500,000 American workers and provides a larger market for American exports than would otherwise be available.

The time that we have bought has been used not only for learning by doing but also for learning by more conventional and academic means. The results of a vast amount of research are helping us to understand the development process, our interest in it, and what we can do to influence it.

Nature of the development process

Revolutions are by definition disorderly affairs. A supposedly law-abiding country like the United States, witnessing the culmination of a hundred-year struggle to liberate its own colored minority, should not be dismayed by the untidy, drawn-out course of events elsewhere. Excesses will continue to occur and opportunities will be missed. Unreasonable demands will be made and reasonable people—hearing them from the comfortable vantage point of a home in the suburbs or a seat in Congress—will be shocked.

What I have said about revolutions in general applies to the ebb and flow of the specific revolution politely called development. Development involves the top-to-bottom transformation of whole societies. It means fundamental changes in traditional values, motivations, institutions, and patterns of behavior. It normally requires inspired leadership and a redistribution of political power. It has economic, psychological, and sociological, as well as political aspects. At best, it will be an erratic, two-steps-forward, one-step-backward, one-step-sideways movement. It is a long-term job for which there are as yet no blueprints and few generally accepted guidelines. Nevertheless, the United States response must be more mature than "Stop the world, I want to get off."

Development, we now know, depends primarily on the will and capacity of the people of the developing country far more than on natural resources or imported supplies. The wish to develop, unfortunately, is more widespread than the will to develop, and we know relatively little about how to translate the wish into the will.

Development is a process rather than an end. Our aim should be to facilitate the unfolding of the process to the point where the local population will not only be desirous but capable of improving its lot, will have some confidence in its ability to do so, and will be earning enough foreign exchange to pay for its growing volume of imports without special subventions from abroad. Gross national product, per capita income, and other economic indexes in the developing country should move upward, but salvation does not lie in increasing these to the highest degree. The larger pie must have more to it than a strengthened upper crust.

A decent sharing of the increased wealth; the elimination of discrimination based on race, color, or creed; higher literacy rates; improved educational facilities; broader and better-informed participation in political life; and efficient and humane administration—these, too are vitally important.

There is no assurance that economic growth will be accompanied by desirable social and political changes or vice versa. Nor is it certain that self-governing, self-sustaining peoples will be prepared to live harmoniously with either their neighbors or the United States. It merely seems more likely than that frustrated, insecure, starving populations will do so.

Outside aid strategically applied can ease the transitional period. The type of aid and the spirit in which it is offered are important, but the fact that it takes more than money to launch the development process does not mean that money is unimportant.

The nature of the development cycle is such that the balance-of-payments deficit of the developing country swells before it shrinks. At the very early stages of development, as explained in the *Report of the Council of Economic Advisers*, technical assistance may be the nation's principal need. As the country acquires the skills and institutions enabling it to help itself, however, its capacity to invest is likely to grow more rapidly than its ability to save. Moreover, for some time at least, it must obtain from abroad the great bulk of the manufactured and semi-manufactured goods that it uses in establishing new industries and raising incomes. Consequently, its requirements for imports rise rapidly.

India is a prime example of this stage of development. It is strategically located, has the largest population of any nation in the non-Communist world, and is making impressive progress without sacrificing its democratic institutions. But it is critically short of foreign exchange. India consequently serves as a dramatic reminder of the perils of assuming that money doesn't really matter. Greece, on the other hand, provides evidence that the need for extraordinary assistance does not last indefinitely, and that major beneficiaries of foreign aid can and do become self-supporting.

The prospects for an early decline in total requirements for extraordinary assistance are slim indeed, but every success story will inspire some of the stragglers. It is not unreasonable, therefore, to envisage a gradual reduction in the number of recipients and a gradual increase in the number of contributors.

Where is the money to come from? It is ironic that when defense expenditures were mounting and disarmament seemed decades away, there was much talk about devoting a portion of the savings from disarmament to development. Now that defense expenditures may actually be leveling off, however, "realism" has taken over and aid appropriations are shrinking.

United States interest
in international development

In domestic affairs, the politician who subordinates the concerns of his constituency to the welfare of the nation as a whole is hailed as a statesman. In foreign affairs, however, the man who fails to put the domestic welfare first—ahead of the welfare of the world as a whole—risks being called a traitor. Foreign policy, therefore, tends to be justified at home on the ground that it serves the national interest in a fairly immediate and tangible fashion. This very justification makes it suspect abroad. Why, it may then be asked, should others honor us or be grateful to us for pursuing an essentially selfish course of action? Yet, so ingrained is nationalism and so muddled the state of the world today, that altruism is almost equally suspect.

The nations of the world have had very little experience in looking at their problems from a truly international viewpoint and seeking accommodation on the basis of the welfare of all. Meanwhile, each country must convince itself that a proposed activity serves its national interest.

The national interests of the United States and the developing countries are not identical and there is little point in pretending that they are. They do overlap, though, in ways that permit both sides to benefit, each in its own way, from the type of relationship that has been evolving.

The United States interest in international development has been spelled out several times and zestful readers can write to me, care of this publisher, for references to those statements. They vary considerably in persuasiveness, but in a pluralistic society like ours it is not necessary for people to agree on the reasons behind an action if they can agree on the action itself.

Co-existence with totalitarian regimes will, I hope, always be difficult for the United States. Our objective must therefore be to keep the alternative of non-totalitarian paths to development open for as long as possible to as many as possible. Our values cannot be imposed on others or imparted on a take-it-or-leave-it basis. Continuous contact and adaptation are necessary if the values of a free society are to have relevance and appeal in the new nations. Their political and economic systems will never become carbon copies of ours, but we can live with a wide range of non-totalitarian, or decreasingly totalitarian, political and economic systems.

The conventional economic arguments for United States participation in the development process are valid though overworked. We are, of course, helped by having foreign markets for our products, and rich countries make better markets than poor countries. We can use imports from many sources, and the sources should be reasonably secure and stable. The developing countries are in truth the economic "new frontier." But the United States can maintain full employment and a high standard of living at home with a very low level of imports and exports, if it chooses to do so. Should it?

Arnold Toynbee has described the impulse to protect wealth, if one has it, as one of the natural human impulses. "It is not particularly sinful, but it automatically brings a penalty with it that is out of proportion to its sinfulness. This penalty is isolation. It is a fearful thing to be isolated from the majority of one's fellow-creatures, and this will continue to be the social and moral price of wealth so long as poverty continues to be the normal condition of the World's ordinary men and women." [2]

Participation in international development programs is a way of breaking out of the isolation in which we would otherwise be dwelling. Such participation helps us to live at peace with ourselves as well as with others.

[2] Arnold J. Toynbee, *America and the World Revolution*, Oxford University Press, 1962, p. 101.

Moral arguments have gone out of fashion and humanitarianism does not occupy a prominent place in international relations. Nevertheless, it is not contrary to the national interest to follow the dictates of our conscience. The inequality that exists between nations, the grinding poverty that permeates so many nations, is no longer tolerable within the borders of a modern, progressive nation-state. This inequality is corrected within a country like the United States or Great Britain by continuous transfers of wealth from the richer citizens to the poorer citizens and from the richer areas to the poorer ones. The world, it has been said, has become too small for fellow-feeling between man and man to stop at political frontiers.[3]

In addition to the moral and economic arguments, important military and political considerations could be mentioned. Even the most convincing presentation of the American interest in promoting development offers little guidance regarding the proper geographic and financial scope and operational techniques of the effort. The situation confronting the United States in Vietnam as this chapter is being written illustrates the unpalatable alternatives we are doomed from time to time to face.

Agenda for the future

If we are clear enough about the nature of the revolution in which, willy-nilly, we are participating, we should be able to develop an agenda for the future based on a viable blend of long-term and short-term considerations.

The immediate job appears to be to take stock of our situation, to prevent further backsliding, to make sure that we use the full arsenal of instruments at our disposal, yet also to realize that our influence is limited. The next item of business is to make the necessary resources available to the less-developed countries with maximum incentives to use them productively,

[3] "The Vienna Declaration on Cooperation for Development," Theodor Körner Foundation, July 1962, para. 2.

while minimizing the usual strains between donor and re-
cipient.

Military aid cannot be dispensed with—Communist China's
probes into India show why—but making the appropriations
directly to the Department of Defense should, without divorc-
ing military aid from other instruments of American policy,
enable the Agency for International Development (AID) to
concentrate more exclusively on international development.

The United States is not obligated to help nations that do
not want American help or have no interest in helping themselves. We can probably afford to be more hard-boiled than we
have been in choosing and retaining clients. Nor, now that we
are no longer the sole source of aid, need we supply every kind
of assistance sought. There are surely some things that we do
better than others do them, and some that it is more in our
interest to do. These priority tasks will suffer so long as we allow
ourselves to be diverted into providing an almost infinite range
of services. Development assistance, moreover, can be harmful
as well as helpful, and will be if it enables receivers to postpone
for too long painful adjustments that they will sooner or later
have to make.

There is no merit in stoically bearing burdens that others may
be induced to share. A more rational division of labor is needed
between bilateral and multilateral programs (that is, between
United States, British, or French national agencies and United
Nations, Inter-American, and European-Economic-Community
agencies). Elsewhere I have suggested some guidelines for the
expansion of multilateral efforts.[4]

The kind of policing of foreign aid engaged in by the General
Accounting Office, with its periodic revelations about roads and
airports that serve no visible economic purpose, is utterly inappropriate to anything as sensitive as the development effort.
American ingenuity is capable of devising less heavy-handed

[4] Robert E. Asher, "Multilateral Versus Bilateral Aid: An Old Controversy Revisited," *International Organization*, Autumn, 1962, Brookings
Reprint No. 66.

methods of safeguarding the integrity of its bilateral programs.

In any event, we cannot vest the entire responsibility for promoting development in a handful of public agencies. A total effort requires total involvement. It has become platitudinous to call for greatly enlarged roles for private business, for trade union and professional groups, for women's organizations, universities, foundations, municipalities, etc., but it is no less necessary because it is platitudinous. Research on the interrelations of economic, social, and political development must also be stepped up and provision made for incorporating research findings into operational activities at the earliest possible date.

Fostering the development of democratic institutions is a top priority field for both research and action. The Communists have a vast network of cultural societies, friendship clubs, political parties, and student groups; democrats appear unnecessarily squeamish about communicating their ideology and maintaining intimate contacts with kindred souls in other lands.

A new look at the methods of financing development is needed. One of the entrenched myths of the postwar era is that loans have character-building virtues lacked by grants. It is perfectly feasible to design a grant program that includes disciplinary features analogous to those alleged to be inherent in the loan process, but does not make comparable demands on the limited foreign-exchange earnings of the developing country.

Moreover, the balance-of-payments deficit that developing countries normally encounter need not be met entirely with loans and grants. Aid is not nobler than trade and there is much to be said for amending the ground rules governing the conduct of international trade so that more of the foreign-exchange requirements of the developing countries can be earned through international trade. The ardent desire of the developing countries for such amendments was amply demonstrated at the United Nations Conference on Trade and Development in Geneva during the spring of 1964.

The present international monetary arrangements also need attention. The development of Puerto Rico has not been hampered by periodic foreign-exchange crises, and bolder attempts might be made to build international institutions to the point where other underdeveloped areas can obtain comparable freedom. A small step in the right direction was taken in 1963 when the International Monetary Fund created a new "facility" for helping member countries that experience temporary declines in export earnings due to circumstances beyond their control.

We would be missing the boat completely if we thought of either the long-range or the short-range tasks primarily as challenges to our technical ingenuity. We can do all the right things with respect to monetary policy, trade, aid, and military support, and still stumble badly because of faulty political attitudes. Failure to appreciate the intensity of opposition in the less-developed world to the South African policy of apartheid, to the policies of Portugal in Angola and Mozambique, or to nuclear testing in the Sahara, will cost us dearly.

At the same time, we must devise more effective ways of enlisting the collaboration of developing countries in safeguarding human rights within the lands that they themselves control. The Charter of the United Nations calls not only for the maintenance of international peace and security and the promotion of higher standards of living. It demands with equal eloquence the promotion of "universal respect for, and observance of, human rights and fundamental freedoms for all."

Great powers have the capacity to inspire as well as to intimidate. The successful prosecution of our war against poverty and prejudice at home will provide a better climate for its successful prosecution abroad. The struggle of American minority groups for integration has its counterpart in the struggle of the less-developed countries for integration in the nascent world community. There is one important difference, however. The less-developed countries are not minority groups. They contain an overwhelming proportion of mankind. Their aspirations, though not necessarily realizable today or tomorrow, cannot for a century be gainsaid.

America

in a Pluralistic World*

AMITAI ETZIONI

THE future historian, writing about our decade with the wisdom of hindsight, may assert that few members of the 1964 Administration realized, or at least publicly acknowledged, the full political significance of two events that occurred in 1963. The installation of the "hot line" and the signing of the Test Ban Treaty, although, of limited significance in themselves, marked (he will write) the end of the age of bloc-politics and the beginning of the "pluralistic" period.

The "hot line," a communication link between the White House and the Kremlin, was widely acclaimed for its function of averting accidental war. But almost no one saw in 1963 that it could also be used to disown an action of one's allies at a moment's notice. The USSR could instantly inform the United States that it did not approve, let us say, of a new Chinese attack on India. The same line could be used by the United States to disassociate itself from any rash move on the part of France, Germany, or any other ally. No wonder that requests from NATO allies to have a "hookup" with the line were po-

* The thesis of this article is elaborated in my Winning Without War, published by Doubleday in May 1964.

184

litely, but firmly, turned down.

Similarly, the main significance of the treaty for partial cessation of thermonuclear tests is not the reduction of fallout or the limited damper it puts on American and Soviet development of nuclear weapons (which continues in laboratories, simulation-computers and underground testing), but the fact that it was an attempt of the two nuclear giants to prevent the birth of more nuclear dwarfs, and to slow the growth of those already born.

The reason why the full potential of these two preliminary steps was not exploited, nor even fully understood, even after the 1963 *detente* in Soviet-American relations, is a familiar one. In 1964, the Administration is trying to solve 1954's problems—and it viewed 1968 in terms of 1948. More specifically, our foreign policy was and is still formulated in terms of a duopolistic strategy, based on the assumption of a bipolar concentration of world power (East and West), with other countries in a residual category ("non-aligned"). The main objective of our policy is still to contain Communist expansionism, in the hope that the frustration produced by Western countermoves, combined with internal pressures, will produce a "mellowing" or even disintegration of the Communist system. These changes in Communism are to be encouraged politically by a united Western counterbloc—and militarily by a combination of a nuclear deterrent, conventional forces, and the newly added subconventional (or "counterguerilla" and "counterinsurrectionist") forces. The global distribution of power, according to this strategy, can be stabilized through a nuclear balance of terror, with the two giants in a stalemate, neither able to break the other. Moreover, policies of gradual expansion and roll-back cannot be vigorously followed because of the fear of triggering a nuclear war.

The dialogue in Washington is largely limited to variations on this theme; some insist that we need more missiles, others that we have more than enough. Some feel that there is room for some arms-control measures, others doubt that very much.

Some still look for an opportunity for a military victory; others believe that such a concept, in the age of big bombs on a small planet, cannot even be defined. But, as a whole, a duopolistic, (two-bloc) balance-of-power (or stalemate) represents both a widely held political forecast and the prevailing strategy; East and West are still the key concepts of most Washington thinking.

But, in fact, every single component of this formula has changed since it was enunciated in the late Forties. The technology of weapons puts at the command of both sides a military power that surpasses all imagination and which, in the long run, cannot possibly be held in check—the most carefully designed, closely guarded system has an occasional breakdown. The probability of a breakdown of the nuclear balance of terror might be small, but the magnitude of disaster that would occur is so large that the system simply cannot be lived with in the long run. Hence, the strategic question is how much longer the United States (and the USSR) can prudently delay serious attempts at arms reduction and strengthening of global institutions?

While there is considerable disagreement among Kremlinologists as to what degree the USSR has mellowed, there is little doubt that profound changes have taken place both domestically and in its foreign policy. The West must now answer the question: what will it offer to the USSR when it has mellowed "enough," what strategy will replace containment when there is nothing left to contain but the drive of those who have vested interests in this position? What conditions do we require the USSR to meet before it will be found to be as fully eligible for membership in the international community as, let us say, France?

Equally important as the changes within the Soviet Union have been changes in the blocs. They were never as integrated and united as we liked to believe. The history of NATO is one of crises and unfulfilled commitments, and the Sino-Soviet conflict has a longer history than we at first realized. As long as our

European allies and the Asian allies of the USSR were weak, there was the kind of unity that results from a single center of hegemony in each bloc (though the extent of our hegemony never remotely approached that of the Soviet Union). In both alliances, however, this kind of hegemony is gone forever. Washington likes to put all the blame for the crisis of the Western Alliance on one man, but we should note that the French nuclear force was initiated before de Gaulle returned to power and will very likely outlive him. Also, while Germany is at the moment our favorite ally on the continent, the day is just around the corner when it will have both the power and the desire to pursue a more independent foreign policy. The Sino-Soviet conflict will surely have its ups and downs, but there will never again be a united Communist bloc as there was in the early fifties.

We must, then, face the fact that the world of the seventies will have several centers of power, not two. These will not be equal in magnitude; the United States and the USSR will probably continue to stand out as nuclear giants. Nor will all the blocs treat all the others as equally remote. But matters concerning world order will no longer be decided in two capitals; the trend is back to a period of five or more big powers, and several emerging ones. This promises more maneuverability, and complicates the considerations of each power. It is an especially unhappy change for the two superpowers, who ran the show from the late forties to the late fifties.

What might United States policy be when Washington finally sees that no mixed-crew ships, tariff cuts, or summit meetings of Western heads of state will patch up the Alliance? What will follow a fuller recognition of the dangers of nuclear war, the limits of arms control, and the fact that the East is also deeply divided? The answer cannot be readily given in terms of forecasting history. But, if we write an "optimistic scenario" assuming a better United States–USSR understanding, we can foresee the development of a new American strategy for the pluralistic world, following the precedents of the "hot line" and the 1963 Test Ban Treaty. I like to call it the "strategy of competition"; the rest of this article is devoted to outlining assumptions on which the strategy is based.

Replacing the current bipolar strategy with a strategy of competition would promote forces, inside Communist as well as non-Communist countries, that are committed to a world of peaceful competition. Under this strategy, Communist countries need not be expected to refrain from advancing the values they believe in, so long as they limit the means employed to nonlethal ones. The West, too, is not committed to a static concept of peaceful coexistence, but is free to promote progressive, democratic forces, likewise through nonlethal means.

The strategy assumes that differences of belief and interest between the United States and the USSR cannot be resolved. But it also assumes that it is not essential to resolve these differences; what is needed are effective limitations on their expression, so as to avoid escalation to the level of armed conflict of the confrontations that will continue to occur.

The new strategy assumes that competition is desirable, because it tends to bind the competitors to one set of institutions within which the competition is conducted, and to advance the values in the name of which the competition is conducted, for example, development. It is assumed that the long-run stabilization of the world order requires a re-allocation of global wealth in favor of the "have not" countries, and that interbloc competition is a most effective propelling power toward such re-allocation.

Similarly, the evolution of global institutions essential for the long-run solution of our international problems is accelerated by the quest of both sides to develop machinery to formulate the rules of the competition and to enforce them. In short, dynamic peaceful competition is very much preferable to static peaceful coexistence.

While the long-run aim of the strategy of competition is world peace through world law, the strategy itself is within the realm of power politics, like the bipolar strategy it seeks to replace.

Both aim at improving the standing of the United States in the global content, and at the evolution of systems which will protect the American and other peoples from nuclear war. These objectives, we believe, can be "harmonized" with those of other big powers, since (a) some dangers are universal (especially nuclear annihilation); (b) some are shared by the United States and the USSR but not by other powers, especially the challenge to their bloc status by their respective allies, which leads the two powers to formulate arrangements to their advantage in terms of universal values and institutions (for example, the ban on nuclear testing); and (c) the criteria for scoring points in the areas in which there is a direct contest between the United States and the USSR (for example, which is developing "better"—India or China?). There is no sign that the stock of prizes to compete over in the third world will be exhausted by the time the contenders tire of the competition.

More specifically, the following assumptions are involved in a strategy of competition:

a. *The USSR and the Soviet-led Communist camp* are viewed as permanent members of the international community. That is, despite crises in agriculture, a deficit in its foreign trade with non-Communist countries, and other difficulties, it is not expected that the Soviet regime will collapse under its own weight, or under the pressures the West can bring to bear by withholding trade, through the Voice of America, and the like. Secondly, it is assumed that it is morally unacceptable and militarily ill-advised to try to break the USSR by military power, which would involve American initiation of a nuclear war. Third, it is assumed that the USSR either has mellowed enough or might mellow enough in the foreseeable future, particularly if encouraged by Western efforts, to continue to liberalize internally and to follow a foreign policy compatible with the standards of a stable, peaceful world community.

It is not assumed that the USSR has lost its global ambitions or messianic urges, but rather that developments in the technology of weapons have brought the USSR to realize that military advances are exceedingly dangerous. There are signs that the Russian people are growing increasingly tired of life in a garrison, and that the government is interested in shifting resources to raise the standard of living even further. The acceptance of the impossibility of massive military gains, and a desire for the reduction of international tensions necessary for domestic improvements, might lead the Soviets to be genuinely interested in limiting their expansion efforts to non-military means. We cannot rely on the word of the Soviet, or anybody else, for such a limitation; but we can follow a strategy that will test these assumptions without undue risk, and we can build forces that would encourage developments and institutions that would discourage tendencies toward regression.

Peaceful competition is preferred over peaceful coexistence precisely because we assume that the Soviet Union and its followers are not free from global ambitions, and that seeking to block all expressions of such ambitions by a rigid duopoly makes global accommodation unduly difficult. We will surely benefit from insisting that every power can appeal to all people— including those who live behind the Iron Curtain—through aid, trade, and communication of ideas, as long as no violence is used and no instigation to violence is involved. We have no reason to fear such a contest with the USSR, and the USSR might be more ready to accept this kind of limitation of the contest than a total and global *status quo*.

b. *Assumptions about Communist China and the Chinese-led camp.* Ostracizing China encourages aggressive forces inside China, leaves it few options to alliance with Russia except isolation, and makes most worldwide arms control and reduction schemes unworkable. Gradual engagement of China in the world community, through opening the routes to travel, trade in nonstrategic materials, membership in the UN, etc., might keep China from re-consolidating its relations with the USSR and bring closer domestic liberalization and mellowing of its foreign policy. Internal collapse of the regime cannot be counted upon, and military moves against China might result in a war with the USSR, just as a Soviet attack on France would bring us into a war with Russia.

As long as the USSR is not involved, China is a weak power vis-à-vis the United States. Hence it cannot, or could not in the foreseeable future, follow a highly aggressive foreign policy which the USSR does not approve. Despite bellicose talk, China did not invade Taiwan, come openly and massively to the aid of the Vietcong (on the scale of United States assistance to the Vietnamese government), or drive deep into India. At least half a generation will pass before China—without massive help from the outside—will have the industrial base for an expansionist foreign policy, backed up by large-scale production of nuclear bombs and missiles (a few bombs do not make a nuclear power). This period should be used to bring China at least as much into the international community as Russia is today.

There is much to be gained from encouraging the entrance of China into the global competition with the United States and the USSR. We should not insist, in the rigid bipolar tradition in which our policy was formulated, that whoever is not with us is with Russia. Nor can we refuse to see that—as in other polycentric situations—whoever is competing with my foremost rival, is helping me, whether he knows and likes it or not. Absurd as it may sound to the present generation of American strategists, Communist China is rendering great services to the United States in this way. Gradually introducing China into the world community would increase these services. To illustrate, a Communist China in the UN would either require the two leading Communist countries to agree upon positions, which they have found rather difficult, or regularly to vote differently, demonstrating the Communist split on the most conspicuous public stage in the world, as well as splitting the Communist and pro-Communist vote.

c. *Assumptions about France and other Western allies.* The United States will always have a special affinity with countries that share its Christian, democratic, social-welfare tradition, no matter what their foreign policy. But the expectation that the retirement of one man could re-establish United States hegemony in the Western Alliance and heal its cleavages is difficult to substantiate. The French nuclear force is not likely to melt away or be given up. While France is likely to be weakened in the succession crisis that will follow de Gaulle's departure, future leaders of France will find it difficult to renounce the image of glory as a world power that has been revived by the General. France must be viewed as a permanently independent power.

Britain has much to gain from playing the role of the great international mediator, and she is likely to continue to move slowly in a more independent direction—as already indicated by her trade with Cuba despite a "Western" blockade, and by her support of a "soft" line in the disarmament negotiations in Laos and in Berlin. It cannot be assumed that Britain, in or out of Europe, will serve much longer as an American anchor.

West Germany, at the moment the European backbone of NATO and the hub of American efforts to re-establish its hegemony in the Western Alliance, might become the next black sheep of the Alliance. It is growing in economic military power and is increasingly intent on using it to bring about "reunification." This goal, which was until recently a slogan to which politicians paid lip service, might tomorrow be the motive for a deal with Russia, a military move against the East German government, or both.

In short, the Alliance—drawn up in the days of a much more direct Soviet threat in Europe, a much greater credibility of the American protection, and a much weaker Europe—is becoming ever weaker. No "Grand Designs" will reverse this trend; one does not paste together fifteen nations into a federation to suit the latest designs of the State Department.

The United States reaction until now has been to invest more and more in stillborn efforts to patch up the Alliance and delay the initiation of policies that would take cognizance of the pluralistic trend of the world. Recognition that the wheels of history cannot be turned back would bring to a halt the training and arming of Europeans with nuclear arms, which undermines the 1963–64 Soviet-American *détente* and provides additional power to Germany. Measures such as the internationalization of the routes leading to West Berlin, recognition of the border between Poland and West Germany and some arms-control scheme in the area might yield considerable Soviet concessions in exchange. We should no longer delay considering these steps out of fear that they will hinder the patching-up of an alliance that is anyhow in serious disarray.

d. *The emerging pluralistic world deeply affects our assumptions about the United Nations.* The UN was to be an instrument of the world community. In effect, it served for years as an instrument of Western foreign policy, as the West commanded an almost automatic majority for its resolutions. But the UN has changed; now the representatives of the Southern Hemisphere—Latin America, Africa, and Asia—can outvote the Northern ones any day of the week. Since, for reasons of their own, many of these countries tend to favor better United States-USSR relations and the strengthening of the UN, a new role for it is evolving. The UN can no longer be used in the narrow service of Western interests, but it can function as the institution which develops the rules and the machinery to limit the global competition to nonlethal means and to provide opportunities for the peaceful settlement of disputes.

As long as there are nation states, it is unreasonable to expect them to regard the UN as something above and beyond power politics and national interests. But national interests are not eternal; they change with time and circumstance. An increasing number of the smaller powers are coming to identify their interests with the strengthening of the UN and of the world community and institutional network of which it is the center.

We often voice support for a gradual increase in the functions and power of the UN. There is no reason we should not pursue this policy more vigorously in the new age. Negotiating outside and around the UN not only weakens it, but makes us more sensitive to our real and pseudo-allies in NATO and less responsive to third countries and other blocs. Working through the UN makes our policy more truly global, in line with our duties as a world leader. This is a mantle that was thrust upon us, but by now we should be getting ready to wear it with fewer sighs and groans.

The suggested change in United States foreign policy can be translated into a myriad of policy shifts and adaptations. Few of these policy recommendations are new; some are known as steps that have been rejected in the past—for example, trade with Communist China—because they did not fit into the bipolar framework. These proposals ought to be re-examined now, in the light of the new strategic outlook. There are other measures that we have advanced but that the USSR has flatly rejected in the past; some of these might be much more acceptable in the context of a new policy. Policies tried unsuccessfully in the past might prove more effective in the coming years, either because they fit better into a pluralistic than a bipolar world (for example, settlement of the Berlin issue), or because the solutions were advanced only halfheartedly in the past (for example, various arms-reduction measures). All these varied proposals have often been discussed and cannot be reviewed within the limits of the space available here, nor is it necessary to do so. Those who can make the transition from outmoded conceptions molded in the forties to a strategy of competition taking into account current realities will readily see the specific policy suggestions that follow. Those who rigidly adhere to obsolete conceptions can hardly be expected to support such proposals. Now, more than ever, foreign-policy debate focuses on the strategic outlook. It is no longer a question of a specific adaptation or adjustment. A strategy based on a bipolar world is defunct in a world that is becoming pluralistic. The advancement of freedom and justice and the achievement of a durable peace call for a strategy of peaceful competition which will be both conducted in the framework of global institutions, and seek to advance their evolution.

Political Action at the Crossroads

The Presidency
at the Crossroads

JAMES MACGREGOR BURNS

The Presidency is the most paradoxical agency of American government. For one thing, it was the least planned part of our carefully laid out governmental system. The Founding Fathers defined the power of the President vaguely; said nothing about a cabinet or staff assistants; and, of course, had little conception of the vast bureaucracy over which the President would come to preside.

A second paradox of the Presidency is the refusal of the people—and of political scientists—to come to grips with the colossal power that now reposes in the White House. We solemnly analyze the niceties of the checks and balances among President, Congress, and Courts, and the ultimate check of the voters, at a time when the President can unleash a nuclear holocaust that would obliterate the checks and balances, the Constitution, and the voters. We have given power to the President precisely in the area where his rash action might be uncheckable and irreversible—that is, in foreign and military policy—and we carefully fence him in in those areas where Presidential errors could be limited and reversed—notably in domestic fiscal policy.

197

The President has always been the practical agency that American leaders have used, and voters have endorsed, to cope with urgent demands for governmental action. From Jefferson's purchase of Louisiana—unconstitutional by his own admission—to Lincoln's conduct of the war, to Franklin Roosevelt's provision of destroyers to Great Britain, to Kennedy's dispatch of troops to Oxford, Mississippi, the President has supplied an infinitely expandable and flexible reservoir of governmental power.

It is Congress that has lagged in confronting the major domestic and foreign policies of our century; the very branch that the Founding Fathers had expected to be the more active and creative department of government has come to be assessed mainly in terms of its effectiveness in passing the President's program. We hear a great deal of criticism of the *President* in this country but not very much criticism of the *Presidency*. Certainly the President has been allowed to organize the top level of his executive department pretty much as he wishes. Congress, however, proceeds under a continuous barrage of criticism as an institution, and the crucial question raised about our national legislature is less its effectiveness than its capacity to reform itself—or at least to put its two houses into some kind of order.

For some years, many of us have preached the need for Congressional reform, while—at least in my case—lacking much confidence in the power of Congress to reform itself. I had hoped that John Kennedy might have won in 1964 in such a heavy sweep that he would have brought into Congress enough Kennedy Democrats not only to enact his program, but to reorganize Congress to make it a more democratic, responsible, and effective body. The tragedy in Dallas marked the end of this possibility for Kennedy. Lyndon Johnson assumed his legislative responsibilities with a sure and skilled hand. He put his personal standing with Senators behind the Kennedy-Johnson program. He also benefited from popular identification of the program with the fallen President.

Unless Johnson can bring about sweeping Congressional reform, we are headed back to a period of politics as usual as the two conservative Congressional parties combine to block or stall Presidential programs, especially programs requiring the heavy spending of money. But how long can politics as usual serve us, or even survive, in a time of heavy and persistent demands on our political system? I can think of no situation that better exemplifies Hans Morgenthau's comment that "we are living in a world that is characterized by unprecedented change both in quantity and quality, and our modes of thought and action are limping far behind what those changes require of us." We are, I believe, approaching a crossroads in the organization of national power and a crossroads also in our thinking about the shape of our national government.

The point is this: since the very beginning, the American people have tended to embrace the Madisonian formula as the orthodox and legitimate model for organizing our national government (and our state governments as well). We have tended to ignore another, competing model, which I have labeled the Jeffersonian model. Under this second model, strong leaders try to carry out their programs with the cooperation of their party in Congress; the majority party is well enough organized to serve as a bridge between the President and his majority in Congress; the majority party does not have the power to obstruct the President's legislation but only the right to carry the issue to the people; and the issue is resolved at the next election. The Jeffersonian model, in short, is that of strong leadership, responsible parties, majority rule, fair elections (which assumes a healthy atmosphere of a free press and civil liberties), and a vigorous opposition eager not only to win power at the next election but to present an alternative program on which it would govern if elected.

Central to the Jeffersonian model is the concept of strong Presidential leadership. This must be emphasized, for as a result of a long dalliance of political scientists with the dream of responsible political parties, the crucial role of leadership has tended to be subordinated to the concept of a democratically operated two-party system. Let me repeat—leadership is central to the Jeffersonian model (as Jefferson himself demonstrated); without leadership, all the rest of the model collapses.

In pursuit of the dominant Madisonian model, Americans have tended to see audacious uses of Presidential power as "exceptions to the rule"—something that has to be resorted to in emergency situations, but is intrinsically dubious and dangerous. Only because of repeated emergencies has the Presidency emerged as the crucial instrument of power it is. It is clear, however, that for the rest of this decade, and probably for the rest of this century, the United States will confront a series of crises at home and abroad. The question I pose is: will the Jeffersonian model become the exception or the rule? If chronic crisis indeed faces us, and if this means a further enhancement of Presidential power, and if this becomes the common pattern of the next few years or even decades, should we continue to look on Presidential power as an exceptional and questionable activity?

Perhaps we should revise our concepts, perhaps we should reassess our thinking, and see Presidential power as it really is—a wholly democratic way of dealing with the problems and crises of government, assuming that the rest of the Jeffersonian model stands intact—a strong party supporting and restricting the President, an effective opposition party, and a pluralistic society protecting civil liberties.

Americans are slowly coming to recognize the fact that the Presidency has been historically a vital weapon for protecting and expanding individual civil liberties and civil rights, rather than a threat to them. Here again is a place where we must revise our orthodox thinking. The framers of the Constitution feared a strong executive as a possible engine of tyranny. They were thinking in terms of historical figures who had seized governments and dictated to the people. The framers also still smarted under the executive authority, often exaggerated, of colonial governors and other minions of the Crown. They expected that Congress would be the great bulwark of the people's liberties, because Congress was so directly representative of the people. But things have turned out much differently. Again and again it has been the President who has acted to defend civil liberties and civil rights—most notably in this century. It has been Congress that has either threatened minority rights and individual liberties through legislation, or has tolerated such onslaughts against civil liberties as were represented by McCarthyism and the Un-American Affairs Committee. Above all, the President has symbolized the fact that freedom needs to be protected against both arbitrary governmental and arbitrary private power, and that freedoms can be expanded both through private action and through public action.

The most relevant case in point is civil rights. In the last thirty years it has been five Presidents, from Roosevelt to Johnson, who have pressed ahead on a program of broadening civil rights through legislation. It has been Congress that has resisted such an effort, largely because of the influence of Southerners in the power structure of both Houses. The startling reversal of what was expected of these two branches of Government is due to circumstances too complex to go into here, but the fact of the reversal can hardly be disputed.

The conventional wisdom has it that, even though the President may take leadership on such matters as civil rights, the very power of the Presidency represents an ominous threat to the maintenance of the people's liberty. The arguments are fourfold:

First, the contention that the Presidency may be filled by either an incompetent of the Harding type, or a demagogue of the Huey Long or the Joe McCarthy type. Perhaps the best answer to this double-barreled argument is the simplest one: in the twentieth century we have had only one Harding in the White House, and no Huey Longs or Joe McCarthys. Indeed, either because of the caliber of the men elected to the White House, or because of the influence of the Presidency on the incumbent, this has been a century of strikingly effective Presidents, or at least of highly capable "near-greats." Even the three Vice-Presidents who have been elevated to the Presidency during this century have turned out to be unusually able men—and this is doubtless true of Lyndon Johnson as well.

A second conventional concern about the American President is that, as Professor Edward Corwin said in 1941, the Presidency might become dangerously personalized, in two senses: overly dependent on the accident of personality and lacking independent advice from organs of Government over which the President had no control. But, with the enormous development of the staff system since Corwin's time, it is hard to see the Presidency as personalized today. Certainly Presidents would deny it; men like Roosevelt and Kennedy have felt the restraints and limitations of the bureaucracy as a whole and of the cluster of permanent civil servants who go on from Presidency to Presidency. We hear much about the "lonely President"—and doubtless in certain crucial hours he does feel very alone. But actually the President is surrounded by men and, even more, responds to the advice of the many men with whom he has had to work to gain his office and to administer it. The President cannot take day-to-day action without operating through a bureaucracy that has been built up over many years, and which embraces a whole set of restraints and safeguards in itself.

A third traditional charge against the Presidency is that it is an unrepresentative office. The President, it is said, simply represents popular majorities—and, indeed, popular majorities that are distorted by the workings of the Electoral College. Congress, on the other hand, it is held, represents the great consensus of the nation because of its ability to respond to the special needs and pressures of a tremendous variety of Congressional districts in fifty states. Whether or not the President is unrepresentative and Congress representative depends of course on one's definition of democratic representation. Congress does tend to represent more of a consensus, though a consensus greatly distorted because of its overrepresentation of rural and conservative interests. The President does perhaps overrepresent the urban, liberal, labor, ethnic minority groups in the nation, both because of their sheer number and because of the winner-take-all impact of the Electoral College.

To attempt to resolve the question of the Presidency as a representative institution would take us beyond the confines of this essay. Actually, however, representation as viewed by the conventional wisdom is essentially irrelevant to the issue. The greatness of a President has not been his mirrorlike representation of the people but his responsibility to the future. The great Presidents, like Theodore Roosevelt with his conservation policies, or Woodrow Wilson with his belief in international organization, or Franklin Roosevelt with his dedication to Western unity against the Axis, or John Kennedy with his vision of a grand new design, have looked beyond immediate majorities to the place they would like to hold in history. Or perhaps they discerned that one way to achieve majorities in elections would be to keep an eye on the likely hindsight of history.

Our conventional thinking about the Presidency will be tested and challenged even more in the future than in the past, because of the tests that lie ahead. The simultaneous impact of heightened civil rights struggles at home and repeated cold war crises abroad, combined with our failure to resolve the Congressional deadlock, means that the Presidency will become more embattled than ever during the late 1960's. We have seen the White House turned into a command post during the two Cuban crises and during civil rights crises; we will see much more of this kind of thing during the remainder of the decade.

Because the Presidency cannot in the long run endure this kind of almost continual crisis, the President—some President —will eventually try, I foresee, to get a grip on his domestic problems at least, so that he can plan against the coming of crisis, instead of always having to cope with the fact of crisis. The great domestic demands on the Presidency in this decade— to the extent that he tries to anticipate crises—will be fiscal. The question will be, given a continuing stalemate in Congress, whether the President will be able to act out of some power of his own, or innovate some power of his own, that will enable him to plan against chronic crisis—for example, to carry out a successful war against poverty, and to take steps to tackle the economic and social malaise that lies at the root of the civil rights problem.

There are some omens of this kind of struggle. President Roosevelt told Congress during World War II to take a certain action in the fiscal field, and warned that otherwise he would— and Congress avoided a showdown. President Kennedy asked for authority to change tax rates within certain limits; Congress, of course, denied him this authority, but the question would be very acute in a recession. Lyndon B. Johnson favored civil rights legislation that would give the President the authority to with- hold Federal funds from any program or activity receiving Federal assistance directly or indirectly. Even if Congress should withdraw this authority at a later time, this is one situation where the President may have the whip hand. For, by custom, he has exercised the power not to spend money appropriated by Congress for certain projects (especially military). What if he should leave unspent money—let's say highway money—dearly wanted by the states pursuing segregationist policies or failing to cooperate with Federal civil rights measures?

The outcome may well be a power fight between Congress and the President, with each using its fiscal power to put pres- sure on the other branch. And such a fight would precipitate the gravest Constitutional struggle since the Civil War. The outcome of such a fight cannot be predicted. But one thing is clear. The more embattled the Presidency becomes in the years ahead, the more Americans will cling to it as their central in- strument for guarding national security and expanding the peo- ple's freedoms. But they can cling to this great engine of de- mocracy only if our modes of thought anticipate the pace of change rather than limping behind it.

Making Congress
Work

JOSEPH S. CLARK

THE President of the United States is a man who was generally acknowledged to be one of the most remarkable, colorful, and successful Congressional leaders of our time. Lyndon B. Johnson, as Majority Leader of the United States Senate, had brought the role of legislative leadership to its apex.

Yet, not four months after assuming the Presidency, Mr. Johnson had this colloquy with a reporter in a nationally televised interview:

QUESTION: Mr. President. . . . You have been around Washington thirty years. How is the view from the inside as compared with the view from the outside?
ANSWER: I have watched it since Mr. Hoover's days, and I realize[d] the responsibilities it carried and the obligations of leadership that were there, and the decisions that had to be made. . . . But I must say that when I started having to make those decisions and started hearing from the Congress, that the Presidency looked a little different when you are in the Presidency than it did when you are in the Congress, and vice versa.

That exchange sums up very succinctly the difference in point of view that generally and unfortunately prevails between Congress and the President. As the leader and symbol of what James MacGregor Burns has aptly dubbed the Congressional Party, Lyndon B. Johnson had one view; as the leader not of Congress but of the nation and the American people, President Johnson became the spokesman for what Burns calls the Presidential Party. The antagonism that has existed throughout our history between those two points of view—the Congressional and the Presidential—has resulted in a deadlock in our democracy, and distorted the balance of powers among our three branches of government which the Founding Fathers intended, and which our Constitution envisioned. The startlingly complex and difficult problems of the second half of the twentieth century demand that we resolve that deadlock, that we remedy Congressional hostility towards the Presidency. We must replace Congressional antagonism with cooperation, and debilitation with vitality. We must make Congress truly representative of the will of the American people. And we must make it possible for the majority to work its will in Congress.

Let me make it very clear that the object of Congressional reform is to strengthen the legislative branch, not to weaken it: to make of Congress not a rubber stamp for the President, but a co-equal partner in progress with the President.

Historically, strong Presidents have pulled us through: Jefferson, Jackson, Lincoln, the Roosevelts, Truman, and Kennedy. These men, and others—Wilson, for example, until he was too weak to fight Congress—used the office of the Presidency to the fullest extent possible in the crises they faced in order to deal successfully with problems Congress refused to face, or refused to resolve.

There is no better example than the history of events which led to the Civil War, Congressional recalcitrance and ineptitude of decades resulting in a tragic division resolved by one man stretching the powers of the Presidency to its outermost limits. But the question arises in our day whether we have not gone as far as we can go in our reliance on the President to muddle us through somehow, whether even so astute a man in dealing with Congress as Lyndon B. Johnson could cope with the problems of contemporary civilization successfully without revitalizing the legislative branch. I believe that he cannot; that no President can; that we have reached the point where fundamental questions of peace and disarmament, of population control, of our technological revolution, of the survival of our cities, of civil liberties cannot be resolved without the constructive help of Congress. The President cannot just go it alone.

What, then, must be done to permit the majority in Congress who are committed to the Presidential Party to prevail?

First, a complete re-examination of the rules, procedures, customs, and traditions of Congress, to update and modernize our governmental machinery.

Second, substantial reform of our national election laws, including Congressional reapportionment, campaign fund-raising and financing, and the Electoral College as well as the restoration of genuine two-party competition in our Congressional and Senatorial constituencies.

The first, which is internal or institutional reform, is long, long overdue, but not without precedent in Congressional history. The hallowed traditions and archaic customs of Congress have been revolted against many times and then modified— most recently in 1913; the supposedly sacrosanct rules and mystical procedures have been changed many times—most recently by the Congressional Reorganization Act of 1946. But the successful revolution against the prevailing Establishment led by Senator Kern in 1913 which made possible the enactment of Wilson's New Freedoms, and the reforms recommended by the La Follette-Monroney Committee which led to some improvements in 1946 were far from complete or long-lasting. Congressional reform is more urgent now than ever before.

The main objectives of internal Congressional reform are, specifically, four:

1. To change the party leadership structure so that within both parties and in both Houses a majority will decide party policy

and enforce party discipline.

2. To change the rules and procedures of both Houses so that a majority can act when it is ready to act.

3. To substitute cooperation for competition in the relations between the two Houses, and between Congress and the President, so that legislative recommendation of the President can be voted upon on their merits within a reasonable time after their submission to Congress.

4. To establish and enforce high ethical standards for Members of Congress and its employees.

Changes in the party structure within Congress do not generally require changes in the official Congressional rules of procedure. Just as our two-party political system is not defined in the Constitution, the party structure of Congress is not defined in the Rules of either body. This is the area where tradition, custom, unwritten law, and gentlemen's agreements hold sway —the inner workings of the Senate Democratic Steering Committee or the House Republican Policy Committee, the various party and leadership caucuses, conferences, and committees which constitute the party organization in Congress, and through which the parties make such basic decisions as party policy, legislative priorities, the ratio of one party to another on committees, seniority, and committee assignments. Each of the parties and each of the Houses has developed its own customs and traditions regarding these vital matters.

There is only a crude similarity in the inner structure of the two parties and between the two Houses. Committee assignments for Democratic Members of the House, for example, are made by the Democratic Members of the House Ways and Means Committee; but committee assignments for the Republicans are made by a special Committee on Committees. There is such a thing as a Joint Senate-House Republican Leadership Committee (it produces the Ev and Charley show), but the Democrats have no counterpart. Again, the Senate Democratic

Leadership decided—when Lyndon B. Johnson was Majority Leader—that each new Democratic Senator would be given at least one major committee assignment; the Republican Leadership to this day adheres to strict seniority, and Republican Senators have to work their way up to major committees.

In this jumble of party organization, some parts of the machinery work effectively and democratically, others do not work at all. The result, however, is control of the inner workings of the Congressional institution by a conservative bipartisan minority coalition that I have named the Congressional Establishment—the tight little band of men who, dedicated to the status quo, and determined to maintain their power and prerogatives, guard the citadel against the majority will and prevent Congressional reform.

Space does not permit here a detailed analysis of the way the party machinery is now used to keep the bipartisan conservative coalition in control of Congress,[1] but here, briefly, are some of the suggestions I have made for reform of the party structure:

Regular meeting days for the Democratic Conference of all Senators (the Republicans already do this), with a written agenda and written reports circulated in advance.

Party discipline to the extent that no Member of Congress who refuses to support the Party's Presidential candidate can participate in party conferences. No Congressman unwilling to support the national platform plank of his party in the area of jurisdiction of a particular committee should serve on that committee, much less be permitted to become its Chairman.

The assignment-making committees—the Senate Democratic Steering Committee particularly, which is the worst offender—should consist of members elected for two-year periods, nominated by the party leader but subject to confirmation by the party conference in a secret ballot, and representing a fair cross section of the ideological and geographical representation of the Party in Congress.

A complete overhaul of the policy committees of both parties in

[1] See *Congress: The Sapless Branch* by Joseph S. Clark, Harper and Row, New York, 1964.

both Houses, with the committees of the majority party in each House meeting with their opposite members to develop ways and means for enacting into law their party platform; conferring periodically with the President or his nominees for the purpose of carrying out his legislative program. The minority party policy committtees would also meet to determine their position on the legislative program of the majority, and confer with the President or his nominees on bi-partisan matters such as civil rights or foreign policy.

The next major requirement of Congressional reform is to make it easier for both bodies to act effectively when a majority is ready for action—to remove the obstacles to democracy while retaining adequate opportunity for careful consideration in committee and full debate on the floor of all bills under serious consideration. In the House the problem is not so difficult as in the Senate. Floor action is expeditious and needs no significant change, thanks to the reforms of 1910 when Speaker Joe Cannon was overthrown. The problem in the House is to pry loose from the legislative committees and the Rules Committee bills which are part of the President's program or which are desired by a clear majority of the House. The presently available techniques are inadequate and three methods which worked well in the past but were subsequently abandoned by the House Establishment should be reinstated. Unlike reform of the party structure, these recommendations require an actual change in the rules of the House:

The twenty-one-day rule should be re-enacted under which the chairman of a legislative committee could call up for action a bill within twenty-one days after his committee had reported favorably on it, if in the meanwhile the Rules Committee had failed to grant a rule.

The number of names required to release a bill from a legislative Committee refusing to report it out for consideration by the House should be decreased from 218, as at present, to 150, which was the rule from 1924 to 1935.

The Rules Committee should be deprived of the power to determine whether a bill shall go to a House-Senate conference if one

Member of the House objects on the floor to a motion to appoint conferees, leaving the decision to the whole House.

Reform of the Senate Rules is, in my judgment, more difficult and more urgently needed. For it is in the Senate that the notorious Rule XXII is in force—the rule governing the filibuster, which requires the affirmative vote of two-thirds of the Senators present forty-eight hours after a cloture petition to close off debate has been filed by sixteen Senators. The complications and ramifications of this rule are almost infinite. Instead of amending the rule so that debate can be shut off by a simple majority—as has been unsuccessfully attempted many times in the past—it would be wiser to abandon Rule XXII in its present form and reinstate the right to move the previous question as it once existed in the Senate and as it presently exists in the House and in most state legislatures. This motion is roughly the opposite of the motion to table which is often used in the Senate to end debate immediately without a vote on the merits. The previous-question motion, if carried, required an immediate vote on the merits of the pending bill or other pending business.

The most recent filibuster against the Civil Rights Act of 1964 is famous, the threat of one hangs over proposed legislation, requiring that it be watered down to suit the conservative coalition and frequently resulting in a failure to make a serious effort to pass it at all. It has been frequently and accurately said that the Senate is constantly legislating in the shadow of both the House Rules Committee and the filibuster.

As long ago as July 1960, I submitted to my Senate colleagues proposed changes in the rules of the Senate intended to make more efficient floor action possible, and to modernize our procedures. Some of them—dealing with obsolete technical matters used nowadays only for purposes of delay: requiring the reading of the journal each day unless it is dispensed with by unanimous consent, for example—are relatively unimportant. But most of them are necessary to permit the orderly dispatch of business.

Here, very briefly, are some suggestions I have made for reforming Senate Rules:

No Senator should hold the floor for more than two hours unless he is floor-managing a bill or unless he has unanimous consent of the Senate.

The Senate should adopt a bill requiring debate to be germane when legislation which the leadership wishes to expedite has been made the pending business. The recently adopted germaneness rule is limited to three hours each day, and has not worked in practice. No other legislative body in the civilized world, so far as I know, operates without a genuine rule of germaneness.

A motion to take up a bill reported by a Committee and on the Senate calendar should not be subject to debate when made by the majority leader, but should be voted on immediately. At present such a motion is subject to unlimited debate. Debate on such a motion during the Civil Rights filibuster of 1964 lasted from March 9th to March 30th.

Committees of the Senate should be permitted to meet while the Senate is in session unless a majority of the Senate votes otherwise on a motion, not subject to debate, to prevent such a meeting. At present committees may meet while the Senate is in session only by unanimous consent of the Senate. Thus the legislative mill in the Senate ground to a near halt during the 1964 Civil Rights filibuster.

A majority of the members of a Senate Committee meeting jointly in conference with its House counterpart to iron out the differences in the two versions of a piece of legislation passed by the separate bodies should be in sympathy with the Senate version of matters in disagreement with the House. At present, it sometimes happens that Senate representatives to a House-Senate Conference are not in sympathy with the Senate-passed version of the legislation and therefore find it difficult to argue the Senate's position against House disagreement. Obviously a majority of the Senate's conferees should be able to defend the Senate's position with conviction. You do it by selecting a majority of the membership of the conference committee from those Senators who voted to support the bill and those amendments which the Senate (or the House) adopted by roll call vote.

There are a number of reform proposals applicable to both House and Senate. The first of these, more important than at first appears, is to install electric voting machines in both houses, as has been done in many state and foreign legislatures. A good deal of precious time is lost in Congress answering roll calls: in the Senate each roll call takes fifteen to twenty minutes, in the House perhaps an hour. On a day when eight or ten roll call votes take place, anywhere from two to five hours of valuable time is wasted by the roll call procedure.

Another proposal which could save time and have a more direct bearing on creative legislative action would be to schedule joint hearings of House and Senate Committees on legislation pending in both houses whose consideration is desired by the administration and the leadership. This would eliminate at least one appearance, and possible more, of hard-pressed and overworked administration witnesses like the Secretary of Defense or Secretary of State, who sometimes spend half a month testifying on Capitol Hill. Joint hearings would be especially helpful on appropriations bills, military authorizations, and tax measures. Built-in tradition, not the Constitution, prevents such joint hearings.

A third new procedure which would pay off many times over would be the establishment of a Congressional schedule by the leadership of both parties in both houses in consultation with the President, including a week-by-week legislative calendar, specific deadlines for all appropriations bills, and a regular schedule for recesses and holidays. At present there is no order whatsoever, and very little planning, in the legislative schedule; it is all played by ear mostly according to the tune called by the senior standing committee chairman who is least likely to care whether a positive program of any kind, must less the President's program, is enacted.

It is true that in legal terms the committees of the House and the Senate are mere creatures and agents of their respective parent bodies. But in fact, many committees tend to act more like feudal principalities, "pickling" or indefinitely delaying major bills on which decisions are urgently desired by the President and by majorities in both houses.

What is needed is a procedure by which these majorities can enforce their will on recalcitrant committees. I have introduced in the Senate a proposed new rule by which a majority of Senators, after not more than eight hours of debate, could direct any standing committee in which a major legislative matter is pending to report that measure to the Senate within thirty calendar days, by poll or otherwise, with the recommendation (a) that it be passed, or (b) that it not be passed, or (c) that it be passed with amendments, stating the recommended amendments. A similar procedure ought to be adopted in the House.

When a committee is intent on doing its job, and not on delay, thirty days is ample time for holding exhaustive hearings and considering carefully even very complicated bills. Our national economy simply does not permit us to dawdle over a major Presidential economic proposal, for instance, for fourteen months. In that time, the conditions which the legislation was designed to meet may well be different, and probably worse. It is instructive, I think, that the British Parliament enacted the government's tax proposals in five weeks, while we took over a year to enact ours. I do not overlook the fact that we also drastically changed the President's proposals.

Finally, with regard to internal Congressional reform, there remain the two problems best known to the layman, and in many ways, the most difficult to resolve satisfactorily: the seniority system and Congressional ethics, including conflicts of interest.

It is usually said of the seniority system that the reason it has lasted so long is that despite its obvious drawbacks no one has come up with anything better to replace it, and to a certain extent that is true. The unwritten custom is that length of service in the House and Senate determines eligibility for appointment to committees, and that the member with the longest service on a committee succeeds automatically to a vacancy in the chairmanship. Actually, the latter half of that custom is more scrupulously observed than the former, as I have pointed out in a detailed study of the committee assignments made by the

Senate Democratic Steering Committee in 1963.[2]

Seniority was violated time and time again in assigning Committee seats. But it is the power of the usually elderly, usually conservative, and frequently Southern Committee Chairman that has attracted most adverse comment.

It is not so much the seniority system itself which is at fault but the failure to exercise party discipline in a manner which would require chairmen either to conform to the platform of their party in the area of the committee's jurisdiction—as I noted a moment ago—or resign and seek service on another committee. Thus the remedy to the obstructionism and hostility of Committee chairmen toward the President's program is not to eliminate seniority, but to restrain it by invoking party discipline. Additionally, committee vacancies should be filled, regardless of seniority, with men known to be in sympathy with party policy and well versed in the area of the committee's jurisdiction. A third reform to curb the evil effects of seniority would be to provide by rule that the chairman of all standing committees be elected at the beginning of each Congress by secret ballot of the majority members of the committee. In nine cases out of ten, I believe seniority would prevail, but the tenth case might be crucial, and in the other nine the chairman would obviously bend over backward to be fair in order to minimize opposition. Finally, the autocratic power of arbitrary action now held by many Committee chairmen should be curbed by what I have called a "Committee Bill of Rights." This would provide that a majority of members of a committee would convene meetings, fix an agenda, call up bills for consideration, terminate hearings and Committee consideration, and report bills to the floor. With such a committee bill of rights the Senate Judiciary Committee might not have remained the graveyard of civil rights legislation for so many years.

Public suspicion of Congressional integrity, always smoldering, was fanned into flame in the fall of 1963 by revelations

[2] See *The Senate Establishment*, Joseph S. Clark and Other Senators, Hill and Wang, New York, 1963.

surrounding the financial transactions of Bobby Baker, one-time secretary to the Senate majority, and of Representative John Byrnes of Wisconsin. Despite the widely publicized "Bobby Baker hearings," there has been a good deal of resistance among Members of Congress to passage of "disclosure of possible conflict of interest" legislation, and no more than a dozen Senators have made voluntary public disclosure of their financial holdings. Perhaps the time will come when some kind of resolution, applicable at least to the Senate and its employees, regarding possible conflicts of interest between public duty and private gain can be passed; but the time is not yet. I believe a public airing of private financial holdings and the professional connections of Members of Congress and its executive staff, and a public record of contacts between Congressional offices and the Executive branch on behalf of themselves, their friends, or their constituents is long overdue. I shall continue to press for such legislation in the Rules Committee.

These, then, are the outlines of what Congress must do by way of internal reform to make it possible to make Congress once again a constructive, coequal partner of the Executive and Judicial branches of the Federal government. Congress itself has the power, if not yet the will, to make them.

There is still, however, the problem of assuring that Congress truly represents the majority will of the American people as expressed in national elections. There is reason to believe that today it does not.

The relationship between our political system and the organization, rules, customs, and procedures of Congress is reciprocal. A change in one will very likely eventually produce changes in the other. Today's Congressional performance reflects the process by which its members are elected. Obviously, if there were more two-party districts and states, seniority would be of less consequence; at the same time if we could change the filibuster rule in the Senate and particularly now that we have passed effective voting-rights legislation for all Americans, those presently disenfranchised in the South would revolutionize politics in that region and bring to an end one-party domination of the kind we now have. The election of six conservative Republicans from Alabama and Mississippi is a start in this direction.

External reform in the political process itself is necessary if we are to achieve majority rule both in Congress and in the country. For our principal problem is not, as some maintain, that our system occasionally produces a President of one party and a Congress of another. That is bad enough; but the major problem is rather that the political process results in a continuing and nearly irreconcilable conflict between any Congress and any President, regardless of the nominal partisan composition of the Congress.

The reason is that the Congress and the President are nominated and elected by different processes which produce different results. In one, national considerations predominate; in the other, local considerations. Most presidential candidates are inevitably oriented toward the urban, industrial, international, activist, minority-group position; Senator Goldwater was the exception whose defeat proved the rule. Congress is in all too many cases oriented toward the small-town, pastoral, isolationist, conservative, Bible-belt perspective. And while it has been much noted in recent years that the President can be and usually is elected by the large, industrial states with the prize electoral votes, it is insufficiently noticed that in the last seven Congressional elections an average of less than a hundred House seats changed hands. Thus, while the Presidency is a hotly-contested and sometimes close election, the House remains pretty much the same no matter who is elected President.

The "Congressional Party" thus forms the bipartisan conservative coalition representing one-party districts from both parties. It remained a powerful roadblock to progress in Congress after the country elected a John F. Kennedy President to get the country moving again. Congress sat on most of my legislative programs for three years. The foundation of our two-party system is competition, but it is sorely lacking in most Congressional districts, not just in the South alone. Recent decisions of the Supreme Court in reapportionment cases affecting both the state legislatures and Congress will help somewhat in this area.

The subject of money in politics is, to say the least, difficult. With the coming of television and the increase in the number of voters, campaigns have become fantastically expensive. There is general agreement that some method must be found for securing mass financial support for political candidates. The pernicious consequences of reliance on a few wealthy contributors for large donations are obvious.

In April, 1962, the Presidential Commission on Campaign Costs recommended major changes in our laws dealing with political fund-raising. They suggested that for a trial period—two presidential elections—political contributors should be given a credit against their Federal income tax of 50 percent of their contribution up to $10 or alternatively to claim up to $1,000 in contributions as a deductible item. This would apply only to those gifts made to the national party committees or state organizations designated by them.

These proposals are sound. Tax credit is a better way of securing broad-based mass financial support than a tax deduction (which the Senate Finance Committee recommended in 1963) because it is useful to everyone in all tax brackets, whereas a deduction is useful only to those relatively wealthy taxpayers who file a detailed tax return. Perhaps more significant is the Commission's recommendation that the money be disbursed through National and State Committees, for this would substitute national for local control of the parties' financial efforts and concern and should help to elevate politics in the national scale of values.

Since it is desirable to bring Presidential and Congressional politics closer together, it would be wise to have the terms of Congressmen and Senators coincide with that of the President. The forces of national purpose as opposed to parochialism, the forces of democracy as opposed to oligarchy and plutocracy, and the ability of the President to obtain enactment of the platform on which he ran and was elected would all be strengthened if elections to both the House and Senate were held only in Presidential years. This could be accomplished by a Constitutional amendment increasing the terms of Representatives to four years, decreasing the terms of Senators to four years and eliminating mid-term Congressional elections, thus calling for the election of the entire Senate at the time of each Presidential election.

Some critics of our political system—those who like to point out that under the electoral system we use in Presidential elections John F. Kennedy could have been elected President even if Richard M. Nixon had received more popular votes—periodically ask why we don't do something about our antiquated Electoral College. It is true that under the present system a President can be elected by far less than a majority by carrying a few populous states by a very small majority while losing the smaller states by a landslide. But the efforts to tinker with the Electoral College in recent years have almost invariably reflected the philosophy of the repairmen. Little sentiment has been expressed for what seems the most obvious way to settle the issue: abandon the Electoral College altogether and elect the President by direct national popular vote without regard to state lines. If the President is to represent the nation as a whole, why should he not be elected by the nation as a whole? The major problems of our day, from foreign policy to education to the state of the economy—are national issues, and these are the issues of the Presidential campaign. But at present there is no consensus in Congress or in the country for that or any other solution to the problem of the Electoral College. There seems little chance of reform in the foreseeable future. This should not preclude appropriate steps by each state, however, to insure that the decision of the electorate in that state is faithfully reflected by the presidential electors. There is no excuse today for the "unpledged" election.

Basic to all attempts at electoral reform is the need to remove arbitrary restraints on the right to vote. Voting participation is unusually low in the United States, partly at least because of these restraints. The most serious, of course, is the discrimination practiced against the Negro voter in the South. The civil rights legislation of 1957 and 1960 has already helped. The 1964 act will help more, but there are also a good many other obstacles to voting which, taken together, effectively disenfranchise millions of Americans in today's highly mobile population. About eight million Americans could not vote in the last Presidential elections, for example, because they could not meet local and state residence requirements. Much could be done at the local and state level to eliminate these unnecessary barriers. The time has surely come, nevertheless, for the nation itself to define the right to vote in national elections and to protect that right with appropriate means, either by legislation or by constitutional amendment. The right to vote is so central to the success of our Federal government that to deny the power to establish the qualifications for exercising it is to deny that government the means of maintaining its own integrity.

One final political reform that needs also to be extended is the elimination of political patronage at all levels of government. The case for a merit system for government employees hardly needs further argument. But the unhealthy relationship of the patronage-staffed political machine to the political system itself is sometimes overlooked. By relying on tangible economic rewards—jobs—to create a corps of the faithful large enough to produce victory at the polls, the machine extorts tribute from government, subordinates issues, and debases the political process. It also strengthens the worst elements in the political system by subordinating a mayor's appointive power to a ward leader, a governor's to a county leader, and even a President's to a Representative or Senator. Does it make any sense at all, for example, to have the United States Senate confirm each year thousands of Postmasters?

Those of us who are attempting to improve our political system, to restore our Congress to health, to make it possible for our government to perform effectively and democratically in a world of unprecedented danger must have the support of an aroused public opinion if we are to succeed. No such irresistible popular demand for the comprehensive reforms and drastic changes which I have lightly touched on here exists today. Yet, there are signs that the public is stirring, and that the ineptitude which marked the performance of Congress in 1963, and the famous filibuster over civil rights in 1964, did not go unnoticed. In time, and perhaps sooner than it now appears, I believe the sense of national purpose of the American people will provide the will to break the pattern of the national legislature as it operates today. Already the Senate has begun tinkering with its rules, toying with notions of germaneness, considering the problem of Congressional ethics. This is just a beginning, to be sure. We may hope that the political leaders of this generation, responding to an aroused public opinion, will before it is too late pass those measures and take those steps for reform which are essential to the life of Congress, and hence to the Republic.

The Case
of the Ailing Unions

NEIL W. CHAMBERLAIN

Labor unions today are admittedly—that is, admitted by everyone except themselves—in poor health, but there is disagreement among the diagnosticians as to whether the difficulty is simply tired blood or whether they are seriously ill or even dying. The argument presented here is that their problem is not constitutional but institutional, not organic but organizational. They are a species whose behavior patterns have been so firmly fixed by past environmental conditioning that their capabilities of adapting to new circumstances have become severely limited. The challenge which they face is Darwinian, but they continue to react as though it were the N.A.M.

The unions have been subjected to so much criticism in recent years that, bitterly, they now put quotation marks around those whom they call their friends. But their inability to recognize that some of the criticisms are indeed well-intentioned, and that the suggestions for remedial action which sometimes accompany the appraisal are at least worth considering in the same way that a consultant's recommendations warrant consideration, is additional evidence of their institutional rigidity. They are remarkably thin-skinned and sensitive. Their feelings are as fragile as those of an old maid, except that when offended they break into bluster rather than tears. Few groups on the American scene are as unwilling to engage in self-examination and introspection.

But having said all this, and before launching into a bill of particulars, let me add that there are special reasons why this should be so, and that we would be less than fair to the unions if we did not take a few lines to remind ourselves of how deep go their roots and why change is peculiarly difficult for them.

We sometimes talk as though labor unions in the United States were largely a product of the New Deal-sponsored Wagner Act, recent arrivals on the American scene. In a more fundamental sense they are an offspring of two revolutionary parents—the eighteenth-century political revolutions which established the principle of democratic representation, and the nineteenth-century industrial revolution which created centers of work apart from the household of either the worker or a master, where increasingly large numbers of people were employed. Given large-scale industrial operations, on the one hand, and the representative principle, on the other (the latter more firmly established in this country at an earlier period than in Europe), the conception of industrial democracy was almost predictable.

But at this point special conditioning factors, unique to this country, make themselves felt. There is no need to develop here any catalogue of reasons why the United States has not produced a political labor movement, but two deserve mention. One was the strong ideological insistence on individualism and self-reliance, and its counterpart of a limited role for government to play. The other was the fragmentation of political power in the United States, dispersed among Federal, state, and local governments, with emphasis on home rule. Under the circumstances, and with product and labor markets expanding to a national scale, unions found little payoff in politics and concentrated their efforts on an institution which was more directly subject to their control, collective bargaining.

Collective bargaining, in turn, took form under this special conditioning. It became the private law-making process in industry, dealing with subject matter which in Europe often came under the purview of legislatures. It created its own legislation and codes of laws—but only for a particular company or less commonly, a particular industry. Dealing with special rather than general circumstances, it elaborated the rules which were to govern the rights of its members in their workplaces into documents which got longer and longer, and now in some instances run to several hundred pages. And borrowing from the common-law approach of its English antecedents, these private bodies of law were interpreted and applied in the light of custom and precedent. With the spread of private arbitration as the means of enforcing and applying the body of rules, "past practice" became the arbitrator's guide.

The development of unionism and collective bargaining in the United States thus has roots in some of the most fundamental principles of the culture. Institutionally they have been shaped by such concepts as representative government, the primacy of private over governmental economic decision-making, reliance on precisely worded written private law, and the use of the common-law basis of precedent both in the application of the written rule and in some circumstances not specifically covered by written rule.

The form which has been cast from molds like these is not easy to reshape. The unions and their primary instrument, collective bargaining, embody too much highly valued historical principle to change their behavioral contours very readily. Therein lies their weakness, their brittleness. Their environment has changed, and changed rather fundamentally, but their form and functioning remain rigidly the same. I exaggerate, but the exaggeration is intended to lay bare the problem and not to obscure it.

In countries where labor unions have been more preoccupied with political activity, they have often been cast in the role of revolutionary or radical agents, in some instances making political alliance with such avowedly change-seeking groups as the Communists. But in the United States, where the focus of union activity has been the shop and the company, and where the union has been party to *private* legislative processes in the form of collective bargaining, its outlook has been more conservative than revolutionary. Lacking an effective political arm, it has had relatively little interest in reforming the society which has—finally—made a place for it. The reforms which have primarily concerned it have been internal to the firm, affecting managerial discretion. In particular, it has sought to create job security for its members by a variety of rules and work practices concerning work assignments, job content, crew composition, the pace of operations, and so on. This preoccupation with work practices—*past* practices—has made it a technologically conservative institution, in addition to its political conservatism.

But this philosophy was workable only as long as society was not subjected to the strains of rapid economic change. A formula of conservatism is feasible as long as change comes at a manageable pace, so that there is time for adjustment. But in the post-World War II period change has been coming at an accelerated rate, and the effect has been largely to nullify the unions' reliance on collective bargaining to provide job security for their members, while leaving them still without effective means of political action to secure remedies on a broader front. The unions have thus been stripped of much of their power— not by any concerted anti-union action on the part of employers, though one might think so to listen to labor leaders haranguing their memberships as they cast about for some one or some thing to blame for the state in which they find themselves. The Delilah which has shorn them of their strength is a social phenomenon (which, parenthetically, threatens the security of managements too), namely, the quickened rate with which new scientific, technological, and organizational knowledge is being accumulated and applied.

The phenomenon is frequently summed up in the term "automation," which has become simply a verbal symbol for a much more complicated process which has been labeled by others the "explosion of knowledge" or the "knowledge revolution." We need not explore here the nature and causes of this development. For present purposes, we are interested only in the fact that it has thrust on our private economic institutions a greater *necessity* for creating and initiating new products and new processes than they have known in the past.

With new knowledge being produced in an ever-expanding number of institutions, and with knowledge—once "out" and known—almost certain of being applied somewhere by someone (one's competitors?), the pressure on management to keep current with the latest developments has become irresistible. As a matter of corporate survival, a firm cannot fall behind its rivals and potential rivals either in new products or new processes. The assets which today it manages will continue to have value tomorrow only if they are constantly updated and supplemented. No wonder there has been more emphasis in recent years on accelerated depreciation. The value of current assets must be released—made liquid again—rapidly, before it has been lost through accelerated obsolescence. Thus change—the more rapid introduction of new ways—has become a condition of corporate survival.

The agitation of unionists over the impact of change—"automation," to use the short title which they give it—is understandable. The old job-security provisions of collective bargaining have little value when a firm sells off a whole plant so that it can build—usually elsewhere—a brand-new plant, with the latest processes. Such devices as seniority cease to provide meaningful security when the introduction of automatic equipment cuts in half the number of workers who are needed, or requires new skills which the older employees cannot offer. Union by union, or company by company, one could compile an extensive catalogue of technological changes which have taken place or are about to take place on a scale sufficient to negate the kinds of protective clauses which unions have written into their collective agreements. The conservative emphasis on past practice is little protection when whole processes to which past practice was relevant are swept out to make way for something wholly new.

As yet, the extent of such changes—which some people have dramatized by dubbing it the second industrial revolution—is nothing compared with what looms on the horizon. In particular, we can confidently expect that the computer holds out a likelihood of such extensive application—in small operations as well as large—as to make its current uses only the earliest tentative stages of an evolution which has a long way to go. The social and economic implications of this development are likely to be so fundamental as to make concern over the impact on the labor unions seem like a parochial preoccupation—as we look back from the vantage point of the year 2000, say. But at this point in time this is one of the most immediate consequences, and the subject of our attention in this essay.

Simply stated, the magnitude of the changes which are being introduced into our economic and industrial relations at a pace which is still mounting, even if it cannot be forever maintained, has created a new state of job insecurity. The old private legislative processes of collective bargaining, while not totally ineffective under such circumstances, have lost a large part of their significances. They can no longer provide workers job security by a network of rules and practices which look to the past. And at the same time the unions have not developed any political strength to seek the more radical solutions which the circumstances of our times may require, via public legislative action. The unions thus are playing a role of constantly dwindling importance.

They will always have a role to play, to be sure. As long as some union members are employed on some job, the unions can act as a representative in dealing with management on their behalf. But their function is more temporary and less comprehensive. It is not an antagonistic management which is the cause of their decline, with whom they can again do battle and perhaps win; it is a social phenomenon which is as compulsive on management as on the unions.

In this kind of a situation, the unions themselves stand in

need of radical changes, but the changes which are needed are probably not so compulsive but that they can be resisted, even if that means the enfeeblement of the labor institutions.

First, it would appear that if labor is to be effective in the changing economic order it must create a more unified and more sharply focused political instrument—not necessarily and not even *desirably* a labor party. But if automation—and new knowledge generally—is to be an economic blessing, some rather basic changes in economic society are called for. It is time that some further thought went into the whole question of income distribution, for example—serious, analytical thought, not the soapbox utterances which union spokesmen and sympathizers have been given to. The stale debate between the desirability of private or public expenditures to sustain full employment needs to give way to well-conceived and operational programs making use of both, sufficiently clear-cut to rally public support and be made the object of organized political pressures.

Perhaps as important as anything, the place of education in our society needs extensive re-examination, so that individuals—workers and managers both—do not confront the fact, in their prime, that they no longer possess an adequate knowledge or usable experience on which to project a continuing career development. In the earliest days of labor unions in this country, at a time when they were still politically oriented (though on a municipal and state basis), they constituted one of the major influences in the establishment of public school systems—a magnificent achievement. The time has come when unions again should join forces with others in pushing as vigorously for the overhaul of our educational system to make it a continuing resource throughout the lifetime of every individual, whatever his economic position.

The likelihood that American labor unions will convert themselves into an effective political organization, pressing for a few major social and economic reforms (rather than passing conventional "resolutions" on every aspect of modern society) is not very great. The labor unions in this country, as we have already noted, were molded into institutions representing the particularistic interests of their memberships, along individual company lines. Each union has acquired "organizational autonomy," and the officials of each union are custodians of the strength and power of that union, looking to its perpetuation and growth. Everything which stresses the importance of the functions which the union has been conditioned to perform (collective bargaining) enhances its own greatness. Anything which emphasizes a role which the union is incapable of discharging (institutional reform through political action) undermines its organizational autonomy. It would probably take little short of a threatened collapse of unionism all along the line to induce these particularistic enclaves to create a new and politically oriented institution in which they would play only a submerged role.

What then can unions do if they insist on continuing to concentrate their efforts on collective bargaining, as they have done in the past? Are there internal adjustments which they can make which will increase their effectiveness even in the face of accelerated change? Of course there are.

For one thing, unions must learn that they too, just like business firms, are the managers of assets. In their case, the assets are the skills of their members. Just as business management must be alert to upgrading its physical assets, converting and supplementing them by reinvestment and net new investment *before* they have lost their value, so must union management come to a realization that in the "explosion" of knowledge and its applications, which is bursting all around them, they too must be alert to the improvement and supplementation of the skill assets of their members, in order to maintain and enhance their employability, and long before the loss of a job drives members into frantic and often misguided "retraining" programs aimed at some specific occupation. If a worker's skill value is to be kept high he must have the opportunity of acquiring significant new knowledge *before* the knowledge he has has lost its value.

This calls for quite new kinds of bargaining programs. It would suggest, for example, that unions should make more extensive use of educational advisors and consultants to frame formal, systematic programs dealing with the new technologies and their scientific base, and with the verbal and mathematical skills which they require, offered perhaps on a community basis, or on the company premises, or in programs organized at nearby colleges. Paid time off could be bargained for—a day a week, a week a month, three months every few years, or even a year of formal study at periodic intervals. Such programs would be expensive. They need careful planning, hard bargaining, and perhaps—in view of the current primitive state of the bargaining arts—even strikes to win management acceptance.

The old-line bargaining for a few cents more an hour, carried on as though the union membership were at a poverty level where a few cents was the margin of survival, is obsolete. In terms of straight economic gain to the membership it cannot compare with bargaining programs for upgrading worker skills so that they become more productive, can advance farther along a career line.

To be sure, such programs would run smack into the particularistic nature of American unions once again, since in given circumstances skill training might be indicated which would carry the member outside the union's jurisdiction, raising the double problem of whether the union would want to assist in a process of dispersing its membership and whether the members so trained could find satisfactory entrance into other jurisdictions presided over by unions seeking to conserve opportunities for their own present memberships. But perhaps such jurisdictional problems—symbols of a passing era—could at least be partially met by treaties negotiated between unions, and perhaps in time by merger.

If unions are to become more effective managers of their members' skill assets, this will probably call for a professional kind of management which may not be wholly compatible with the democratic forms of present union political life. Unions have often been criticized for depriving their memberships of the rights of democratic participation in union government. The charge is justified only if one makes the highly debatable assumption that the *functions* which unions are set up to perform, and which are their only reason for existence, can be satisfactorily performed in a town-meeting atmosphere. It may well prove to be the case that effective representation requires a different form of union government, and as long as some accountability of union leadership to the membership is preserved this may be all that one can reasonably expect. Is there really any basis for a double standard as between business and union institutions?

A more professional management of the unions might well consider whether there are not more effective means of mobilizing bargaining power than by the antiquated instrument of the strike, with all the mythology which attends that institution. The "voluntary" nature of the agreement, which the right to strike presumably preserves, is dubious at best in the coercive atmosphere which a strike inevitably produces. Strikes have often been likened to the military phase of union-management policy-making, but few would maintain today that war preserves the voluntary nature of the treaty or agreement which brings peace. What is clearly wanted is an instrument for private decision-making, in contrast to an imposed public settlement, and this the parties should be able to devise for themselves, along lines which still permit the marshaling of bargaining power but which give greater promise of a reasoned settlement.

Finally, we must realize that the impact of accelerated change will not be borne by the unions alone. It is a whole system of economic, social, and political relationships which are being subjected to stress. The behavior patterns of business and the administration and objectives of governmental units are likewise forced to stand the tests of relevance and adequacy in our brave new world, in which the period permitted for adjustment, even to sweeping changes, has been so attenuated.

Labor
in Perspective

EDWARD D. HOLLANDER

I

WHEN militant industrial unionism burst on the American scene in the late 1930's, to many it seemed like the dawn of a new era. Liberals, so long without a political base, envious of the European labor parties and despairing of the American labor movement, suddenly and delightedly found themselves partners in a coalition whose leaders were the labor activists and whose followers numbered in the millions. Those were passionate and glorious days of victories in the courts and at the polls. They were also grim and dangerous days, of strikes and sitdowns, court battles and street battles, even massacres. The labor movement was proudly class-conscious, and the liberals were exhilarated to be allies in the crusading army.

Now, thirty years later, the labor movement is on the defensive, divided within itself, uncertain of its place and its power and even of its future in a world of bewildering change. Some of its old friends who then romantically could see no wrong in it as they basked vicariously in its glory now detach themselves dyspeptically from imperfections they themselves hasten to reveal. Many who should be its young friends see it as a bastion of racial discrimination and an obstacle to civil rights; they have forgotten, if they ever knew, how much they owe it. Politicians ask themselves if they can trust their future to its power at the polls and become correspondingly circumspect on "labor issues."

What has happened to the labor movement as a force in American life? Is it, as some say, ailing? Has the fire gone out of it? Has it become so professionalized and bureaucratic that it has lost touch with its members and with the American community? Is it to become a trustee in bankruptcy for an era that is passing or past? These are questions it has become fashionable to ask, as though "the labor movement" were something self-contained and separate, an institutional zoo in American life.

Actually, the labor movement is neither more nor less than a part of the American community, and any view of it out of this context of place and time is certain to be distorted. Except for brief bursts when it is fired by confrontation with a "class enemy"—like the recalcitrant industrial die-hards of the Liberty League in the late 1930's—it is not class-conscious. Present-day unionists are not so much a "movement" as a lobby. Their working-class politics have been swallowed up in the Democratic Party, and their mutual-aid societies in the United Givers Funds. They are not a "proletariat"; their sons and daughters may as well be clerks or school teachers as factory workers or waitresses. Like other Americans they are preoccupied with getting and spending, with security and comfort, with debt and taxes. They partake of the general hopes and the general fears. (One militant labor leader was heard recently to complain: "How can I get my Wage Policy Committee to approve wage demands when they ask me, 'But what will happen to the balance of payments if the companies push prices up?' ")

"What is wrong (and what is right) with the labor movement" is neither more nor less than what is wrong or right with all of us. Union members are decent, reasonable, idealistic folk, like most Americans; they can, when the occasion demands, rise to the same heights of courage and sacrifice. But they can also, on occasion, be lulled by complacency, pricked by anxiety or panicked by fear, exactly like the rest of us. Given reasonable security and serenity, they are responsive and generous; but if their livelihood is threatened, they react to its defense neither less nor more intelligently or foresightedly than anyone else, whether the threat is from a machine, an import, or a Negro. They will yield voluntarily to the broader public interest as much as other Americans, as willingly or as grudgingly, and they will require as much to be forced, by law or by custom. They will contrive, or connive, to support or enhance their incomes as much as business men, doctors, farmers, using like these, what means are at hand or permitted. No more, no less.

II

The militancy waned in the labor movement when it waned in the rest of us. Two immediate post-World War II events are convenient symbols. The unions, after having been in the main current of American politics through the New Deal and the War, suffered their first jolting political setback when they could not muster one-third of either House of Congress to prevent passage of the Taft-Hartley Act over President Truman's veto in 1947. Taft-Hartley was not the "slave labor act" which the unions called it in a political hyperbole (though it placed restraints on the unions' growth and effectiveness), but its passage introduced a period in which labor has been, and is, politically on the defensive. It has been a period in which American business regained the political initiative (lost in the fiasco of anti-New Deal intransigence) with charges of "labor monopoly," "denying workers the right to work" and similar sloganized appeals to middle-class America. To these were later added the indictment of the unions for responsibility for "inflation," as prices and wages leapfrogged in round after round in the late 1940's and early 1950's. This campaign reached a political climax in a remarkable broadcast by President Eisenhower, pleading for passage of the Landrum-Griffin Act in 1959—the most naked anti-labor expression of an American President in a quarter-century. The unions have been fighting an uphill battle in politics and public relations to this day. "Big labor" has won few political victories, and those mostly defensive, since World War II.

Another postwar sign was the remarkable contract between the United Auto Workers and General Motors in 1948, in the aftermath of a wave of bitter strikes. GM offered and the unions accepted a contract providing automatic annual increases geared to the rising standard of living, plus automatic adjustment to the cost of living, in return for no strikes. By the time this contract was renewed in 1950 for an unprecedented five years, it had set a new mode for big industries and many small ones. Collective bargaining became more and more businesslike, highly technical, and professionalized in the hands of leaders, lawyers, and staff. The union members are about as much involved as stockholders. Though both sides growl ritualistically in courtship maneuvers, sometimes very prolonged and even including strikes, the object for both (as GM said in 1948) is "to make cars and make money." With the possible exception of the 1959 steel strike and the 1963 New York City newspaper strike, there has hardly been an embattled strike since.

This is partly because collective bargaining has become tripartite: the Government is always a tacit partner in important negotiations and an active one when the public interest demands it. Many of the features in today's labor-management relations are remodeled from the War Labor Board. The Government has not hesitated to intervene in various ways to prevent head-on collisions, by lubricating mediation, face-saving formulas, or even legislation to provide a framework for settlement. This is not new: a railroad strike was averted in 1916 by an Act of Congress prescribing an eight-hour day. Today the Taft-Hartley Act provides legal procedures for enjoining strikes if they threaten the public health and safety (a phrase that has been stretched to end strikes only remotely affecting health and safety). The Government has recognized the principle of the UAW-GM contract in "guideposts" for wage and price behavior to prevent price increases and tailor wages to the increases in efficiency of the economy. If the unions and management were willing to accept the Government guideposts, the effect would be to freeze present wage-profit relationships. Although neither labor nor management is willing to accept, both are self-conscious about departing from the guideposts and quick to blame each other. Industrial relations have become more and more like business transactions.

III

In the face of this, the solid and unique contribution of the labor movement to American democracy over the past quarter-century is too easily taken for granted. To appreciate just how great it has been one has only to imagine what would have been lost without it. It was the labor movement that brought American industrial relations out of the jungle warfare that persisted as late as the 1920's. It was at the unions' insistence that grievance machinery was introduced to keep the peace, to rationalize efficiency and protect the rights and dignity of workers from the petty tyranny in the lower ranks of management hierarchs. It was in this way that workers came to accept efficiency because they could share in its rewards and to cooperate in expanding production. (There are many who can recall today the willful acts of sabotage of products by which workers expressed their resentment and frustration before unions provided a means of venting and correcting them.) The processes of collective bargaining have been a powerful force in rationalizing the structure of wages, and the benefits have spread widely through the economy beyond the unionized segments. (By contrast, Southern resistance to unions has prolonged the impoverishment of the South and left it, even after a generation of industrialization, still the seedbed of poverty from which FDR set out to rescue it.)

If it has not always been the crusading force that some hoped for it, as an institution the labor movement has borne more than its share of responsibility for the quality of American society. In politics, in legislation, in standards of leadership, and accountability, the record of the unions bears scrutiny at least as well as, say, business management, and political parties—I would say much better. In the scale from leaders to laggards in social progress, the labor movement certainly ranks with the far-sighted in its advocacy of reforms which politicians have been slow to accept and business has continued to resist even after the fact: not only bread-and-butter matters like labor-relations legislation and minimum wages but benefits for the community at large, such as housing, urban renewal—yes, and specifically civil rights. (Let it not be forgotten that in the long years before the Negro community rose in its own behalf, the civil rights movement depended heavily on a few unions and their articulate and dedicated leaders.) In their pension plans, unemployment benefits, and health services (all obtained through collective bargaining), the unions have pioneered in welfare and health services with standards which the rest of the community has yet to reach.

This brief recital is not offered as a "defense" of labor but as prelude to the question: In the light of its history and its nature, is the labor movement composed and equipped for its role in the years ahead? And what is that role? These are valid questions to ask, as much of the labor movement as of our enterprise economy, our political system, and our society itself.

The most difficult role of the unions will be as trustee and protector of workers' interests—short-range as well as long—in the galloping technological changes that are taking place. In one sense, this is nothing new: for decades unions have been adapting to the short-term dislocations that followed from changes in processes and products, recognizing the long-term benefits to come. If some of the adaptations have been clumsy and a few downright absurd, for the most part labor has been a partner in the steady increase in productivity (that is, output per worker) and the consequent increase in wages and living standards. This, in fact, has been one of the unions' principal contributions to the American economy, notwithstanding the legend of "featherbedding" that has been built around the exceptions. But even in industries which have been the butt of the horror stories of "featherbedding," increases in output per worker have been large and persistent: in the railroads, for example, approximately the same volume of work as in 1949 is being done by about forty percent fewer workers. The question now is not whether unions will accept technological change—they always have—but whether an extension of the same processes of adaptation through collective bargaining and collective rule-making will keep the effects of the "new industrial revolution" of automation manageable and tolerable to the workers and to the society as a whole.

If technology should raise productivity at a rate of five or six percent a year (about twice the historical rate in the American economy but no more than the recent experience in agriculture and some industries), at least three major innovations will be required. First, the destruction or obsolescence of skills and jobs will have to be recognized *explicitly* as a *cost* of technological progress and paid for by the economy like all other costs, not borne by individual workers. It is the responsibility of the unions to represent the workers in assuring that this cost is acknowledged, paid, and equitably borne through prices or through taxes. There is precedent for this: the railroad unions, for example, have established that certain railroad workers made redundant by change will be protected as individuals in their rights to income or to jobs until they retire, die or quit. This is not "featherbedding," perpetuated in work-rules or occupational custom to frustrate efficiency. It is payment of a nonrecurring obligation in recognition that the society which benefits by technological change shall bear its *full* costs.

Second, it will fall to the unions to take much broader responsibility for helping members adapt to the occupational demands of the new technology. For this also, the unions have precedent: in the early days they helped their immigrant members to "Americanize"; and more than a century ago they led the campaign for free public education. Their own programs of workers' education pioneered in adult education. Whether by company money, tax money, or dues money, they must see to it that their members are educated, trained, and, if necessary, resettled for the new jobs, whatever and wherever they may be.

Third, the unions are sternly obliged to lead an unceasing and uncompromising demand for full employment. Just as they were the main force in the campaign which made explicit the national Government's responsibility for the national economy in the Employment Act of 1946, the unions must now demand fulfillment of that responsibility. And this means now much more than is written into the Employment Act. It means the obligation on the Government to take whatever measures are required, radical as they may seem, to cope with the radical consequences that may ensue from the revolution of automation.

Labor's responsibility is double. The problems of technological displacement, difficult as they are at best, simply defy rational solution when there is not enough work to go around. If the excessive unemployment and underemployment of the past decade persist, the arena of collective bargaining will become smaller and the issues more bitter. The unions will find themselves in the impossible and thankless position of trying to protect American workers (the union-resistant white-collar class no less than the blue-collar) by unworkable, unpopular, and uneconomic devices; not only drastically reduced work weeks, enforced vacations and premature retirement, but other devices, however bizarre, to share too little work in an economy that cries for more production and more consumption and an end to poverty. Shorter hours, paid vacations, and adequate retirement have been welcome benefits which labor has realized from rising productivity of the economy. To pervert these goals by using them as devices for sharing the work would frustrate the productivity on which progress depends. The unions do battle not for their members alone but for all of us. If we do not support them in the demand for full employment, let us not be surprised or indignant at share-the-work and share-the-income alternatives.

This double obligation is nothing new to the unions. They had their origins at a working-class lobby in the days when union activity and union leadership were often a short cut to jail. Now that "the working class" is tinged with middle class, too many unions and their leaders have forgotten, like the rest of us. If the unions want to regain the place they once held in American values and ideology, they will need to demonstrate once again that they are the champions of every reform that is necessary to restore the quality of American life. They must be the spokesmen for the one-third of Americans at the bottom of the economic scale, the lobby for the poor, the defenders of the oppressed. They must fight the battles of the defenseless—the workers outside the protection of minimum wages, the migrant farm laborers, the unemployed, the aged, the slum-dwellers on relief.

They must demand and practice respect for civil rights, as the best of them do now. They must mobilize their members— except for the churches, the largest reachable bloc in the American community—to demand the political reforms from courthouse to Capitol necessary to make our governments responsive and responsible. They must demand the quality of education to which they and all of us are entitled. They must force action to clean up our cities and build the homes necessary to depopulate the slums (incidentally, a path to more employment than we have seen since World War II). Anyone looking for a blueprint of responsible unionism can find it in the program Walter Reuther presented in his testimony to Congress on the war against poverty.

This program is one of the heartening signs that the unions are aware of the duties they are called to perform and that they are rousing themselves from the complacency and passivity in which they have drifted with the rest of the body politic. If they neglect these duties, they will appear as the wage-earners' equivalent of the N.A.M. or the A.M.A., and they will remain on the defensive. If in their preoccupation with the narrower issues they slight the broader ones, they will be suspected by voters, brushed off by politicians, and despaired of by liberals. In shedding their class consciousness, they must gain a consciousness of the role that will restore their honored place in mid-century America.

Antitrust in
the Age of Planning

LOUIS B. SCHWARTZ

THE United States is an underdeveloped country which must increasingly resort to national planning to achieve its goals. The antitrust laws are essentially an affirmation of the desirability of what might be called "planlessness," that is, free development of private business subject to the discipline of competition but without centralized direction either by the government or by monopolies and cartels. What is the future of antitrust in an age of planning? To answer this question we must reflect upon the necessity for certain kinds of national planning, and upon the continuing validity of the principle of designed planlessness in some sectors of the economy.

I

The United States is an underdeveloped country. That is, its legitimate aspirations and national commitments vastly exceed available resources. The ratio of American aspirations to resources—and this is the meaningful index of underdevelopment in the political and psychological sense—may be higher in the

United States than in any other country in the world. We would conquer space. We would ring the earth with artificial satellites. We would provide our physicists with billion-dollar instruments to hunt subatomic particles. We would build supersonic planes. We would conquer poverty in our time, and ignorance, and disease, mental as well as physical. Decent American homes will stand where wretched tenements now blot the landscape and twist the lives of millions. Bright schools and teachers are to open the minds of myriads now condemned to subliteracy, perpetually banished from the world of today's skills and culture. We require vast expansion of medical research and care, of hospital facilities, of day nurseries and recreation facilities. Marginal farmers and redundant coal miners are to be relocated, retrained. The very face of the land is to be remade with dams, tunnels, roads, airports, open spaces, new forests. Total or even merely sensible military defense demands its incalculable billions of us. And of all these good things we visualize for ourselves, we mean to provide a share also to the needier nations through generous foreign-aid programs.

But all these splendid aspirations cannot be achieved now or in a generation. We must make choices. We must decide whether homes are more important than roads, a hundred thousand schools more important than moon travel, whether to build first an additional medical school, a 100 BEV accelerator, or an intercontinental missile. The choices to be made are of course much more subtle than "either-or." It is a question of timing in the deployment of resources. Large immediate investments in Project A may be necessary now to supply the requirements of Project B later. Project B may be the most pressing ultimate goal; yet for the present it would be pointless to do more than make a small initial allocation of resources. This is why an underdeveloped country must plan.

Planning must extend to major categories of private expenditure as well as to items normally covered in governmental budgets. The investment projections of A.T. & T. or General Motors are as significant for national development as those of the Tennessee Valley Authority, and make comparable demands on resources. Levels of production of wheat or housing are critical elements in the shaping of our future, regardless of the fact that production is and will remain largely in private hands.

It is astonishing how little planning of national economic goals this country has had. No one has come forward with a rational ordering of goals including estimates of cost matched to specific resources from income and borrowing: not the government, not the major political parties, not the intellectual liberal groups, not the economists. Instead, thought and discussion have focused on abstractions like "growth rates" expressed as a percentage of increase of Gross National Product—as if it were of little importance what kinds of goods and services composed the increase or, for that matter, the base figure. Or there has been what might be called fragmental planning, the uncoordinated announcement by interested groups of their particular demands: for defense, for housing, for education, for medicare, or new prisons and probation services, etc., each estimate made utterly without reference to competing demands. In the aggregate these demands are so unrealistic as to be completely irresponsible and amount to no plan at all. Sometimes we are bemused by what appears to be comprehensive planning but turns out to be mere forecasting of the results of unplanning or of private planning by interested enterprises. I speak here of input-output analysis, which takes as its starting point projected investment and marketing plans of the private sector of the economy, anticipated consumer demands (themselves largely directed by producer decisions and advertising), and government spending. The analysis then derives from these projections a series of quantities of designated types of goods which must be produced if the projections are to be realized. This sort of thing, if it can be called planning at all, has little to do with the selection and ordering of rational objectives; it merely facilitates the logistics of campaigns planned by someone else.

But no-planning is itself a kind of planning. When the Kennedy-Johnson tax-cut handed $11,500,000,000 to tax-payers, there was a pretty fair idea of what the money would be spent for. Most certainly it would not be spent for the achievement of those high-priority national goals reviewed earlier. It would be spent in the pre-existing patterns of expenditure, for automobiles and other consumer hardware, for middle and lower-middle-class clothing and food, for corporate investment, for stock-market speculation and debt reduction. This is not the place to debate the merits of the tax-cut compared to increased expenditures in the public sector as a quick employment stimulator. It suffices here to observe that the preference for the tax cut amounted not only to a refusal by the government to spend in an avowedly planned way, but also a decision to underwrite the *status quo* in national spending patterns.

Why the aversion to national economic planning? Gunnar Myrdal, whose recent book, *Challenge to Affluence*, has as its central theme the necessity for long-range planning in the United States, attributes our lag in planning to irrational fears of governmental intervention and "a general tendency to near-sightedness among both politicians and experts." There is substance as well as inertia and superstition in the resistance to planning. Total planning and control would be an intolerable tyranny. The government, as sole employer, would wield a frightful influence over one's livelihood as well as one's political freedom. Where decisions are made for the whole economy mistakes can be catastrophic, and mistakes are less likely to be revealed than they would be in a pluralistic, competitive economy. National control of production would tend to restrict the variety of goods produced; excessive standardization would offer a lower level of satisfaction to the immensely variable desires of incurably individual human beings. And then there are the inherent weaknesses of large organizations, whether governmental or private: the tendency to proliferate personnel and stultifying red tape, the susceptibility to nepotism and corruption, the inclination of total planners to plan largely for their own survival and aggrandizement.

If planning is essential to achieve our national aims, but total planning is fundamentally objectionable on political and economic grounds, the sensible thing to do is to mark out as clearly as may be the spheres of activity requiring public planning and initiative. In other spheres, the rule of the day should be entrepreneurial freedom under the restraint of effective competition guaranteed by vigorous antitrust law and administration. Without this clarifying discrimination, the drive for essential planning is obstructed by obsolete laissez-faire notions associated with naive or calculating overreliance on competition to make big business serve national goals. Without this clarifying discrimination, progress in antitrust law is hampered by fear of disrupting giant organizations that are, or seem to be, performing vital functions.

Even within the sphere where planning is essential we must try for the largest amount of freedom and flexibility, the characteristic virtues of free enterprise. Planning does not necessarily imply compulsion. The mere public formulation of economic objectives in specific quantities to be achieved in a stated period would encourage private entrepreneurs to align their investment and production programs in accordance with the government's projections. Planning in Scandinavia, France, and India, for example, gives meaningful guidance to the private sector in this way. To the extent that more positive measures are required, there are many techniques that can be employed without resort to bureaucratic regulation of the details of individual business decision on prices, materials, location, and the like. Excise taxes, tariff policy, tax incentives, and special credit facilities can be used to redirect private competitive operations along lines contemplated by a national plan.

In any event, for a long time to come American planning need be no more than a systematic effort to set down our goals, timetable, and budget. It need not even be governmental planning at first. In the universities and among liberal political groups, a beginning must be made. Government can hardly be expected to move ahead of the most advanced public opinion. It is irresponsible and unbefitting for liberals and political scientists to favor programs and expenditures for all worthy goals without recognizing some limits on our capabilities and some order of priorities. What we need are:

1. an inventory of the principal classes of goods and services being produced;
2. a schedule of desirable major shifts in the distribution of our collective energies and resources over the next decade; and
3. proposals for a series of national budgets and programs of taxation, borrowing, subsidies, and regulation, designed to mobilize our resources in capital and labor to accomplish the chosen goals.

II

Although the United States needs more planning at the level of definition of fundamental economic objectives, there are vast domains of business where planning, structuring, is already excessive. It is not planning by government, but planning by the managers of giant private business firms. When a given industry comes to be dominated by a few big companies, the phenomenon known as oligopoly results. Under oligopoly conditions, the large firms, although nominally independent of each other and engaged in rivalry in many respects, manage to arrive at a consensus policy on fundamentals.

Price leadership is the best known example of oligopolistic consensus policy. A key firm in a particular market will announce a price increase. Other major firms will almost immediately match the increase. A particular rival may have lower costs and be in a position therefore to sell below the newly established level; it will typically not avail itself of this advantage, knowing that to do so would merely result in its prices being met by the price leader. The price leader can generally count on having its decision prevail throughout the industry. This is partly because a few big firms are likely to be faced with some common problems, for example, wage increases, movement of raw-materials prices; but the influence of common costs in producing uniform prices is often exaggerated, especially in the case of most heavy industries where unit costs depend largely on how fully the plant capacity is utilized. A more important influence in bringing about industry-wide price uniformity is the fact that a "statesmanlike" business leader will inform himself about the conditions facing his big rivals and their attitudes toward prospective major price changes. There will be a good deal of informal exchange of views through press releases, speeches at trade conventions, and the like, to say nothing of such direct discussions of common price strategy as may take place surreptitiously in violation of the Sherman Antitrust Act.

Thus, when the leader finally announces his decision, he has good reason to believe that his decision will be the industry's decision. He may not be followed every time by everybody, but in this respect his situation in the "administration" of prices does not differ radically from that of an official price regulator, whose rulings may be undermined by a black market or be modified under political pressure if he drastically defies the conventions of the trade. A crucial difference between the private and the public price administrator lies in his constituency. For the private price-maker, the constituency is his fellow traders. The public price administrator must consider not only the trade, but consumers and larger political interests of the nation. Senator Kefauver's hearings on administered prices and the confrontations of Presidents Kennedy and Johnson with the steel industry over price increases sufficiently demonstrate the difference in the criteria of public and private price regulation.

Oligopolistic consensus policy may govern not only prices but also production and technological development. Not one of the Big Three automobile manufacturers offered a small car until after a sizable share of the market had been captured by European producers, whereupon they entered the "compact" market concurrently. American movie producers made an oligopolistic industry response to the appearance of television and the drive-in theater, concertedly refusing to provide them with the best films on early runs.

We come then to inquire why the Antitrust laws do not prevent private regulation of trade and what might be done to vindicate the paramount political interest in large-scale private planning of the economy. The Sherman Antitrust Act of 1890 prohibited essentially monopolization and conspiratorial restraint of trade. These are the primitive and clear cases of private usurpation of power to govern commerce. However, the emerging pattern of American industry is neither monopolistic (in the sense of overwhelming control in a single firm) nor provably conspiratorial. As we have seen, it is oligopolistic, sharing power among half a dozen or fewer great corporations, and its government is by consensus without overt agreement. Congress' concern about oligopoly has so far manifested itself only in a restriction against mergers (Section 7 of the Clayton Act of 1914 as amended by the Celler-Kefauver Act of 1950) and in a few qualified prohibitions against specific anticompetitive arrangements such as price discrimination and exclusive dealing. The great industrial and financial empires already in being are, at most, forbidden to expand further by acquiring other firms in the same field, although they are free to extend their operations by direct investment in new facilities.

The three main lines along which reforms must go are reasonably clear:

1. The Sherman Act prohibition of monopoly must be supplemented by a law directed against excessive concentration of economic power. The law should expressly provide for breaking up existing giant firms to the extent that they manifestly exceed the scale required by technological considerations.

2. Since, under any conceivable deconcentration program, there will remain many very large firms operating unavoidably under oligopoly conditions, the Clayton Act list of

forbidden anticompetitive practices must be extended, and the prohibitions made absolute as to leading firms.

3. The veil of secrecy which surrounds strategic decision-making within the very largest private enterprises must be pierced so that responsible political authorities, if not the public, will be informed about the processes and considerations on which basic industrial policies depend.

The deconcentration program would be patterned on the famous Section 11 of the Public Utility Holding Company Act of 1935. That law required the great utility holding-company empires to reorganize so as to be limited in principle to "a single integrated public-utility system, and to such other businesses as are reasonably incidental or economically necessary or appropriate to the operations of such integrated public-utility system." The Securities Exchange Commission may permit more than one integrated system to remain under common control, where they operate in adjacent territories, and independent operation would entail loss of substantial economies, provided that the combined operation "is not so large . . . as to impair the advantages of localized management, efficient operation, or the effectiveness of regulation."

The proposed deconcentration law should be limited to not more than 100 of the largest enterprises, measured by a formula that gives appropriate weight to assets, volume of business done, and proportion of trade in a given field controlled by the enterprise. The reason for restricting the law to the 100 largest enterprises is not any a priori judgment that precisely the top 100 require deconcentration. The purpose is to confine the task of the regulatory agency to workable size. The number could as well be 50 or 200. Inclusion in the group would in any event raise only a rebuttable presumption of excessive concentration. Huge firms not embraced in the group would still be subject to ordinary antitrust controls supplemented by the extended list of Clayton Act prohibitions proposed below. The following table, from Kreps, *An Evaluation of Antitrust Policy: Its Relation to*

KREPS, AN EVALUATION OF ANTITRUST POLICY: ITS RELATION TO
ECONOMIC GROWTH, FULL EMPLOYMENT, AND PRICES (Study Paper
No. 22, Joint Econ. Comm., 86th Cong. 2d Sess. 1960).

Billionaire enterprises—Business versus governmental, ranked according to size
[Data are for 1958]

BUSINESS ORGANIZATION OR POLITICAL UNIT	REVENUES		EMPLOYEES		ASSETS	
	Amount (millions)	Rank	Number	Rank	Amount (millions)	Rank
Federal Government	$69,117	1	2,405,000	1	$262,056	1
General Motors Corp	9,522	2	521,000	3	6,891	29
Standard Oil Co. (New Jersey)	7,544	3	154,000	8	9,479	15
American Telephone & Telegraph Co.	6,771	4	592,130	2	19,494	7
Great Atlantic & Pacific Tea Co.	5,095	5	145,000	9	647	164
Ford Motor Co.	4,130	6	142,076	10	2,962	60
General Electric Co.	4,121	7	249,718	5	2,398	72
Sears, Roebuck & Co.	3,721	8	205,609	7	2,036	84
United States Steel Corp.	3,439	9	223,490	6	4,437	39
California	2,965	10	114,675	13	24,308	5
Metropolitan Life Assurance Co.	2,911	11	57,554	38	16,282	9
Socony Mobile Oil Co.	2,886	12	43,700	52	3,237	50
Gulf Oil Corp.	2,769	13	56,000	41	3,430	47
Prudential Insurance Co. of America	2,648	14	58,277	35	14,732	12
Swift and Co.	2,645	15	63,906	30	585	166
New York	2,558	16	117,474	12	36,686	2
New York City	2,542	17	254,094	4	22,450	6
Texas Company	2,328	18	52,515	42	3,112	55
Safeway Stores	2,225	19	59,555	34	408	173
Chrysler Corp.	2,165	20	95,846	16	1,338	124
Bethlehem Steel Corp.	2,006	21	140,474	11	2,195	80
Westinghouse Electric Corp.	1,896	22	114,652	14	1,412	117
Standard Oil Co. (Indiana)	1,864	23	46,033	48	2,769	64
Armour & Co.	1,850	24	45,700	49	412	172
E. I. du Pont de Nemours	1,829	25	83,875	22	2,649	65
The Kroger Co.	1,776	26	40,500	55	331	174
Boeing Airplane Co.	1,712	27	92,878	18	605	165
Pennsylvania	1,680	28	80,790	23	16,131	10
Shell Oil Co.	1,666	29	38,572	57	1,648	103
Standard Oil Co. (California)	1,559	30	38,395	58	2,457	70
General Dynamics Corp.	1,511	31	92,900	17	651	163
Ohio	1,478	32	57,883	37	24,630	4
National Dairy Products	1,451	33	44,194	51	558	167
Equitable Life Assurance Society of the United States	1,436	34	11,511	114	9,298	17
Michigan	1,421	35	64,794	29	15,957	11
J. C. Penney	1,410	36	75,052	26	416	171
Goodyear Tire & Rubber Co.	1,368	37	98,264	15	915	155
Union Carbide & Carbon	1,297	38	57,020	40	1,530	107
Douglas Aircraft Co., Inc.	1,210	40	71,925	27	473	168
Procter & Gamble Co.	1,295	39	20,700	93	756	157

KREPS, AN EVALUATION OF ANTITRUST POLICY: ITS RELATION TO
ECONOMIC GROWTH, FULL EMPLOYMENT, AND PRICES (Study Paper
No. 22, Joint Econ. Comm., 86th Cong. 2d Sess. 1960). (*cont.*)

Billionaire enterprises—Business versus governmental, ranked according to size
[Data are for 1958]

BUSINESS ORGANIZATION OR POLITICAL UNIT	REVENUES		EMPLOYEES		ASSETS	
	Amount (millions)	Rank	Number	Rank	Amount (millions)	Rank
United Aircraft Corp.	1,202	41	57,315	39	470	169
Sinclair Oil Co.	1,190	42	23,828	87	1,500	111
International Business Machines Corp.	1,172	43	86,736	21	1,261	131
Radio Corp. of America	1,171	44	78,000	25	734	161
Texas	1,148	45	66,325	28	9,369	16
R. J. Reynolds Tobacco Co. ...	1,147	46	13,135	110	743	158
Illinois	1,111	47	60,801	33	28,609	3
International Harvester	1,098	48	63,206	31	1,026	151
Montgomery Ward & Co., Inc. .	1,092	49	58,152	36	738	160
Continental Can Co., Inc.	1,080	50	51,000	43	688	162
Phillips Petroleum Co.	1,067	51	24,459	82	1,515	110
Firestone Tire & Rubber Co. .	1,062	52	88,323	20	738	159
American Can Co.	1,037	53	49,567	45	837	156
Cities Service	1,015	54	18,100	98	1,288	129
General Foods Corp.	1,009	55	21,012	92	443	170
New York Life Insurance Co. .	926	56	9,374	124	6,707	32
John Hancock Mutual Life Insurance Co.	890	57	17,560	100	5,518	33
Pennsylvania R.R. Co.	844	58	80,727	24	2,963	59
Aetna Life Insurance Co.	832	59	5,345	144	3,551	46
Aluminum Co. of America ...	753	60	44,281	50	1,337	125
New York Central Railroad Co.	740	61	61,678	32	2,603	67
Massachusetts	691	62	39,498	56	8,872	19
Washington	690	63	29,944	69	4,451	38

Economic Growth, Full Employment, and Prices (Study Paper
No. 22, Joint Econ. Comm., 86th Cong. 2d Sess. 1960), sug-
gests the scale of enterprises to be examined under the proposed
law.

The underlying principles of the proposed deconcentration
law differ markedly from existing antitrust law. In the first
place, size itself is treated as a matter of public concern, apart
from any question of "monopoly" of particular markets. A
multi-billion-dollar firm wields enormous power whether or not
it chooses to engross 30 percent or 60 percent or 90 percent of
the business in any particular product or group of products. Its

investment policies alone will have significant impact on national planning and development. Secondly, the proposed law would not carry criminal penalties or subject the firms to treble damage actions; there would be no implication of immorality or exploitation in a firm's being found in a position of such economic power as to entitle the community to demand structural changes. Thirdly, new principles will emerge from experience in administering the law. For example, as the regulatory agency seeks to answer the question whether the existing scale of the firm's operations is technologically justified it may become necessary to distinguish between efficiency in sales-promotional efforts and efficiency in production. I should also look for emergence of the principle that technological gains from very large-scale operations, say at the manufacturing level, are not to be used as a justification for concentrating in the same firm control of raw materials or product distribution on an equivalent scale. On the contrary, the greater the necessary concentration at the manufacturing level the stronger should be the case against vertical integration that gives additional leverage to an unavoidably powerful manufacturer.

For leading companies in oligopolized industries, Congress must strengthen the prohibitions against restrictive practices. The Clayton Act presently reaches only price discrimination, exclusive dealing, and merger. And these are prohibited only "where the effect may be substantially to lessen competition." It should be made clear by statute that the inference of adverse effect on competition can always be drawn from the fact that the company engaging in the practice is a powerful enterprise whether in terms of absolute size or position in a particular market. In addition, the list of practices from which such firms should be barred ought to include the following:

1. *Resale Price Maintenance.* The so-called "Fair Trade" laws are an impediment to free competition in distribution and a costly fraud on the public. The Federal enabling legislation (the McGuire Act) which permits these laws to operate in a number of states by exemption from the antitrust laws should

be repealed in its entirety. This seems unlikely to happen, considering the long and nearly successful efforts of the proponents of "Fair Trade" to incorporate it into Federal law under the euphemism, "Quality Stabilization." Pending the desirable repeal of the McGuire Act, the least that should be done to loosen the grip of powerful enterprises on the business policies of other firms is to forbid them to dictate resale prices or terms.

2. *Territorial Restrictions on Distributors.* A common provision in dealer franchises limits the dealer to a prescribed territory. Its purpose and effect is to prevent dealers from competing with one another. Although such agreements to restrain trade are within the scope of the Sherman Act, the "rule of reason" under that Act has generated doubts and difficulties in enforcement. The Supreme Court of the United States may soon put the practice in a special category of "per se" violations. If it does not do so, the practice certainly ought to be proscribed for oligopolists.

3. *Restrictive Patent Licensing.* Under existing law, a patent owner may refuse to license anyone, or he may license whom he chooses at whatever royalty rate he wishes to set. In addition the courts have sustained, with limits that are too complicated to summarize here, the patentee's right to require the licensee to sell at specified prices, to limit the quantity produced, to confine himself to particular uses of the patent, or to restrict his operations to a specified territory. Much can be said in favor of giving these powers to an individual inventor or firms of moderate size. The situation is altogether different when such powers are exercised by great enterprises whose financial resources alone endow them with much influence over other firms, an influence which should not be magnified by the leverage of restrictive licensing of one or hundreds of patents.

4. *Refusal to Deal.* The time has come for a reappraisal of the right of leading companies to select the persons with whom they will deal. To give that right to a small storekeeper accords with general notions of freedom of association, and his exercise of the right can have very little effect on the community. (I am

not here considering discrimination on the basis of race or color or religion.) It is quite another thing to accord the right to a corporation supplying nationally an extensively advertised commodity. Its refusals to deal have nothing to do with associational preferences of the individuals managing or owning the corporation, but rather with the corporation's desire to impose its commercial policies on other nominally independent entrepreneurs. It will not deal with price-cutters. If it is a pharmaceutical company, it may refuse to supply patent medicines to an aggressive chain of food stores, preferring a cozy, high profit margin distribution through druggists. It may seek to preserve an obsolescent wholesaling system by declining to deal directly with department stores or a mail-order house, or to use a new efficient form of retailing.

We need not go so far as to impose on dominant national suppliers an obligation to serve within the limits of their capacity all customers who are ready to pay or meet normal credit requirements. (French law goes about that far, whereas we reserve such obligations for common carriers and public utilities.) But it should be illegal to refuse to deal where the only objection to the customer is that he follows trading policies which he could not lawfully contract to abandon. Thus, where the antitrust law forbids a supplier to compel his distributor to resell at specified prices, it should be unlawful to refuse to supply the distributor on the ground that he has been or is expected to be a price-cutter.

III

Perhaps the most fundamental of tomorrow's issues in the area of private government of the economy is the issue of the public's right to know how the private government is functioning. As a result of the Securities Act of 1933 and other New Deal legislation, investors and the Securities Exchange Commission know something of the general financial aspects of corporations whose securities are publicly distributed. But we have only occasional incomplete glimpses of the processes by which major operating decisions are arrived at inside General Motors, Standard Oil of New Jersey, A.T. & T., General Electric Co., U.S. Steel Corp., duPont, or the Pennsylvania Railroad. It is not enough to be provided with abstract descriptions of the organization of such firms, accounts of how the company allocates authority among committees, plant heads, or vice-presidents, whether it has a "centralized" or a "federalized" structure, etc. What I, as a citizen and student of political economy, want to know is who wrote which memoranda that led Company V to adopt or postpone an important technological advance or model change, Company W to set its new investment program at half a billion rather than a billion, Company X to buy a controlling interest in giant firm A rather than B, Company Y to extend operations to South Africa rather than India, Company Z to announce a major price increase. I should like to know the considerations advanced and the alternatives rejected. I should like to know what commercial or investment bankers or insurance executives were consulted or had a voice in the decision. I should like to know the basis for personnel policies, for key appointments, for executive compensation, and for general labor policy.

This is not a proposal to require annual reports calling for this information from all big corporations. That would be burdensome and probably unrevealing. What I have in mind rather is a series of spot checks or case studies to be carried out by either a Congressional Committee or by the Federal Trade Commission. Investigations would be conducted in a spirit of dispassionate enquiry rather than in a flamboyant, adversary fashion. Hearings, if held at all, would typically be private, and every possible protection afforded against disadvantageous disclosures to competitors and others. But hearings are a clumsy, inconvenient, expensive form of official inquiry, involving attendance of corporate executives and their advisers in Washington and the painfully slow exposition by question-and-answer of information already known to the committee staff. Better than hearings would be audits conducted within the offices and files of the subject corporation, as official examiners audit the accounts and credit policies of banks.

The very knowledge of the possibility of an outside review would tend to introduce into major corporate decisions a degree of rationality and explicit consideration of the public welfare that may be lacking at present. At the same time, management would be left completely free to make its own decisions with all dispatch. The degree of governmental intervention resulting from the occasional post-audit here suggested would be far less than was proposed in the price-notification bills growing out of the Kefauver hearings on administered prices. These called for official public hearings before a price increase could be made effective "in industries where most of the output is produced by relatively few firms."

It requires little imagination to anticipate the anguished outcry which will greet the suggestion that our political representatives should have an occasional peek through the velvet curtain that surrounds high corporate policy. Once more the death of private exterprise will be announced by those whose power would be mildly circumscribed. But private enterprise would not die any more than the public utility industry expired with the enactment of Section 11 of the Public Utility Holding Company Act of 1935, widely denounced in its day as the "death sentence." Indeed some of us who fancy ourselves as the true defenders of the faith in private enterprise believe that it can be maintained only if the line between what is private and what is of public concern is respected by both sides.

Is there a legitimate public concern with the major decisions of giant firms? Adolf Berle for a generation has led a chorus of affirmative response to that question, although he rather preaches self-restraint to corporate managers than prescribes devices for assuring accountability. Certain it is that, if the people of the United States come to recognize that great industrial and financial combines are to some extent agencies of "government," they will not indefinitely tolerate Star Chamber government or government in which they do not have a share.

The Breakthrough
to Modernity:

The Kennedy Legacy and Public Opinion

JOHN P. ROCHE

I⊤ was difficult, if not impossible, in the first weeks after his death to attain any real perspective on the accomplishments of John Fitzgerald Kennedy. Now that more than a year has passed, it is important for us to turn to the task of critical evaluation. To the American historian of the future, who can rely only on the cold record, the Kennedy Administration may appear quite insubstantial. The Ph.D. candidate in 1980 will probably begin his dissertation by saying that President John Kennedy had less than three years in which to make his mark and that one can never know what triumphs might have marked his last five years in office. He will then turn to the legislative record and to the accomplishments of the Administration in foreign affairs and, I suspect, indicate at some length that Kennedy was not a "great President," that his domestic policy was strangled in Congress and that his foreign policy had one major success—Cuba in 1962—to balance the failure of the "Grand Design" for an Atlantic Community, the Alliance for Progress, the Bay of Pigs and the withering away of NATO and SEATO.

In objective historical terms the young man will be essentially correct. It is going to be as difficult to substantiate the proposition that John Kennedy was a magnificently talented politician twenty years from now as it would be to demonstrate that a pitcher who spent the years 1961–63 warming up in the bullpen had the greatest curve of our time. By this—the only meaningful standard—Kennedy hardly ranks in the majors. He was a stylish loser.

Yet at the basic level of American political reality, the young man will be profoundly wrong. His legislative statistics and sour observations on the Grand Design will be unimpeachable, but what he will probably overlook is the impact of John Kennedy on American opinion, on our self-image. In a word, his *style*, in which there lay concealed a politics of modernity. We are not here talking about superficial mannerisms, but about a fundamentally new approach to the nature of politics. The "Thousand Days" marked a sharp transition in American attitudes: a whole series of issues were buried and a new set emerged to replace them. The '40's and '50's were characterized by a universe of political discourse which had its roots in World War II and the postwar collapse of the "Grand Alliance"; between 1961 and 1964, the whole international system founded on bipolarity began to crumble. It was Kennedy's genius that he realized the extent to which our foreign policy was dying from hardening of the categories, and he set out to lead the American people to a new formulation of the alternatives.

Before we examine the Kennedy Breakthrough, it is important to recreate the mood of the preceding era, particularly as it shaped the responses of the liberal community—a term used here to include both the stalwarts of organized liberalism and the broader reaches of inert commitment to the liberal value system.

The depressed years

Liberals have been accused of holding a naive faith in the progressivism of the American people. Historically there may have been some merit to this charge, but it appears to me that some of our recent problems have arisen from the converse, from an over-addiction to a secularized version of the doctrine of Original Sin. The 1950's, and particularly the presidential election of 1952, tended to generate a profound liberal pessimism ultimately based upon an unarticulated distrust of public opinion.

The 1950's were indeed a hard decade for liberalism. I suspect that many liberals have not yet recovered from the deadening impact of the 1952 election. For twenty years the liberal movement had enjoyed that wonderful feeling of exhilaration that accompanies victory; Truman's 1948 triumph, in particular, seemed to indicate that there was a Cosmic endorsement for the objectives of liberal Democrats. Then came Korea, McCarthyism, and November, 1952.

We all died a little on that somber November night as we learned that the Age of Banality had begun. And I suspect that we all began, at various levels of consciousness, to question the viability of the democratic process. The fearful beatings we took in the early '50's tended to encourage a seige mentality. We had been brutally whipsawed: can one ever forget being simultaneously denounced as pro-Communist for "losing China" and as a "war party" for intervening in Korea?

The 1952 election results appeared to indicate that we had lost what we had blissfully assumed was a permanent majority among the American people for the forces of Enlightenment. Yet in retrospect it seems clear to me that the remarkable aspect of the 1952 election was that Stevenson did as well as he did: while in macroanalytical terms the American people were counting on Eisenhower to get them out of the front lines and back to normalcy, when one got down among the detailed figures he could learn that the election was anything but a repudiation of liberalism. (Even among Irish Catholics, who were allegedly raving with the McCarthyite virus, 55 percent of the votes were cast for Stevenson.) While Eisenhower carried 297 congressional districts, the Republican candidates for the House were victorious in only 221. And Stevenson, running against a picture on the American wall—the Liberator of Europe—still amassed more votes than any previous *winning* candidate for President.

Liberal pessimism was, of course, reinforced by the terrible drubbing Stevenson took in 1956. Eisenhower hardly deserved to win, but neither did Stevenson, bereft of the intellectual vitality of his '52 campaign. The long and the short of it was that in characterological terms we went "underground." We continued to express ourselves and to advance vigorously unorthodox positions on such issues as the recognition of Red China, anti-Communist legislation, or nuclear testing, but the old punch was gone. We spent an unduly large proportion of our time talking to each other—and the rest in the psychologically satisfying but essentially negative task of excoriating the Eisenhower administration. But we did not undertake the task of public education or stimulate a climate of opinion in which vital questions (such as the absurdity of the Dulles doctrine of "massive retaliation") could be canvassed.

In other words, we took the Eisenhower victories of '52 and '56 as evidence that we had lost contact with the American people, and this conviction undermined our élan, our will to fight and above all to provide the vanguard for new political ideas and formulations. And this happened concurrently with the exodus of our friends from the political communications network and from office in the national administration; we no longer had the privilege of going to the White House or the Department of State to put our case. We felt lonesome and alienated—a fact which, I suspect, contributed to the fantastic increase in assaults by liberal intellectuals on the horrors of "mass culture."

The consequences of this defeat syndrome were many and varied, but the key one for our purposes here was that in its reaction to an alleged reactionary rigidification of American opinion the liberal community tended to become hermetic and to a considerable degree non-political—a large segment took refuge in cultural elitism and abandoned the masses to their materialistic revels.

It should be pointed out that liberals are not the only people who are haunted by the past. The Kennedy and Johnson administrations, for example, have continued to treat the issue of recognition of Red China as if it were a blockbuster, although I am convinced the fuse was pulled out of that explosive question years ago. Red China was an explosive quantity in the early 50's for two reasons: first, it was an alleged byproduct of the "sell-out" of Chiang by State Department "Communists"—one episode in the "twenty years of treason" fantasy. Second, Chinese Communist soldiers were killing Americans in Korea. On both counts the American people were justified in their concern, although this legitimate anxiety was converted into demagogic currency. Yet last year, before the elections, Barry Goldwater indicated that if he were elected President he would be willing to permit negotiations with Peking.

This is an important consideration and deserves emphasis. Because liberals are issue-oriented, they sometimes delude themselves into believing that politics is—or should be—an intellectual enterprise. This leads to what I have called the "hyperthyroid theory of democracy," the view that nobody should ever take a position on anything until he has studied the facts for himself and reached an independent judgment. I would be the last person to depreciate the role of intelligence in the political process, but I would strongly argue that an intelligent approach to political decisions can quite reasonably involve the application of the division of labor. The notion of 190 million Americans engaged in technical research on the problems of a test-ban treaty is in fact rather terrifying, for it would indicate an absence of that trust in leadership which is the necessary foundation for any stable society.

The Kennedy-Nixon debates are a case in point. Does anyone seriously think that the watchers were scoring the results with a copy of *Time*'s current events test? They were scoring it, but in an entirely different fashion. Intellectual evaluation was, of course, part of the total, but essentially the watchers were attempting to determine—on the basis of a whole range of considerations both conscious and unconscious—which of these men could be trusted with the destiny of the Republic. And before the angry reader accuses me of anti-intellectualism, he should meditate on the ironic fact that if the franchise were restricted to college graduates, Richard M. Nixon would have been elected President of the United States.

Those who decided to vote for John Kennedy after watching him on the Great Debate were not registering their support for the specific propositions he advanced, which were not much out of the ordinary, but were naming him their opinion-executor. Effectively they were saying that Kennedy (or Nixon) was the man to whom they delegated their decision-making in national affairs or international affairs—just as, at a different level, congressmen also exercise delegated trust. A failure to understand this key proposition led to much pessimism about the possibilities of American ratification of the test-ban treaty. In Chicago in December of 1962, I told a Turn Towards Peace audience that if President Kennedy strongly endorsed the treaty, public opinion would support him overwhelmingly and it would go through the Senate with at least 75 votes, well over the necessary two-thirds. I was promptly accused of naïveté and elitism, that is, of believing that public opinion was manipulated from the top rather than generated from the bottom.

But in this context, "manipulation" is hardly the right word. What is involved is trust, and an inability to appreciate this concept and its vital consequences has crippled the peace movement. When a "peace candidate" rode forth in the fall of 1962, he did so with the commendable mission of informing the public on the crucial issue of war and peace. The difficulty was that to the average voter—who strongly believes in peace—the essence of a "peace candidate's" message seemed to be: "The President and the Congress are eager to see us all blown up." In other words, he attempted to cut the bond of trust between the population and its political leaders, and failed completely. The public trusted John Kennedy in the Cuban confrontation—and in the test-ban negotiations; after all, he was elected to handle precisely such questions.

This detour leads us back to the problem in the early 50's. Then precisely the opposite development occurred: the "public" (again a statistical fiction) *lost* faith in its political leaders, and transferred its trust to Dwight D. Eisenhower. It would be nice to blame this transfer on History or some other transcendent factor, but I regret to say that—while I think the decision the electorate made was wrong—there was a real foundation for public concern and dismay. From 1950 on, the Truman administration was a shambles and liberal forces in the political sector were in fearful disarray. True, the Republicans were playing dirty, but most Democrats were not inclined to fight. When Truman vetoed the McCarran Internal Security Act of 1950, for example, only ten Senators supported him; and the appalling Internal Security Act of 1954 passed 79–0.

At this point let us close the books on the past. The lesson, however, should be clear by now: the overarching importance of liberal leadership in the political sector and the secondary character of cultural or purely issue-oriented emphases. Contrast, for instance, the tremendous battle the liberals fought against McCarthyism in the society at large with the collapse of anti-McCarthyism in the political arena. This curious situation encouraged the pessimism of European observers, who, assuming that Washington, D.C. was the United States, announced that McCarthyism was carrying everything in its path and the nation was on the brink of the abyss of fascism. In fact, as I then noted, McCarthyism was not an organized political movement with deep roots in the country, but a psychosis that thrived on the disorganization and timidity of its opponents, and on the opportunism of the so-called "conservatives," Democratic and Republican, who were glad to employ any stick to beat the liberal dog.

The Kennedy Breakthrough

Examples of what I have called the Kennedy Breakthrough can be drawn from a number of areas of domestic and foreign policy, but I shall confine myself to two instances drawn from each. In foreign relations, Kennedy inherited the Manichean universe of John Foster Dulles and Dean Acheson. Dulles' foreign policy was in fact a logical extension of Acheson's: "liberation" was always implicit in "containment," though Truman and Acheson had the prudential sense not to convert operational logic into a *reductio ad absurdum*. In essence, Dulles was a caricature of Acheson. More important, the policy which Acheson and Kennan devised in 1947 was designed to cope with immediate Soviet expansionism, to mobilize American opinion to a "hard line" which was absolutely necessary in the context of the times. Ironically, just as Stalin died, Dulles became President of the United States for Foreign Affairs and set to work to "correct" the policies of the five previous years. With a fixated legalism, Dulles seemed to think that he could at the appellate level reverse the decisions made at the trial; for six years he rebriefed the past and in his dream-world took Stalin to the "brink."

But Stalin was dead and Dulles' exercises in brinkmanship were fantasies, founded—as Hans Morgenthau noted at the time—on the archaic premise of nuclear monopoly. One may suspect that Khrushchev only learned that he had been humbled at the brink from subsequent Dulles memoirs in the *Saturday Evening Post*. Indeed, Dulles' *de facto* foreign policy must have encouraged the flexible Soviet leader, who—one suspects— decided early in his career that Dulles confused rhetoric with action. During the Hungarian Revolution, for example, the Soviets were obviously in a quandary (put bluntly, they were afraid —and understandably so—of an American response to military intervention in Budapest) until Dulles thoughtfully took them off the hook by assuring Khrushchev that the United States would not intervene in the internal affairs of the Soviet bloc. From this point on, Khrushchev had Dulles tagged as a moral isolationist—a spiritual America Firster—who would never risk Chicago to save Budapest. Only in this fashion can we explain the expansion of Khrushchev's political vocabulary from that time on to include, almost as a standard incantation, the threat of a "hail of rockets" to those nations who persited in anti-Soviet coalitions.

In short, American foreign policy as it emerged from the 1950's was an eerie compound of high-flown anti-Communist morality and operational cowardice. The American people had been (willingly) lulled to sleep by assurances that the forces of Satan were cowering before the Sword of the Righteous. Indeed, I can not find one instance in the eight years of the Eisenhower Administration when the people were told by their leaders that real risks were present, that the road was perilous. The threat of Communist expansion had allegedly been exorcised. But Khrushchev, who had survived many purges and knew a risky road when he saw one, was not fooled; on a perfectly solid empirical basis, he calculated that in any confrontation the United States would take all steps short of action that would risk a thermonuclear exchange. As he put it to Robert Frost and several other visiting Americans, "the United States is too liberal to fight." Since it was in his power to define the "risk" of thermonuclear war, he was able to shape American foreign policy.

Thus Kennedy inherited a policy that consisted of ferocious abstract attacks on the wickedness of Communism and tactical paralysis. From the short-range viewpoint of the American "man in the street," this was ideal: he could rejoice in the ferocious rhetoric and relax. It made the neo-isolationists happy because it warmed their hearts to hear an American Secretary of State "tell off the Reds"—and yet justified budget cutting. It even warmed the hearts of the group I once called the "Eisenhower Marxists," whose dialectical sense led them to support the President as a "peace candidate," *i.e.*, a loser in the cold war.

The essence of any sane American policy in 1961 was an absolute reversal of priorities: a diminution of chiliastic rhetoric and calls to immediate "total victory" and a stepping up of concrete, tactical responses to the endless Communist probes. Above all, Kennedy had to change the universe of discourse by convincing the Soviets that nuclear war must be abandoned as an instrument of policy because it was a real possibility. And he had to bring home to the American people that Communism could not be exterminated if we so willed, unless we were ready to go down in a common grave; that massive resurrection would be, for most of us, the precondition to massive retaliation. In sum, he had to obtain freedom of maneuver by escaping from the trap of Soviet nuclear initiatives—the "hail of rockets"— and from the ideological bonds created by rigid, hard-line, millennial anti-Communism. In specific terms, he had to ask the American people to trust him with their destinies in a war of maneuver—not Armageddon—where it might be necessary to stop short of "total victory," where it might be imperative to negotiate with the "enemy"—even to do business with the "enemy" where tactical demands might require retreat in the interest of long-run objectives.

He achieved these objectives in two superbly organized campaigns: the first against the Soviet Union in October of 1962, and the second against the frozen American Right in the struggle for the Test-Ban Treaty. The Cuban confrontation is surely the most remarkable application of political physics the world has ever seen: the Soviet miscalculation was met with precisely determined optimum force responses, there was no chauvinism, no howling for total victory, no effort to mislead the American people about the gravity of the crisis. Initially, imitating Soviet tactics in East Germany, we simply tore up the roads to Cuba and prepared for gradual escalation of the pressure; from the outset Khrushchev was provided with room for retreat. The Soviets were clearly terrified; they were used to Dulles—who would have left the missiles in Cuba, organized a Caribbean Security Treaty, and denounced the evils of Communism before the American Legion.

This halfway house between defeat (which would have left the missiles in Cuba or brought a nuclear holocaust) and total victory (which would have seen the elimination of the Castro regime) brought the Chinese out screaming: the Chinese Right in the United States and the Chinese Left in the Soviet bloc. But the American people, who had knowingly put their lives in the balance for almost a week, were prepared to accept the President's prudential guidance, that is, they abandoned the Goldwater Standard of anti-Communism.

This became clear during the prolonged battle for Senate approval of the Test-Ban Treaty. The Chinese Right brought out all the old drums and beat them frantically for six months. The President and his advisors in Congress and the Administration mounted a coldly rational campaign: the treaty was not presented as a miraculous cure for Cold War tensions but as a beginning, a first step; the Soviets were not billed as reformed sinners, but as partners in a quest for mutual interest—survival; there was no apocalypticism—only a sober appeal for common sense. And against the opposition of great congressional barons, public opinion gradually mobilized behind the President. The Gallup Poll, for example, indicated a fantastic growth in favorable opinion between July and September, 1963—a surge of pressure so great that it led to a vote of 80–19. The conclusion was obvious: the American President was dealing with The Enemy and the American people were willing to trust him with the unfortunate, undesirable, but necessary task. The Chinese Right had called the spirits from the murky deep, had invoked all the magic in the arsenal of the 50's, but the spirits from the murky deep had not responded: the ship of state had finally broken out of the ice-pack of McCarthyism.

It is important to note that Kennedy's policies here, as elsewhere, were not "liberal" in the usual ideological sense of that word; indeed, one could argue that his notions of how foreign policy should be conducted were, if anything, in the classic tradition of statecraft as represented in our time by, say, George Kennan and Sir Harold Nicolson. The significant thing is thus not the content of his policy, but the fact that he won public acceptance for a diplomatic posture that has traditionally been associated with aristocratic regimes and unrepresentative elites. Kennan, for example, writes off the possibility of restrained maneuver, arguing that a democratic society must take its ideology neat, must be fed on moralism to get it to accept commitment. It was Kennedy's genius, his style, that the American public was willing to send him out to handle the incredibly delicate task of maintaining freedom and peace in a contingent universe.

A final contrast, perhaps, will emphasize the point: When in 1958 President Eisenhower announced over TV that we might have to consider the possibility of undertaking certain conceivable warlike actions in the Formosa Straits, the public response was quantitatively and vigorously negative—before the State Department suppressed statistics, communications were allegedly running on the order of 500 to 1 against. On the other hand, the reaction to Kennedy's statement on the Cuban blockade was overwhelmingly favorable. Eisenhower had painted himself into a strategic corner by his constant refusal to challenge the American people, particularly by his suggestion in the 1952 campaign that the Korean War was a Democratic blunder. Again at the time of Hungary and Suez he prescribed tranquilizers—his role was to exorcise the turbulent past. Without for a moment suggesting that he was right in calling for a policy of (ambiguous) vigor in the Formosa Straits, I would suggest that any concretely vigorous foreign policy he might have suggested would have received the same negative response. He was in the position of a man who has become a prisoner of his own press releases. Kennedy, in contrast, sensitized American opinion to the perils of the nuclear age and carried his constituents with him—nervously but with commitment—to the abyss in the most awesome display of democratic solidarity since the

Battle of Britain.

On the domestic scene, much the same process occurred, though less dramatically. The conduct of foreign relations was ideally suited to Kennedy's "style": traditionally the President has far greater scope for initiative in the international sector than at home and far less attrition from Congress. [I suspect that, despite his years in the House and Senate, Kennedy was really quite bored by Congress: he was never a good listener unless he could set up the conversational options, and his congressional career must therefore have contained a good deal of cruel and unusual punishment. And in the handling of domestic policy, the President must to a considerable degree throw himself on the mercy of the national legislature; he has a good deal less "power" in this context than is ordinarily realized.]

It must be conceded that Kennedy never really developed an effective relationship with Congress. For one thing, he suffered from what Sören Kierkegaard called the "paralysis of knowledge"—he knew too much about the congressional capacity for sabotage to commit himself to a militant challenge to legislative power. Yet at the same time it was perfectly clear to those who knew him that he considered Congress something of an overgrown kindergarten, an appalling barrier to the creation of an efficient, modern government. Unlike Harry Truman or Lyndon Johnson, he had never been an "insider," a member of the club—secretly he may have felt that such membership was equivalent to high status in the Society for the Preservation of the Whooping Crane.

Thus his legislative program was quietly strangled in the House Rules Committee or in the anterooms of the Senate, and the bills that emerged were often far removed in substance from those that he proposed. However, despite the pathetic legislative record of the Thousand Days, there is another aspect which must be taken into consideration—the impact of Kennedy's views on American public opinion. Alas, we can never know whether this impact would have been reflected in Congress, say, 1965–66, but I suspect that the groundwork that the President did would have brought delayed but substantial rewards. Again let us look at the breakthrough in two areas: fiscal policy and civil rights. And again, let me make clear that while Kennedy's efforts contributed to a "liberal" climate of opinion, he was not in my opinion proceeding on any ideological guidance system. He simply wanted to eliminate from American politics and administration a collection of inefficient, dysfunctional fairy tales.

The first superstition to be brought under public scrutiny was the moral wickedness of deficit spending and the whole notion of the inherent godliness of the balanced budget. Here the President, with the aid of a series of charts, attempted to bring Keynes to the consciousness of the American public via a TV lecture. It was (as he commented wryly to me) a "C-minus performance." Nonetheless, for the first time a President of the United States impeached the validity of the most deeply rooted economic myth in our collective consciousness. It seems difficult to believe, but until 1962—despite all the empirical data that has been accumulating for the last quarter-century—the balanced budget had maintained its sacramental standing in American politics. Of course, if the average citizen adopted the principle of the balanced budget, the economy would probably collapse: he is in hock for his house, his car, his refrigerator, his boat, his kitchen stove—all purchased today on the premise of future affluence. And the investment policies of business are predicated on similar optimism and willingness to take a risk. But somehow the realities of economic life have never been permitted to intrude into the virginal atmosphere of economic myth: the United States government is not even permitted to organize its budget on a rational basis like that employed by, say, A. T. & T. If it did, the annual deficit would diminish if not disappear!

Kennedy, with his customary intellectual ruthlessness, seized the nettle, proposing major tax reductions with the concomitant of an unbalanced budget as a technique for stimulating long-range economic growth. The clamor was fantastic: the banshees wailed in the hills, solemn legislators predicted that the creditors would evict us from the country, Henry Hazlitt and Raymond Moley held the deathwatch for American capitalism in *Newsweek*. But eventually (after Kennedy's assassination) the principle was enacted into public policy. True, Lyndon B. Johnson did rush to the rescue of classical mythology by demanding "economy" in government, thus eliminating the most effective form of economic stimulation—direct government expenditure —in favor of the indirect techniques of leaving expansion in corporate and private hands (where the savings factor can act as a massive restraint). Yet the deed was done, the precedent established. Kennedy made it clear that in his opinion the emperor had no clothes, and it is doubtful whether all the incantations that classical economic fakirs intone can ever restore the myth to its pristine position.

Kennedy's part in the civil rights breakthrough was far more passive than his role in fiscal policy or international affairs. While it was always clear where his sympathies lay in this matter, he seemed for too long a time to cherish the unrealistic hope that a reconciliation was possible between the Southern white politicians and the Northern liberals, one which could prevent a public confrontation, a blowup. Tensions within the national Democratic coalition, which led to some Southern defections in 1960, could be increased to the point where the antique alliance would fall apart—and with it, perhaps, would vanish his majority in 1964. Moreover, Kennedy had, in my judgment, one great blind spot: he was simply incapable of understanding extremism. The day he was shot, he had spent an hour in the plane pressing two Texas Representatives on the Birchers and the radical right—persistently he returned to the same question: "What do they *really* want?" In other words he insisted that all irrational behavior must be founded, somewhere, on a rational basis. Similarly, he seems to have assumed at the outset that the Southern Democrats were merely putting up a militant racist front in order to establish a hard bargaining position, that they didn't *really* believe the tasteless anachronisms they promulgated.

The outcome of this presidential restraint was a tremendous effort on the administrative level to work the civil rights issue out below the threshold of political visibility, an effort which culminated with the dispatch of the Attorney General to Birmingham, Alabama, literally to "fix the ticket," that is, get the reasonable brokers together in a room and hammer out a face-saving compromise. The Attorney General apparently got an education in Alabama: he was alleged to have said on his return that it was like "going to another country." John Kennedy and his brother here confronted the thing which above all others makes a modern, urbane utilitarian nervous: raw ideology unmitigated by any rationality or willingness to compromise.

The President had no temperamental fondness for moral civil wars, but whatever his reservations the fact remains that once the genie was out of the bottle, he shifted his whole approach and threw his influence behind a strong civil rights bill. In addition, he announced flatly (with none of Eisenhower's reservations) that there were no two ways of looking at the civil rights matter: the white supremacists were simply wrong. Although it is difficult for one who was urging the President in season and out to raise the battle flag and exercise moral leadership to admit it, there were undoubtedly great benefits that accrued from Kennedy's low-key handling of the civil rights issue. Most important perhaps was the impact of his flat, factual, unadorned, unemotional statements on public opinion. He made the whole quest for equality sound so *sensible*, so commonsensical, while racists appeared worse than immoral—they were stupid Neanderthalers trying to hold back the tide of modernity. The great American public, which more often than not tends to react suspiciously when called to the moral barricades (and, alas, not without reason), picked up the President's position.

We liberals, who have been fighting for civil rights over the years, have every reason to be proud of our accomplishments—I for one refuse to flagellate before the image of St. James Baldwin for the alleged sins of "white liberals"—and it is clear to me that our travail was necessary before the American people would treat racial equality as a meaningful component of national idealism. But if we were necessary, we were not sufficient —we could not go it alone. And I suspect that when the history books are written, it will be seen that the final civil rights breakthrough occurred under the (curiously reluctant) auspices of President John Kennedy.

The challenge of an open future

If I am correct in my reading of the state of mind of contemporary public opinion, the time has come for a basic reassessment of the liberal posture. It seems apparent to me that John Kennedy's Thousand Days closed the books—in a psychological sense—on much of the recent political past: closing in the process many of our accounts, as well as those of our opponents. He brought us into the modern world and in a symbolic way the reaction to his murder indicated a new mood of public maturity. To the great dismay of European ideologues—to whom ironically the excesses of the McCarthy era were proof of American puerility—we did not launch a great hysterical witch hunt for "conspiracy," but rejected social paranoia for the commonsense assumption that the deed was done by an isolated psychotic. Those of the far Right and the millennial Left who have patiently cultivated the seeds of a conspiracy theory have been left arguing with each other on whether Kennedy was killed by the Communists for double-crossing his master Khrushchev or by the C.I.A. for signing the Test Ban Treaty; the cracked drums are beating in a void.

Liberal essays characteristically end on a note of exhortation, and this one will be no exception. As a historian and political scientist, I can trace a diagnosis of the breakthrough to modern politics and indicate the open-ended quality of American politics in the middle 1960's. But as a committed liberal activist, I regret that I can supply no institutional prescriptions, no certain chart of where we should go from here. In short, I can issue negative injunctions with some confidence—I know what we *shouldn't do*—and in my historical capacity I am afraid that we are in for perilous times, that we run the risk of becoming ideological dinosaurs unless we respond to the challenge of the open future.

I must therefore end on an abstract note—with apologies, since my views may be a bit embarrassing to my utilitarian friends who get nervous when anyone talks about morality. But either we are moralists or we are nothing, and the nub of our dilemma is that the times imperatively require a rebirth of liberal morality, or of liberal political theory, to use a less loaded term. Over the past half-century we have exhausted our stock of ideas, those we inherited from Victorian liberalism and Victorian socialism, and unless we are prepared to spend our time as social and political plumbers, playing with the pipes and unclogging drains, we must turn to the task of reformulating our premises. This is not a call to "repudiate" anything—we need theory, not polemic—for the historical fact is that with the weapons we held we took the United States away from the Yahoos and created the foundations of a decent society. We are suffering from the failure of success, a classic problem in the history of political theory.

We stand, in conclusion, at the threshold of a new era with a public that has transcended the New Deal, the Fair Deal, and the Catatonic Fifties, an era in which the categories "liberal" and "conservative" as we know them may have as much meaning as Whig and Tory. It is our obligation to take the grand principles of our tradition, the great ideal of a self-governing community living in justice and freedom, and apply them radically and without trepidation to novel circumstances. Put another way, we must reassert our political function of the offensive, climb out of our defensive redoubts, and justify our noble claim as prophets of democratic morality.

CONTRIBUTORS

HANS J. MORGENTHAU is Albert A. Michelson Distinguished Service Professor of Political Science and Modern History at the University of Chicago and Director of its Center for the Study of American Foreign and Military Policy. He is the author of *Politics in the Twentieth Century, Politics Among Nations, The Purpose of American Politics,* and many other books and articles.[1]

STANLEY H. LOWELL, formerly Assistant United States Attorney and a former Deputy Mayor of New York, is Chairman of the New York City Commission on Human Rights. He is a board member of the Urban League of New York and the National Committee Against Discrimination in Housing.[1]

JOSEPH L. RAUH, JR., a Washington attorney and General Counsel to the United Automobile Workers, was National Chairman and is presently Vice-Chairman for Civil Rights and Civil Liberties of Americans for Democratic Action.[1,2]

LEON H. KEYSERLING, a consulting economist and attorney, is the President of the Conference of Economic Progress; he was Chairman of President Truman's Council of Economic Advisers.[1,2]

ROBERT R. NATHAN, a prominent New Deal economist under President Roosevelt, is now a consulting economist.[1,2]

EMILE BENOIT is Professor of Economics at Columbia University and co-author with Kenneth Boulding of *Disarmament and the Economy.*[1,2]

[1] A member of the National Board of the Americans for Democratic Action.
[2] A National Vice-Chairman of the Americans for Democratic Action.

CHRISTOPHER JENCKS is a Contributing Editor of the New Republic and a Fellow of the Institute for Policy Studies.

ERIC LARRABEE, author of The Self-Conscious Society, has been Managing Editor of Horizon and American Heritage. He is now a free-lance writer and regular contributor to Harper's Magazine.

NORTON E. LONG is James Gordon Professor of Community Government at Brandeis University and research associate at the Joint Center for Urban Studies of MIT and Harvard University. A widely-known student of urban problems, he is the author of The Polity.

HUBERT H. HUMPHREY, the Vice-President and former Senator from Minnesota, is the author of two recent books, War on Poverty and The Cause is Mankind. He was National Chairman and is presently a Vice-Chairman of Americans for Democratic Action.

PAUL SEABURY is Professor of Political Science at the University of California and author of Power, Freedom and Diplomacy.[1,2]

ROBERT E. ASHER, a former Special Assistant to the Assistant Secretary of State for Economic Affairs, is an international relations specialist with the Brookings Institution.

AMITAI ETZIONI, Associate Professor of Political Sociology at Columbia University, is the author of Winning Without War and other books.[1]

JAMES MacGREGOR BURNS is Professor of Political Science at Williams College and the author of John Kennedy: A Political Profile and The Deadlock of Democracy.[1]

JOSEPH S. CLARK is the Senior Senator from Pennsylvania and a former Mayor of Philadelphia. He is the author of Congress: The Sapless Branch and The Senate Establishment as well as a contributor to many magazines.[1]

NEIL W. CHAMBERLAIN is Professor of Economics at Yale

[1] A member of the National Board of the Americans for Democratic Action.
[2] A National Vice-Chairman of the Americans for Democratic Action.

University and the author of *Sourcebook on Labor, Collective Bargaining,* and other books.

EDWARD D. HOLLANDER is a consulting economist and Chairman of the National Executive Committee of Americans for Democratic Action.[1]

LOUIS B. SCHWARTZ is Professor at the University of Pennsylvania Law School and the author of *Free Enterprise and Economic Organization,* among other books.[1]

JOHN P. ROCHE, Professor of Political Science at Brandeis University and author of *Shadow and Substance, The Quest for the Dream,* and other books, is National Chairman of Americans for Democratic Action.[1]

[1] A member of the National Board of the Americans for Democratic Action.